THE COMEDY AND TRAGEDY OF THE SECOND EMPIRE

LECTOR HOUSE PUBLIC DOMAIN WORKS

THE COMEDY AND TRAGEDY OF THE SECOND EMPIRE

EDWARD LEGGE

ISBN: 978-93-5614-077-6

Published: 1911

© 2022
LECTOR HOUSE LLP
TM

LECTOR HOUSE

LECTOR HOUSE LLP
E-MAIL: lectorpublishing@gmail.com

NAPOLEON III.

BY ALBERT BRUCE-JOY.

From the cast taken by the Sculptor, by permission of H.I.M. the Empress Eugénie, immediately after the Emperor's death, January 9, 1873.

Mr. Bruce-Joy's bust has never been exhibited, and was specially photographed for this book in June, 1911.

Frontispiece.

THE COMEDY & TRAGEDY OF THE SECOND EMPIRE

PARIS SOCIETY IN THE SIXTIES INCLUDING LETTERS OF NAPOLEON III., M. PIETRI, AND COMTE DE LA CHAPELLE, AND PORTRAITS OF THE PERIOD

BY

EDWARD LEGGE,

AUTHOR OF "THE EMPRESS EUGÉNIE: 1870-1910"

1911

I DEDICATE THIS VOLUME
ON HIS EIGHTY-SIXTH BIRTHDAY
TO THE
EMINENT STATESMAN AND HISTORIAN OF
L'EMPIRE LIBÉRAL
ÉMILE OLLIVIER
PRIME MINISTER IN 1870
LOYAL FRIEND OF NAPOLEON III.
AND
GRAND OLD MAN OF FRANCE

*   *   *   *   *

Ab honesto virum bonum nihil deterret.

A NOTE

30 juin, 1911,

Monsieur,

Non-seulement j'accepte avec plaisir la dédicace dont vous voulez bien m'honorer, mais je vous remercie des termes beaucoup trop bienveillants dont vous vous servez à mon égard. Je vous remercie aussi de l'envoi de votre livre, que je me ferai lire, et dans lequel, je suis sûr, je trouverai beaucoup d'intérêt.

Agreez, Monsieur, mes sentiments les plus cordialement sympathiques.

Émile Ollivier.

[Translation.]

June 30, 1911.

Sir,

Not only do I accept with pleasure the dedication with which you are good enough to honour me, but I thank you for the much too kind terms in which you refer to me.

I thank you also for sending me your book, which I shall have read to me, and in which I am sure I shall find much that is interesting.

Accept my most cordially-sympathetic sentiments.

Émile Ollivier.

[The book referred to is "The Empress Eugénie: 1870-1910." London: Harper and Brothers. New York: Charles Scribner's Sons. 1910. Owing to M. Olliver's somewhat impaired vision, books and documents are read to him.]

PREFACE

I⊤ is due to the readers of "The Empress Eugénie: 1870-1910," that they should know how that volume was received by the British and American Press. Leading critics like Mr. Courtney, "Daily Telegraph"; Mr. Richard Whiteing, "Manchester Guardian"; and Mr. Tighe Hopkins, "Daily Chronicle," devoted much space to their analyses of the volume, as did the able reviewers of the work in the "Morning Post," "Daily Mail," "Evening Standard," "Scotsman," "Illustrated London News," "Observer," "Athenæum," "Church Times," "Catholic Times," "Onlooker," and many other influential and widely-circulated journals. Two editions were exhausted in this country and the United States. A remarkable, and severely-critical, article appeared in "La Grande Revue" (Paris), from the pen of the celebrated author and publicist, M. Gérard Harry, a strong anti-Bonapartist, who deprecated what he considered the excessive praise bestowed upon the Empress Eugénie. I had a distinctly "good Press," and to that fact I attribute the success of the work, a French edition of which will be issued by the eminent Paris firm of Pierre Lafitte et Cie. The written words of Napoleon III., hurriedly jotted down at the hazard of the pen on his way from Sedan to Wilhelmshöhe; of General Fleury by the side of the captive; of the Empress, and those about her, addressed to Mgr. Goddard—all these documents, it was agreed by the Press, threw new light upon the period of the Second Empire.

One of several appreciative American critics did not appear quite satisfied with the evidence authenticating the Empress's "Case," the elaborate statement justifying Her Majesty's severely-criticized political and domestic acts. If any doubt existed on that point I will now remove it. The assertions contained in that document were indeed those of the Empress herself, and would never have been published without her express approval and sanction.

Sovereigns who have been traduced do not "rush into print" with signed denials of accusations published to their discredit. They adopt other means of repelling attacks upon their honour, and sometimes upon their morality. Thus, the Emperor Napoleon, during his captivity at Wilhelmshöhe, wrote with his own hand a detailed explanation of his policy as the Ruler of France. It would not have been convenable—not in accordance with his dignity or with the rigid etiquette which guides Sovereigns even in their most trivial actions—for the Emperor (who had not then been formally deposed) to have issued that statement with his signature appended to it. The Duc de Persigny refused to "father" the document, and it was sent forth as "by the Marquis de Gricourt," although, as General Count von Monts assures us, the Emperor was the actual author of the pamphlet,[1] and gave the

---

[1] This has been confirmed by M. Émile Ollivier in the "Revue des Deux Mondes"

General a copy of it. Some extracts from the Emperor's "Case" are printed in the present volume.

The Emperor's letters to the late Comtesse de Mercy-Argenteau display the workings of his mind during the crisis of his life as only intimate correspondence could do. This gifted and charming woman's letters to Napoleon III. are in the Empress's possession, and will probably, like all other correspondence, remain unpublished "until fifty years after Her Majesty's death." The Emperor's letters came into the possession of Herr Paul Linderberg, of Berlin, by whose kindness I am privileged to print them in this volume.

English people who had held the Emperor in holy horror took a different view of him when they made his personal acquaintance. Lady Westmorland, for instance, "had always felt a great antipathy for Napoleon III.; to her he was a clever 'scoundrel.' In 1863 her son was a guest at Compiègne, and there he became seriously ill. She went over to bring him home, and not only did she acknowledge the Emperor's kindness, she was won by his personal charm, and recognized, as Queen Victoria had done, the evidence of his high-bred instinct: 'He tried to put others at their ease, and he is always himself a perfect gentleman.'"[2]

The Emperor, who lavished millions of francs upon others, was himself very economical. The bills of his fournisseurs show that he had his hats done up for four francs and his coats for fourteen francs. "Napoleon III.," says M. André Lefèvre, "entering France with one or two million francs of debts, left it with twenty, thirty, or fifty millions owing to France.... We must not allow even the mummy of Chislehurst to sleep in peace." A beautiful sentiment, essentially French.

I have essayed, with the help of others, to paint the Pale Emperor as he was, and the Empress as *she* was, and is, and Paris Society as it was. Of those who knew both, some will agree, others will disagree, with me; but it is not for this little coterie that I write. I write for the English-speaking peoples all over the world.

As in my first volume, "The Empress Eugénie: 1870-1910," the object primarily aimed at was to narrate the lives of the Imperial Family in England, I was precluded from dwelling upon the Reign. In the following pages I have endeavoured to portray some aspects of the Court and of Paris Society between 1852 and 1870. These are necessarily only bird's-eye views; brief, however, as are these parts of the imperial story, I hope they will convey an idea of the real life of the period. It was very gay—not a doubt about it. Was it an "orgy"? One can hardly think so. Everything was New. To the severe critics—the "sea-green incorruptibles"—the Emperor was an "adventurer," the Empress an "adventuress," Society "rotten."

The descriptions of Fontainebleau and Compiègne are mainly derived from a work by M. Bouchot,[3] whose encyclopædic knowledge is only equalled by his fascinating style. Other details of life at Compiègne are from the brilliant pen of the Marquis de Massa, whose unexpected death in 1910 robbed Paris Society of one of

---

(1911).

[2] "Quarterly Review," April, 1910.

[3] "Les Élégances du Second Empire." Par Henri Bouchot. Paris: À la Librairie Illustrée. 1896.

its wittiest and most delightful figures. (The Marquis furnished the Imperial Theatre at Compiègne with many humorous saynètes, and was in great favour with the Emperor and the Empress.) From a lecture delivered in 1910 by the Marquis,[4] and from his entertaining and always reliable "Souvenirs," I have selected some amusing items. The telegrams sent by the Emperor and Empress in August, 1870, form a history of the war up to the eve of Sedan. These despatches are taken from the fifth volume of M. Germain Bapst's remarkable historical work, "Le Maréchal Canrobert," the eminent publishers of which, MM. Plon-Nourrit et Cie., have very generously authorized me to reproduce them. M. Bapst's running commentary on the dissensions of the Generals, Ministers, and politicians is deeply interesting, and I have quoted largely from it, convinced that it will be as fresh to English as it was to French readers. The picture of the Empress, so vividly sketched by M. Bapst, reveals her in a new light. Although critics are against me, I hazard the assertion that throughout that month of August she displayed most of the qualities of a competent Regent—qualities possessed by no other Empress or Queen of the period, with the single exception of Queen Victoria. But she strove to accomplish the impossible. No human power could convert inept Generals into strategists and tacticians, nor double the strength of the French forces, nor remedy the defects of organization. Every factor that makes for success was lacking, or we should not have a distinguished French soldier writing in 1910:

> The authors of most of the works inspired by the war of 1870 have too willingly yielded to the temptation of looking for the guilty, and fixing them with the blame for all our reverses. In turn they have chosen for scapegoats the Emperor Napoleon III., that dreamer, straying into the field of politics, that idéologue, punished in excess of his faults by the pitiless decrees of destiny; Marshal Lebœuf, so fatally lacking in foresight; the Corps Législatif, so badly inspired in its contests with Marshal Niel; the Generals who succeeded each other in the command of our troops, from MacMahon to Bourbaki; and, finally, the Government of National Defence, especially its Delegates. How few have recognized the fact that the French army and our rulers in 1870-71 were purely and simply, with their qualities and their defects, the representation, the faithful image, of the nation![5]

It was a Frenchman, again, who wrote: "The German schoolmaster was the real conqueror of France in 1870, for he it was who had for years developed in the hearts of the children the idea of Teutonic greatness."[6]

I recall, without in any way endorsing, a quaint reason seriously advanced for the French defeats: "Don't blame your late Emperor because the Germans thrashed you; the cause lies far deeper: it is due to the sneakishness of your male

[4] "La Cour des Tuileries" (Conférence prononcée à la Société des Conférences le 17 janvier, 1910). Paris: "La Revue Hebdomadaire" (Plon), 1910. "Mes Souvenirs et Impressions." Par le Marquis de Massa. Paris: Calmann-Lévy.

[5] General Palat, author of "La Guerre de 1870-1871," completed in October, 1910. In seventeen volumes. Paris and Nancy: Levrault et Cie.

[6] Péladan, the "Figaro," March 19, 1910.

population."[7]

Quite recently I read in the Press that only two or three days before the outbreak of war Count Bismarck declared that he had no idea there would be a conflict. If he really said so (I do not credit it), he spoke in a very different strain in January, 1868, to a prominent German socialist. "War," he is alleged to have said, "is inevitable." And he continued:

> It will be forced upon us by the French Emperor. I say that clearly. He is an adventurer, and will be forced into it. We have to be ready. *We are ready.* We shall win, and the result will be just the contrary to what Napoleon aims at—the total unification of Germany outside Austria, and probably Napoleon's downfall.[8]

That prediction—assuming it to have been made—was fulfilled to the letter. Germany was ready—France was not. It is to be noted that M. Émile Ollivier's new volume—the fifteenth!—is devoted to this question of preparedness or unpreparedness, for the work is entitled "Were we Ready?"[9] The veteran Prime Minister (the last) of Napoleon III. deals with three points—the military preparations, the diplomatic preparations, and the first war operations, down to the morning of August 6 (before the Battles of Wörth and Spicheren):

> The conclusion is that, from the military point of view, we were sufficiently ready to conquer, and that, despite formal promises, no alliance was concluded by August 6. Finally, that if, from July 31 until August 6, we had adopted a vigorous offensive on the side of the River Sarre [*i.e.*, at Saarbrücken] we should have gained that first victory which would have changed the conditions of the struggle.

This will strike many as a splendidly-audacious proposition; yet it is neither audacious nor new. The two hours' fighting at Saarbrücken on August 2 was entirely to the advantage of the French force (overwhelmingly superior in numbers) under Frossard; but the "victory" was not followed up, and thus proved wholly fruitless. M. Ollivier is, therefore, entitled to this expression of opinion, over-sanguine as some war critics may deem it; and his view must be received with respect, even by those who differ from it.

The "great years" of the Reign were 1855, when Queen Victoria and the Prince Consort (the Princess Royal and the Prince of Wales with them) returned the visit paid to them by the Emperor and Empress of the French; and 1867, when "all the Sovereigns" were the guests of the imperial pair. The events of the latter year were brilliantly and amusingly recorded by that most vivacious chronicler, M. Adrien Marx, in "Les Souverains à Paris,"[10] from which I have translated some salient passages.

---

[7] Author of an article on French Children in "Blackwood's Magazine," December, 1871.

[8] "Reminiscences of Carl Schurz." London: John Murray. 1909.

[9] "Etions-nous prêts?" Par Émile Ollivier. Tome XV. Paris: Garnier. 1911.

[10] Paris: E. Dentu. 1868.

In "L'Impératrice Eugénie,"[11] one of M. Pierre de Lano's vigorous and much "documented" works relating to the Second Empire, there are to be found many tableaux vivants of the epoch—mordant pages, glowing with colour, of that "Exotic" society which, more than aught else, tended to bring the Second Empire into disrepute; and impressions of the imperial lady which are nothing if not frank and unconventional. The extracts which I have made from M. de Lano's valuable work cannot fail to be appreciated by impartial readers, who, perhaps, will be startled by the audacity of this highly-original and exceptionally-gifted author.

Two recently-issued works—one by M. Irénée Mauget,[12] the other by M. Gaston Stiegler[13]—strongly appealed to me. To the first I am indebted for some diverting material; to the second for the delightful picture of the Emperor intime in the early days of the Reign and the grim story of the Orsini "attempt," into which M. Stiegler has infused a few deft touches of romanticism.

The "papers" of my valued friend Mgr. Goddard have again provided me with much material otherwise unobtainable, and have left me with a reserve for future use.

Immediately after the death of the Emperor Napoleon III. at Camden Place, Chislehurst, the Empress Eugénie permitted Mr. Albert Bruce-Joy to take a cast of the head of His Majesty. The sculptor later executed the bust. In June, 1911, at my request, Mr. Bruce-Joy courteously allowed a photograph of his beautiful work to be taken for reproduction in this volume. As the distinguished sculptor worked from the mask taken with his own hands, there can be no question of the perfect fidelity of the portrait. The Empress Eugénie has graciously accepted a photograph of the bust, which I had the honour of sending to Her Imperial Majesty in June.

On May 7, 1910, Queen Alexandra graciously allowed Mr. Bruce-Joy to take a cast of the features of King Edward VII.; and the sculptor's bust of our late beloved Sovereign was a prominent feature of the Royal Academy Exhibition in 1911. It was executed for Manchester University. Mr. Bruce-Joy's most recent work is a colossal bronze statue of the late Lord Kelvin.

Prince Roland Bonaparte has again been very generous in sending me some very finely executed photographs, for which I tender His Highness my respectful thanks. These are (1) H.R.H. Princess George of Greece, the Prince's only daughter (née Princesse Marie Bonaparte); (2) the deeply-regretted Marquise de Villeneuve-Esclapon (née Princesse Jeanne Bonaparte, Prince Roland's only sister); and (3) Prince Roland himself, in the costume of President of the Geographical Society of France. These photographs are primeurs. The portrait of the charming and gifted Consort of Queen Alexandra's nephew is particularly à propos, for Princess George was the solitary member of the House of Bonaparte present at the Coronation of King George V. as (with Prince George) a Royal guest.

I have to thank Messrs. Russell and Sons, Baker Street, for their kindness in

---

[11] Paris: Victor Havard. 1894. London and New York: Harper and Brothers.

[12] "L'Impératrice Eugénie." Paris: Sociétés des Publications Littéraires Illustrées. 1909.

[13] "Amours Tragiques de Napoléon III." Paris: Albin Michel. 1910.

specially preparing, and, allowing me to use in this volume, the beautiful picture showing the Empress Eugénie on board the royal yacht with our beloved King Edward, Queen Alexandra, and other Royal personages, when, in 1902, the late King reviewed the fleet. This is the only picture of the kind ever taken, and will be treasured as a souvenir of the affectionate relations between the Empress and the principal members of our Reigning House. Of the latter Messrs. Russell and Sons have taken hundreds of superb photographs during the last forty years.

In my quest for suitable portraits of the Second Empire period I have been greatly aided by that universally-popular lady, Mrs. Ronalds, who, with charming courtesy, placed her valuable collection of imperial, royal, and other photographs (all autograph) at my disposal. These include rare pictures of the Emperor Napoleon, the Empress Eugénie, and the Prince Imperial, enriched with their signatures. Unfortunately, I could only avail myself of this generous offer to a limited extent, for I have been confronted by an embarras des richesses. The portraits I selected are those of Mrs. Ronalds and her sister, Miss Josephine Carter. Of their beauty and esprit the chroniclers of the epoch speak in the most flattering terms. Mrs. Ronalds enjoyed the distinction of being a guest of their Imperial Majesties at the Tuileries.

Miss Carter represented "America" at the magnificent fancy-dress ball given in 1866 at the Ministère de la Marine. Other ladies appeared as "Europe," "Asia," and "Africa," and I have it on the authority of a surviving eye-witness of this notable fête that the costumes of the fair representatives of the "five" quarters of the globe were "gorgeous." Miss Carter was carried on a large platform by twelve of her compatriots dressed as Indians. She was seen reclining in a hammock suspended from two palm-trees. Her dress was artistically embroidered with emblems of the victorious Republic, and her corsage was studded with diamond stars. On her beautiful golden hair she wore a Phrygian cap. In the cortège of "America" were many charming American women, distinguished (as was "Maud") by "dead perfection." "Oceania" was represented.

I have been so fortunate as to obtain from the Vicomte de La Chapelle some exceptionally interesting reminiscences of Napoleon III. and the Prince Imperial, as well as a curious story of Marshal Bazaine. His father—one of the comparatively few survivors of the Bonapartist régime—was, as I well remember, one of the stanchest and most valued friends of the Emperor, who made him his political and literary collaborator and confidant. I have also to thank the Vicomte de La Chapelle for the portrait of his father (the venerable Comte de La Chapelle) and the picture of the Emperor on the field of Sedan.

The welcome co-operation of the Vicomte de La Chapelle—a popular figure in legal, City, and social circles—has enabled me to print a number of letters written by his aged father to the Emperor Napoleon. I have given an outline of the Comte de La Chapelle's career, and I will not dwell upon it further here except to say that he was the trusted and valued collaborator of the august Exile from 1871 until the unexpected happened on January 9, 1873. But I must mention the invaluable services which he rendered to Napoleon III. at a time when His Majesty did not know where to turn for money. I noticed this question in my previous volume,[14] and in proof of the correctness of my assertions quoted a letter written by the great house of "Barings," and published in the "Times," denying the absurd statements that they had invested immense sums on the Emperor's account. The accuracy of what I wrote in 1910 is now further confirmed by my valued friend the Comte de La Chapelle, whose letters to the Emperor on the subject of his financial embarrassment I am now privileged to make public. It was the Comte de La Chapelle who, by his influence, energy, and devotion to Napoleon III., succeeded in raising large sums for the personal use of the Emperor and to keep the Bonapartist cause going. The name of one of these generous helpers is very well known to me, and in the early seventies it was familiar to the commercial world generally. These letters form a most interesting chapter in the Emperor's amazing career.

The Comtesse Edmond de Pourtalès, with the most charming and kindly grace, sent me, at my earnest request, a very rare photograph of herself, taken in the later period of the imperial reign. The Empress Eugénie will, I am confident, be gratified at seeing the portrait of this great lady—the most lovely of all the belles dames who surrounded Her Imperial Majesty in the years of her splendour, and one of the very few surviving intimate friends of the still radiant châtelaine of Farnborough Hill.

The proprietors of the well-known and deservedly popular Paris illustrated paper, "Femina," have been exceedingly generous in this important matter of pictures. But for their good offices I could not have given the delightful and piquant portraits of the Empress Eugénie in various costumes, or the large picture of Her Imperial Majesty at La Malmaison, with portraits of M. Franceschini Pietri and Comte Joseph Primoli. Certain difficulties arose in the preparation of these historically valuable pictures, but these obstacles were overcome by the great goodwill and liberality of the proprietors of "Femina," to whom I shall always be grateful for their kindness.

During the Terrible Year a "Times" leader-writer took as his text for a powerful essay some extracts from the Reports of Colonel Stoffel, French Military Attaché at Berlin (1866-1870), to his Government; and in the course of his article he did not hesitate to assert that it was a puzzle how anyone who had read those documents could ever have dreamt of plunging France into a war with Prussia. After reading M. Franceschini's letters to Stoffel the puzzle would appear greater still were it not now, thanks to M. Émile Ollivier, matter of common knowledge that the Emperor and his Government were goaded into a declaration of war by the French Press and by the nation en masse. These letters (from which, by the great courtesy of the director of the "Revue de Paris," I have been able to give extracts) are in every way remarkable, but their main importance lies in the fact that they were written by M. Pietri. In 1866, as later, he was the mouthpiece of Napoleon III. When he wrote to Colonel Stoffel he expressed not only the Emperor's views, but his own. He shows us that Stoffel's opinions were highly valued by the Emperor and by Marshal Niel, then Minister of War. Both Sovereign and War Minister set special store upon the

---

[14] "The Empress Eugénie: 1870-1910." London: Harper and Brothers. New York: Charles Scribner's Sons. 1910.

Military Attaché's Reports. The Emperor could not hear too often from him. M. Pietri was always urging the Colonel to write. The Emperor dictated to M. Pietri questions which Stoffel was required to answer. The Prussians, in their campaign against Austria, in 1866, used the needle-gun for the first time in warfare, and M. Pietri sent Stoffel funds wherewith to purchase one of the new rifles for the Emperor. These lettres révélatrices are further remarkable for their ardent patriotism and wide knowledge of political and military affairs. It is hardly too much to say that in these epistles M. Franceschini Pietri shines as the Admirable Crichton of Bonapartism. Sometimes he is amusingly audacious and delightfully humorous, but always he is "the Emperor's man" to the backbone. With a few hundred of such letters it would be possible to construct a history of the Second Empire which only the publication of the Empress Eugénie's Memoirs could rival. And perhaps the Secretary's letters would be the more historically interesting of the two.

Proof-sheets of the chapter, "Prince Napoleon's Policy," were sent to His Imperial Highness's Secretary, M. Beneyton, and returned to me by that gentleman with his wonted courtesy. If I mention these incidents, it is simply to show that I have always taken the utmost pains to secure absolute accuracy in all which I have written concerning the Imperial Family. Similarly, I based my exposé of the forged "Mémoires de l'Impératrice Eugénie" on the written statements courteously furnished me by M. Franceschini Pietri in January, 1910.[15]

I have been honoured by the letter of M. Pietri conveying the Empress Eugénie's thanks, and also by these gracious communications:

SANDRINGHAM, NORFOLK,
June 29, 1911.

DEAR SIR,

I am commanded by Queen Alexandra to thank you very much for the excellent photograph of the Emperor Napoleon the Third's Bust, which Her Majesty is very glad to have.

Believe me,
Yours truly,
CHARLOTTE KNOLLYS.

PARIS. 10, AVENUE D'IÈNA,
30 juin, 1911.

CHER MONSIEUR,

J'ai recu votre aimable lettre du 27 ct., ainsi que la photographie du buste de l'Empereur Napoléon III. et les paragraphes sur la représentation de la Maison Bonaparte aux fêtes du couronnement de S.M. le Roi Georges V.

Je me suis empressé de remettre le tout à S.A.I. Monseigneur le Prince Roland Bonaparte, qui me charge de vous en remercier vivement, et de vous dire combien Elle a été sensible à cette délicate attention.

Veuillez agréer, cher Monsieur, l'expression de mes sentiments les plus distingués.

G. FAUSSEZ DES MARES.

TRANSLATION.

PARIS, 10, AVENUE D'IÈNA,
June 30, 1911.

DEAR SIR,

I have received your amiable letter of the 27th inst., and also the photograph of the bust of the Emperor Napoleon III. and the

---

[15] Vide "The Empress Eugénie: 1870-1910." London: Harper and Brothers. New York: Charles Scribner's Sons. 1910.

paragraphs referring to the representation of the House of Bona-parte at the Coronation fêtes of H.M. King George V.

I hastened to hand the whole to H.I.H. Monseigneur Prince Roland Bonaparte, who directs me to warmly thank you, and to tell you how sensible he is of your delicate attention.

Accept, dear sir, the expression of my most distinguished sentiments.

G. FAUSSEZ DES MARES.

I have selected for detailed treatment 1867. In that year the Emperor Napoleon and the Empress Eugénie entertained three Emperors, eight Kings, one Viceroy, five Queens, nine Grand Dukes, two Grand Duchesses, two Archdukes, twenty-four Princes, seven Princesses, five Dukes, and two Duchesses. The Prince of Wales (King Edward VII.), the Duke of Edinburgh, and the Duke of Connaught were of the party. While 1867 is generally considered to have been the "great year" of the Imperial Reign, M. Hanotaux[16] inclines to the opinion that "the climax of Napoleonic glory" came in November, 1869, when the Empress Eugénie inaugurated the Suez Canal—ten months before Sedan.

---

[16] "Contemporary France," by Gabriel Hanotaux. London: Constable. 1907.

CONTENTS

LIST OF ILLUSTRATIONS

CHAPTER I

THE EMPRESS'S GIRLHOOD

It is August, 1840, and from the balcony of the Delesserts' house a fair-complexioned, golden-haired girl of fourteen looks down on a man escorted by two gendarmes. Dishevelled, unkempt, in his shirtsleeves, the prisoner, who has been fished out of the salt water, passes out of sight, unaware of the child's wistful looks and the sympathetic glances of her sister and their mother. Perchance he sees Goldenhair wave her handkerchief.

Mme. Delessert's husband is Préfet of Paris. The ladies on the balcony are the Comtesse de Montijo and her daughters. The man in custody is Prince Louis Napoleon, the derided, but unabashed, hero of the Boulogne "attempt"; and he is two-and-thirty.

The daughters of the Comte and Comtesse de Montijo made their acquaintance with Paris when they were not more than four or five. It was about 1830 or 1831 when the family went to reside there for a while. Prosper Mérimée, whose name can no more be kept out of the history of the Empress than could Mr. Dick suppress the mention of King Charles's head, was there, and his friend of the British Museum, Dr. Panizzi, was kept informed of the strolls on the boulevards of the little Eugénie, and of her liking, not only for the author of the story of "Carmen," which Bizet was later to set to music, but for the sweets given to her by Mérimée.

The Montijos seem to have been then in only fairly easy circumstances. Three or four years later their fortunes improved, the head of the family having died.

Eugénie's education begins at a celebrated convent school, on whose books she figures as Eugénie Palafox, a name used by her for a score of years.

At the Sacré-Cœur, Rue de la Varenne, the little Montijo is supremely happy. Her holidays and those other days when she is allowed "out" she spends with her mother's friend, the Comtesse de Laborde, at a country house at Passy, where a park runs down to the Seine. Mme. de Laborde has promised Madame mère to make Eugénie's school life as pleasant as possible, and she fulfils her promise to the letter. The Comtesse de Laborde has three daughters, all well married, all charming mondaines: Mme. Delessert—who, as the wife of the Préfet, is a personage—Mme. Bocher, and Mme. Odiar. Eugénie is in the good graces of this captivating trio. But the lady to whom she is particularly attached is the Comtesse de Nadaillac, daughter of Mme. Delessert, and grand-daughter of the Comtesse de

Laborde.

At the age of eleven (in 1837) she makes the vows imposed upon communicants, in the stereotyped phrase, "La fille de la Comtesse de Téba (Montijo) fit sa première communion," in the chapel of the convent school. Soon—in March, 1839—there comes a hurried departure for Spain, whither her parents had returned a short time previously. Her father has died, and the child's Parisian "schooling" is over. For some little time before the loss of their father Eugénie and her eldest sister, Francisca, familiarly "Pacca," had been in the charge, in Paris, of an English governess, Miss Flowers,[17] who accompanied them to Madrid at the time of the Count's death. Mérimée wrote: "No one would credit the regret I feel at their departure" (from Paris). I will note only in passing that Eugénie's education was "finished" in this country at a school at Clifton, Bristol.

Having ceased to be a schoolgirl, the Señorita Eugénie de Montijo undergoes a transformation. She is, and for some years will remain, in her teens. At fifteen she is bewitching. In the saddle, what a charming and picturesque figure! Madrid has no such fearless rider. There is no particular evidence that now and then she gallops through the streets riding à califourchon; but legend has it so, and in this case legend may possibly not wholly err. In the forties she is heedless of criticism, perhaps because only her rivals can find it in their hearts to malign her. As yet she is not seen in the hunting-field. She little recks that ten years or so later she will be arousing the undisguised hostility of her sex at the imperial chasses at Compiègne.

The Señorita would hardly be Spanish were she not much in view when all Madrid foregathers at the bull-fights. Like her companions, she has her favourite toreadors, and is lavish of her rewards—gold and flowers. Matadors and picadors do her homage. She is coquette to her little finger-tips. A smile from that sunny face and a word from those rosebud lips are eagerly contended for, and she is not slow in according both. Meanwhile the élégants group themselves around her as thick as bees round the tulips and honeysuckles. In those Southern climes, if anywhere, flirtation is one of the fine arts. The Señorita Eugénie—"Ugenia" in her own language—is not the least ardent disciple of the genus flirt. She coquettes with this Duke and that Duke. He of Ossuna and he of Sesto (Alganices) are rivals. There is yet a third Duke—Alba—over whom she essays to cast a spell; but, alas! the course of true love is diverted—perhaps unconsciously—by Pacca, the beautiful sister, and she it is who becomes Duquesa. Around this episode of unrequited love how many "histories" have been woven, mostly apocryphal! "Ugenia," some would have us believe, resorts to what she thinks is a phial of poison, and awakes from her torpor to discover—oh, horror!—that she has swallowed a portion of the disgusting, but harmless, contents of a blacking-bottle!

No salon in Madrid was more frequented than the Comtesse de Montijo's. The daughters were not the only magnets. Madame mère was a woman of esprit, and had a genius for making friends and keeping them. "Theatricals" drew all Madrid to the house. Eugénie was seen in De Musset's "Caprice," with the enamoured Duc de Sesto in the cast. The summers—or a portion of them—were passed on the Montijo property at Carabanchel.

[17] This lady was at Chislehurst when, in 1873, the Emperor passed away.

Every great lady in Madrid has her circle of young and middle-aged men, known as "pollos"—literally, chickens. Among the Comtesse de Montijo's "pollos," all more or less smitten by the radiant Señorita Eugénie, was General Espartero's successful rival, General Narvaly, Duke of Valencia, short, dark, a stern soldier, as supple in the young lady's hands as the youngest and most impressionable of her "pollos." A lady well known in social London, the wife of a foreign diplomatist, and gifted with the pen of a ready writer, drew this somewhat caustic portrait of the future Empress when she was the most-discussed personage in Madrid:

> Hardly a week passed without some fresh anecdote being circulated of which Eugénie de Montijo was the heroine. She justified curiosity and courted censure by her disregard of conventionalities; and she certainly possessed the Alcibidian temperament which craves for notoriety. She wielded her sceptre of society queen with no light hand, and her favourites of to-day were discarded by to-morrow's caprice. In her own house she was seen devoting herself for the whole evening to the entertainment of some obscure musician, hanging on his arm, speaking to no one else, and finally dropping the curtains over a window recess to which she had led him; but the following week, if the poor infatuated wretch came confidently to bask in the intoxicating favour that had bewitched him, he was received with a supercilious arching of the lovely eyebrows. This idol could look at him as if he were a total stranger, and glide away from him with the coldest inclination of her head.

The variegated life of the Spanish girl who was destined to become Empress of the French—her life between the ages of fifteen and twenty-six—has never been, and never will be, described in detail. They were "Wanderjähre," years of travel, visits to modish Continental resorts, and one or two sojourns in England. Once, in the summer of 1851, she and her mother (but not "Pacca") attended a Court ball at Buckingham Palace—an incident which Queen Victoria may have recalled in one or other of her numerous meetings with the imperial lady, but not recorded by the Queen in her "Leaves" or her "Letters." The presence of the Spanish ladies among the Queen's guests was, however, noted in the official list, the compiler of which, or the printers, effectually mangled the names of both. A week later Lord Malmesbury saw them at Cambridge House, Piccadilly, the town residence of Viscount and Viscountess Palmerston, now, and for many years past, the Naval and Military Club. Mlle. de Montijo struck Lord Malmesbury as being "very handsome"; with the "flair" of a modern journalist, he noted her auburn hair and her "beautiful skin and figure." He would have earned our thanks had he given us the names of the social sponsors of the Montijos in London. It was our Great Exhibition year, and we may be certain that the ladies were among the hundreds of thousands who flocked to Paxton's huge glass palace in Hyde Park, the exact site of which is probably unknown to all but the fogies of 1911.[18]

[18] The Exhibition building was erected at the western end of the park, midway between Rotten Row and the Ladies' Mile.

A resort which found much favour with the mother and daughter was Eaux-Bonnes, in the Pyrenees. At the hotel honoured by their presence was an observant gentleman who for a full fortnight had the felicity of dining in the company of the fair Spaniards. He was therefore, according to one of his friends, who made attractive "copy" of it for a Belgian paper, able to "coldly study" the younger lady. "C'est une très belle et très jolie femme, qui tiendra fort bien sa place, attendu qu'elle a, comme on dit, le physique de l'emploi."[19]

---

[19] "She is a very beautiful woman, who will be well able to maintain her position, inasmuch as they say she is 'made for the part.'"

CHAPTER II
THE BOYHOOD AND YOUTH OF NAPOLEON III

FEW English readers are, I imagine, familiar with the boyhood and the adolescence of Napoleon III., whose centenary fell on April 20, 1908. It is true that Blanchard Jerrold has given us, in his "Life of the Emperor" (four volumes, published in 1874 by Longmans), an admirable and detailed history of the unfortunate Sovereign who drew his last breath at Chislehurst in 1873; but, perhaps owing to the abundance of other material officially placed at his disposal, Mr. Jerrold devoted only a few lines to the eight years during which Philippe Le Bas was the tutor of the future Emperor.

Luckily, M. Stéfane-Pol has recently produced a volume of the greatest value, entitled "La Jeunesse de Napoléon III.,"[20] containing the hitherto unpublished correspondence of the Prince's tutor, Philippe Le Bas (of the Institut), with many original illustrations, some from the Prince's own pencil, others by Queen Hortense and by artists familiar with Arenenberg.

"Prince Louis Bonaparte," wrote Alphonse Karr, in "Les Guêpes," "born in Paris in 1808, educated abroad, knew neither France nor its ways. He spoke our language with difficulty, with a very strong German accent. His early youth has left no souvenir, even in the mind of his most complaisant biographers."

Even his partisans confine themselves to generalities, stupidly inaccurate. "Although far from France," says M. Stéfane-Pol, "we read in a contemporary publication describing the coup d'état, 'the education of the young Louis Napoleon Bonaparte was entirely French. His mother imbued him with a love of his natal land, and his father taught him, at an early age, to sacrifice everything—life, honours, and fortune—for the holy and sacred cause of the people; taught him, too, to dare and to suffer all things for the triumph of such great interests. Later, his parents, in order to complete his education, confided him to the care of M. Le Bas, son of the Conventionnel of that name, from whom the Prince acquired the wisest and most solid Republican principles.'"

Charles Louis Napoleon Bonaparte, youngest son of Louis Bonaparte, King of Holland, and of Hortense de Beauharnais, was born on April 20, 1808. He was Napoleon I.'s nephew, and the Empress Joséphine's grandson. He was baptized at the Palace of Fontainebleau by Cardinal Fesch, uncle of Napoleon I., and held at the font by the Great Emperor himself. In the *Moniteur* of April 21 his birth was thus chronicled:

---

[20] Paris: Félix Juven.

Yesterday (Wednesday) Her Majesty the Queen of Holland was happily delivered of a Prince. In conformity with Article XL. of the Act of the Constitutions of the 20 Florial, year XII., his Serene Highness Monseigneur the Prince Arch-Chancellor of the Empire was present at the birth. His Highness wrote immediately to His Majesty the Emperor and King, to Her Majesty the Empress and Queen, and to His Majesty the King of Holland, informing them of the event. At 5 p.m. the certificate of birth was received by His Serene Highness the Prince Arch-Chancellor, assisted by His Excellency M. Régnault de St. Jean d'Angély, Minister of State and Secretary of the Imperial Family. In the absence of His Majesty the Emperor and King, the infant did not receive any Christian name; this he will be given by a later act, in accordance with His Majesty's orders.

Napoleon I. and Joséphine had been divorced previous to the birth of the child, whose godmother was Marie Louise, Napoleon's second consort. At the time of his birth the parents of the future Napoleon III. were living apart. "I am sorry Louis is not here," said the mother; "this infant would have reconciled us."

It was said that the King of Holland was not the father of the young Louis Napoleon.[21] It is difficult, however, to adduce proofs of that assertion. There is one fact concerning which there is general agreement. There was no physical or moral resemblance between the brother of Napoleon I. and the son of Hortense de Beauharnais. The infant had neither the face nor the character of the Bonapartes; on the contrary, he was the image of his mother, whose large heart, as well as many other characteristics, he inherited. Ambition and superstition were the principal features of the life of Queen Hortense. "She inspired her son," said Henri Martin, "with a fanatical faith in his destiny," and circumstances developed in both mother and son a firm belief in their lucky star. With the exception of the King of Rome, Louis Napoleon was the only Prince born under the imperial régime—the only one whose birth was greeted by military honours and the people's homage. Was not that (asks M. Stéfane-Pol) a presage of his destiny? A family register, devoted to the children of the imperial dynasty, was deposited at the Senate as the grand-livre of the right of succession. The name of Prince Louis was the first to be inscribed in it, with all the pomp of a consecration. What better auspices could there have been for an aspirant Emperor?

Later, when the Duchesse de Saint-Leu (Queen Hortense), mother of Prince Louis Napoleon, occupied the leisure afforded her by her exile in roaming through Switzerland with Mlle. Cochelet, she had no object in view except that which chance offered. "All our distractions during these wanderings," wrote Mlle. Cochelet, "were confined to searching for four-leaved shamrocks, to which were attached various ideas. 'If,' said the Duchesse, 'I find a four-leaved shamrock, it will signify that we shall return to France before very long, or that I shall receive a letter from my son to-morrow,' and so on." The author does not add, "Or perhaps I shall

---

[21] The King himself is asserted to have declared that "not a drop of Bonaparte blood flowed in the boy's veins."

reign through my son," but that is implied in most of the wishes of the ex-Queen of Holland.

In 1834 Louis Napoleon and his mother travelled in Italy. They had been in Rome for some time, when one day Hortense consulted a negress, a somnambulist, who, according to M. de La Guéronnière, had produced some remarkable phenomena. A clever magnetizer sent the negress to sleep, and presently, in response to the eager questions of Hortense, the somnambulist exclaimed suddenly, as if inspired, "I see your son happy and triumphant. A great nation takes him for chief." "For Emperor, you mean, do you not?" asked the mother breathlessly. "For chief," replied the somnambulist. Hortense could not obtain from the negress anything more satisfactory, but the prediction was confirmed subsequently by what the doyen of Paris priests said to Louis Napoleon, then President of the Republic: "Monseigneur, the will of God will be fulfilled quand même."

Louis Napoleon was imbued with all his mother's superstitious ideas. One of his friends having asked him why the attempt at Strasburg had failed, the Prince smilingly furnished an explanation which doubtless accorded with his fatalistic instincts—a wheel of his carriage had come off between Lehr and Strasburg! But his instincts required guiding, and Hortense was not equal to the task. While she was making lint for the wounded and weaving patriotic romances to cheer the faint-hearted, the mother of the future Emperor (then Queen of Holland) inculcated in the young Louis those bellicose ideas which were quite foreign to his calm and dreamy nature. "Supposing you had not a sou in the world to call your own," she said to her eldest boy one day, "what would you do, Napoleon, to gain a livelihood?" "I should go for a soldier," was the reply. "And you, Louis, what would you do?" "I should sell violets, like the little boy who stands at the gates of the Tuileries," answered the child whom Destiny had marked out for an Emperor. There was something in this boy's character to reform, and his mother set about the task, invoking the aid of all around her—amongst them Napoleon I. and Mme. Bure, the faithful nurse, who was jealous of the attention bestowed upon the boy by Mme. de Boubers and the Abbé Bertrand.

Henceforward the young Louis made considerable progress. Although he was always extremely sensitive, he longed to share the dangers of others. Renault, imitating Mlle. Cochelet, tells this story of him:

> At this time Prince Louis Napoleon was seven years old. One day, on the eve of the departure for that fatal campaign which, after two striking victories, ended with the disaster of Waterloo, Napoleon I., accompanied by Marshal Soult, entered his cabinet. He appeared sad and thoughtful. The tones of his voice, sharp and emphatic, revealed the preoccupation of his mind. Suddenly a child slips into the room. His features are stamped with grief, and he vainly struggles to restrain his emotion. He approaches, kneels before the Emperor, and, laying his head and hands on Napoleon's knees, bursts into tears.
>
> "What is the matter with you, Louis?" exclaims the Emperor,

in a tone showing his annoyance at being interrupted. "Why have you come here? Why are you crying?"

The child, frightened, can only reply with sobs. By degrees he becomes calm, and then, in a sweet, sad voice, says: "Sire, my governess has just told me that you are leaving for the war. Oh! do not go—do not go!"

The Emperor could not but be touched by this solicitude, for the child was Prince Louis, the nephew whom he loved above all others.

"And why do you wish me not to go?" asked the Emperor sadly. Then, passing his hand through the child's golden curls, he said: "Mon enfant, it is not the first time that I go *to the war*. Why should it trouble you? Never mind; I shall soon return."

"Oh, my dear uncle," said the boy, again bursting into tears, "those wicked Allies want to kill you! Oh, *uncle, let me go with you!*"

For a time the Emperor did not speak. Taking the child on his knee, he pressed him to his heart and embraced him warmly. The Emperor was deeply moved, but presently, when he had steadied his voice, he called, "Hortense! Hortense!" And as the Queen came hurrying into the room, Napoleon said: "Here, take my nephew out and give his governess a severe scolding for thoughtlessly putting such words into his mouth and exalting his sensibility." Then, after addressing the boy affectionately, the Emperor, turning to Marshal Soult, who was labouring under deep emotion, said vivaciously: "Embrace him—he will have a good heart and a beautiful soul. He may be the hope of my race."

Hortense must have relished these last words. Are not great captains regarded as oracles? When, at Paris, as at St. Leu, some of the visitors discussed metaphysics, or grouped themselves around La Bédoyère, reading Racine or Shakespeare; when others posed to Garnerey for their portraits, and others played billiards, Louis Napoleon and his brother listened open-mouthed to the tales of heroism which Mlle. Cochelet was instructed to tell them. Later, in the land of exile, while the Duchesse de St. Leu and her suite played diabolo—one room serving as salon and salle à manger—and when the only book at their disposal was a volume of "Anecdotes de la Cour de Philippe-Auguste," discovered, after a long search, by the Abbé Bernard, the ex-Queen of Holland would watch her sons playing at soldiers with the common children. And the day came when she saw Louis at the military school of Thün learning how to command, and then at Rome, at the house of his grandmother, Lætitia Bonaparte—scenes which enabled her to record the story of Prince Louis Napoleon's youth.

The character of the Prince, according to Mlle. Cochelet, was amiable, timid, self-contained. He spoke very little, and Le Bas (his tutor) adds that he was naturally distrait and inactive. Thus he always remained. Those who most flattered

Napoleon III. never concealed, in rhetorical phrases, the evident inertness of his physical nature; morally, he was a docile slave.

> His look of inertness and apparent insensibility is only the mark of an ardent and powerful inner life. His eyes are dull, but they are as deep as the thought in which they are plunged, which appears now and again as the flame leaps from the hearth. His forehead is as sombre as fate, but it is large, like its conception. The lips are white, but fine, delicate, discreet, only sufficiently opened to allow of the escape of sharp and precise expressions of a reflecting and ordered will. His speech is indolent and slow, but he is sure of himself, and his apparent indifference is but the excess of his self-confidence. Audacity veiled by timidity, firmness dissimulated by mildness, inflexibility compensated for by goodness, finesse concealed by bonhomie, life under the marble, fire beneath the cinders—in a word, something of Augustus and of Titus under the look of Werther, that type of German dreaminess: such was the appearance of Louis Bonaparte.[22]

M. de La Guéronnière finds, in this portrait which he gives of the Prince, a justification for the various appreciations formulated of his mind and character. But do we not see, on the contrary, in the portrait a simple play of antitheses, a fantastic interpretation of that which appeared to be the evident reality?—which is to say that Louis Napoleon was a young man of average intelligence, without mental unbending, and characterized by an absolute lack of willpower. Like all who hesitate and dream, he finished by attaching an idea to himself and adopting it, in order not to be submerged by other ideas. Thus he deserved the title of "doux entêté" given to him by his mother. But his impassiveness, his stiffness, were only timidity, and his resolutions to act showed themselves only after delays or with sudden coups, which emphasized his weakness.

He had doubtless a certain fatalistic power of resistance, but this side of his character only showed the absence of an active mind; the enterprises of Stratford and Boulogne do not contradict this view. As to the coup d'état, one might explain it by many causes foreign to a ripe will. Besides, was not the coup d'état predicted by the "Grand Albert," and did not that prediction give the rein to the superstitious docility of Louis Napoleon Bonaparte?[23]

However this may be, whatsoever his faults may have been, we must recognize in him who was Napoleon III. one quality: he had a heart. Even his adversaries knew this, and some of them—those who were sincere—admitted it with a good grace. The words of Georges Sand, written when the Prince was a prisoner in the fortress of Ham, would have remained true if events, stronger than his apparent energy, had not let loose against him hatreds at once tenacious and justified. "Two or three of us," she wrote, "often talk about you, and we always say, after

---

[22] M. de La Guéronnière.

[23] At the Bibliothèque Nationale there is an interpretation of the "Prédiction Miraculeuse du Grand Albert sur Louis Napoléon Bonaparte," published two years before December 2, 1851 (the date of the coup d'état).

recognizing the dangers which would follow your accession to power of any kind, 'He possesses the gift of making himself loved; it is impossible not to love him.'"

Le Bas, who knew the Prince better than anyone else, speaks of his excellent heart, and quotes examples of the sensitiveness and the generous instincts of him whom his mother and the Abbé Bertrand long called "notre petit oui-oui."

The character of the child reflects, in an exaggerated form, the qualities and the defects of those by whom he was surrounded. It is sufficient to peruse the letters of the Abbé Bertrand to understand the lightness and the inconsistency which vitiated the education of the future Emperor Napoleon III. The Republican Le Bas, on the contrary, enunciated more severe, and at the same time more generous, ideas, which his pupil transmitted into Utopian reveries. Later, the Prince's initiation into military studies gave him a taste for the profession of arms, and inspired him with the secret hope of continuing, by modifying and even socializing it, the work of Napoleon I.

The docility of the child bent under the influence of his preceptors, as it had previously given way under that of his mother and the intimates of the household. But, besides this, the fashionable life, the soirées, the concerts, the drawing-room theatricals, and the organization of lotteries, as well as the excessive walks and drives, disarranged the carefully-elaborated programmes of education, so that the personality of Prince Louis could not prevail against the numerous changes of scene, to say nothing of the drawbacks to study caused by the life in exile and the uncertainty of what might happen at any moment.

It would be a curious study to examine the writings of Napoleon III., and to ascertain who amongst those by whom he was surrounded in his youth inspired him with the thoughts which he has put into his book, "Idées Napoléoniennes." That work, his essays on military subjects, and his "Extinction de Paupérisme," all reveal the accurate memory of the former pupil of the camp of Thün, and show how well he recollected the lessons of Le Bas and the advice of the ambitious Hortense, while they also give evidences of that futility for which the Abbé Bertrand was to some extent responsible.

"Slave of the souvenirs of his childhood," wrote the Emperor, "the man obeys all his life, without doubting them, the impressions which he received when he was young, and the experiences and influences of which he has been the object."[24]

If (concludes M. Stéfane-Pol) circumstances had not been stronger than the free-will of Napoleon III., those impressions, experiences, and influences, many and various as they were, would never have brought about the unheard-of metamorphosis of a man of heart and delicacy, if not of reason, until popular sentiment, refusing to analyze him in order to arrive at a result, finished by execrating him.

---

[24] "Idées Napoléoniennes."

CHAPTER III

FROM LONDON TO HAM VIÂ BOULOGNE

BETWEEN 1839 and 1848 Prince Louis Napoleon (allowing for the six years which he spent at Ham) resided mostly, if not entirely, in London. In the first part of those years—on his arrival here from Switzerland, which he had left under pressure of Louis Philippe's Government—he lodged at Fenton's Hotel, St. James's Street,[25] soon removing to Carlton Terrace, Pall Mall. In 1846, upon his escape from Ham and his return to London (May 27), he stayed for a while at the Brunswick Hotel, Jermyn Street; then changed his quarters to King Street, St. James's, where he was living when he acted as a special constable during the Chartist riots.[26] From King Street he wrote (February 15, 1847) to a friend, M. Vieillard:

> For the last fortnight I have been installed in a new house, and for the first time in seven years I enjoy the pleasure of being at home. I have assembled here all my books, my albums, and family portraits—in a word, all the precious objects which have escaped shipwreck. The portrait of the Emperor, by Paul Delaroche, is very fine. This generous present has given me great pleasure, and forms the most beautiful ornament of my salon.

An intimate friend of the Prince (the pseudonymous "Baron d'Ambès") asserts that Louis Napoleon "left Lord Cardigan's house to occupy Lord Ripon's, Carlton Gardens. He did not lose by the change."[27] His drawing-rooms were "full of glorious souvenirs and sacred relics. There were portraits of the Emperor, the Empress, and Queen Hortense; the ring of the 'crowning'; the ring worn by Napoleon I. at his marriage with Joséphine; the tricolour cashmere scarf which he wore at the Battle of the Pyramids; the portraits of all the members of the imperial family; the famous talisman of Charlemagne, found in his tomb at Aix-la-Chapelle, and sent to Napoleon by the cathedral clergy in 1804; a medallion with two portraits, painted by Isabey; and other marvels, doubly dear to him who religiously preserves them."

The Prince drove or rode every day. His cabriolet, driven by himself, soon became familiar in the West End; in the Ladies' Mile it was much remarked, for the Prince soon made a number of friends, well-known men and pretty élégantes,

[25] The site of the Royal Societies Club, which (1911) numbers among its members a Bonaparte (Prince Roland).

[26] The Prince is also said to have had lodgings at one time at Waterloo Place.

[27] "Mémoires inédits sur Napoléon III." Par le Baron d'Ambès; Recueillis et Annotés par Charles Simond et M. C. Poinsot. Paris: Société des Publications Littéraires Illustrées.

some of whom were to be seen at Lady Blessington's. "In London he visited only important personages. He was an assiduous frequenter of the libraries, and a good customer of the booksellers. He now (1840) published his volume, 'Les Idées Napoléoniennes,' a résumé of that programme of democratic empire which he always upheld."

About this time De Persigny appeared among the authors. His "book" was a very small one, but it was read in Paris by everybody, for it was a cleverly-written account of a "visit to Prince Louis" (it was so entitled). It was published anonymously, but people soon gave a name to it. De Persigny, it seems, had read Vertot's "Révolutions Romaines" (a favourite book of Napoleon I.), and discovered a parallel between Prince Louis, nephew of Napoleon, and Octavius, grandnephew of Julius Cæsar. De Persigny's work touched the Prince, whose hopes were revived by its emotional passages.

Louis Napoleon's attempts—first at Strasburg in 1836, and next at Boulogne in 1840—to arouse France to a sense of his merits were signal failures, so farcical as to cover him with ridicule in a country where that defect is popularly supposed to "kill." He was a laughing-stock, yet he survived both contempt and obloquy, to say nothing of six years' imprisonment. In the Strasburg plot the Prince was assisted by a lady (of the same age as himself) who called herself Mrs. Gordon, and who was born Bruault-Eléonore Bruault. She had been a singer, and had received lessons in Paris from Rossini. Some time in the year 1836, beautiful and poor, she was in London, where she came in contact with De Persigny, who probably introduced her to the Prince. After the fiasco at Strasburg she was quick enough to burn all compromising documents before the police could seize them. Moreover, she contrived to get De Persigny, disguised as a cook, out of the town. He reached London safely, and narrated the story of the "attempt" in a pamphlet published in London and in Paris. Fleury joined De Persigny in London; they shared lodgings, belonged to the same club, and were presently joined by the Marquis de Gricourt.[28]

For his attempt to make the troops at Strasburg mutiny in his favour Louis Napoleon was deported to America, where he arrived on March 30, 1837, after a long voyage, which he fully described in letters to his mother. At New York, on the evening of his arrival, the Prince dined with two American Generals, his brothers-in-law, and others, and later met his cousins, Achille and Lucien Murat and Pierre Bonaparte. Achille Murat was employed at the post-office; Lucien was married to a school-mistress; Prince Pierre was leading a gay life. The illness of Prince Louis' mother brought him back from the United States. He reached London on July 10, 1837, and, by means of a passport borrowed from a Mr. Robinson, got to Arenenberg early in August, after frequently evading the Continental police. Queen Hortense died on October 5, consoled in her last moments by her son's presence and Dr. Conneau's promise that he would never leave him.[29]

One night in the first week of August, 1840, the walls of Boulogne-sur-Mer

---

[28] The nominal author of a remarkable pamphlet written at Wilhelmshöhe by Napoleon III.

[29] This promise Conneau kept. He shared the Prince's captivity at Ham, and heard the last words Spoken by Napoleon III. on January 9, 1873: "Etiez-vous à Sedan?"

were placarded with proclamations signed "Napoleon." These "posters," which had been printed in London, were headed respectively, "To the French People," "To the Army," and "To the Inhabitants of the Department of the Pas de Calais" (Boulogne, of course, included). The "proclamations," couched in very lofty terms, aroused no enthusiasm, but much merriment; they were really as amusing as anything in "Charivari." "Soldats, aux armes! Vive la France!"—so ended the appeal to the troops.

Then, on the same wall, the Boulogne burgesses stared their hardest at a "Decree" which they read without a thrill. "Prince Napoleon, in the name of the French people, decrees as follows: The Dynasty of the Bourbons-d'Orléans has ceased to reign" (excusez du peu!) "The French people has entered into its rights. The troops are relieved from their oath of fidelity;" with much more similar rhodomontade. Without a tremor—doubtless with many a wink—Boulogne read that M. Thiers was appointed President of the Provisional Government, and that all who showed energetically their sympathy for "the national cause" would be recompensed "in a striking manner" in the name of the country! One would like to have seen the faces of the conspirators when the "proofs" of these grandiloquent pronunciamientos were taken to Carlton Terrace. How unenterprising of the *Times*, the *Herald*, and the *Post* not to have obtained early copies! Nor could those journals have suspected that the Prince between times—between gallivanting at Lady Blessington's, riding one of his two saddle-horses (there were three others) in the Row, and "beating the town"—the aspiring, talented, and pertinacious Nephew of the Uncle, had devoted himself to the onerous task of "developing his programme"—

1. Alliance of the Empire and the Democracy.
2. Free Trade.
3. The Principle of Nationalities.

All admirable ideas, and all to be carried out one day, but not by entreating Strasburg troops to mutiny, or by "landings" at Boulogne-sur-Mer.

The Boulogne expedition was planned at Carlton Terrace in June, 1840. A steamer, the *Edinburgh Castle*, was purchased for the Prince, ostensibly for the use of "some gentlemen who wanted to cruise on the Scottish coast" (the name of the good ship seemed not altogether inappropriate). Guns were bought at Birmingham. Uniforms were brought over from the "Temple," in Paris—all but the buttons; these were bought in London, and sewn on by Dr. Conneau! "Servants" were imported from France; they had all served in the army.

Between August 3 and August 5 the *Edinburgh Castle* made four trips to Boulogne. On the night of the 5th the vessel was anchored off Wimereux. All told, the imperial force numbered sixty-two, including thirty ex-soldiers (the "servants"). Ammunition, money, and horses were all taken safely across the Channel. And there was a live Eagle, symbolizing the return of "the other." Money had been offered to the douaniers, who scorned the proffered bribes—a bad omen. The audacious conspirators went through Boulogne, shouting "Vive l'Empereur!" They tried to get the 42nd Line Regiment to "rise," but the honest fellows turned deaf ears to the charmers. A detachment of that regiment attacked the conspirators.

The Prince wanted to die at the foot of the Column of the Grande Armée, after "running-up" the imperial flag, but he was dragged away. Pursued by a handful of the National Guard, the conspirators took to their heels and made for the beach. The Prince and some of his friends jumped into the sea, hoping to regain "the lugger." They were "shot down like ducks." One was fatally wounded, another was drowned, others were badly hit. It was said that a bullet grazed the Prince "without hurting him." Louis Napoleon, De Persigny, Dr. Conneau, and Mésonan were picked up by gendarmes, dragged into a boat, and taken to prison.

These things happened on August 6. On the 7th, in the afternoon, the *Moniteur* published a statement, signed by the War Minister, Cubières, that the conspirators had been "driven into the waves, which vomited them up again. Louis Napoleon and all his adherents have been captured, killed, or drowned." The Prince, on the 9th, was taken from the château at Boulogne to the fortress of Ham. On the 12th he arrived in Paris in a carriage, escorted by departmental gendarmes and men of the Municipal Guard. He was kept, until his trial, in the strong-room of the Conciergerie, three gaolers never leaving him. Even his valet, Charles Thélin, was not allowed to see his forlorn, but not dejected, master.

While the Prince was under lock and key his ever-faithful valet wrote to a friend in London the subjoined letter (cited by Baron d'Ambès in his very remarkable volumes):

PARIS, À LA CONCIERGERIE,
August 21, 1840.

MY DEAR FRITZ,

You will have sent to Mr. Farquhar the letter which the Prince left with you on his departure from London [for Boulogne]. It contains his instructions to sell everything except the toilette articles of His Highness and of those persons who left them [at the Prince's residence]. As to the cabriolet and the horse, the two sets of harness, and the sporting gun, Mr. Farquhar will doubtless have already told you that they were the Prince's gifts to him. The Prince thinks that the housemaids and the kitchen servants have been discharged with a month's wages [in lieu of notice].

You will remain in the house, with Lord Ripon's chambermaid, until further orders. The Prince will allow you £4 a month, besides what you are now getting, for your board. You are to preserve all the English newspapers which have appeared since the Prince's departure, and send them to him when he asks for them. Keep in the house the articles belonging to other persons, and put the name of each on the trunks and packages. Arrange all these things so that they may be sent off when you get orders about them. See that the lodgings of these gentlemen are paid, and tell all the tradespeople to apply to Mr. Farquhar for payment of their accounts.

You are to buy two leather trunks at £3 each, and put in them all the things which are in the wardrobe in His Highness's bed-room, with the two pairs of sheets, the two pillows, and the towels in the same room which are marked with an "N" and a crown. Put with them also the two little nécessaires de toilette, the boots, shoes, etc. The two trunks should be got ready for sending away at any moment. You are to take for yourself the old red shooting [or hunting] coat, the leather breeches and the white breeches, the large boots, the green overcoat, the green trousers, the hunt-ing-boots, the large brown overcoat, the two vieilles du matin, and the hats. In the dressing-room you will find a brand-new hat.

I left in my room a leather trunk containing my things. You will find in a drawer a little box containing some papers and other things which I highly value. Take great care of them. There is also in my wardrobe some linen for shirts. Take care of my paletot, my trousers (if there are any), and my little nécessaire. Do what you like with the rest of the things.

Adieu, my dear friend. The Prince is quite well.

CH. THÉLIN.

On September 28, 1840, Prince Louis Napoleon and some of his fellow-con-spirators were tried at the Luxembourg before the Cour des Pairs, M. Pasquier pre-siding over the tribunal. Fifty-five persons had been arrested at Boulogne, but only twenty-two were proceeded against. The Prince was defended by the ablest advo-cate of his day, Berryer, whose brief was marked with a fee of £600; with him were MM. Marie and Ferdinand Barrot. M. Jules Favre defended other of the prisoners.

After President Pasquier had begun the "interrogation of identity," the Prince rose and requested permission to read a short written statement in his defence. He began: "For the first time in my life I am allowed to raise my voice in France and to speak freely to Frenchmen."

Towards the end of his address he said: "A last word, gentlemen. I represent before you a principle, a cause, a defeat. The principle is the sovereignty of the people; the cause that of the Empire; the defeat, Waterloo. The principle you have recognized, the cause you have served, the defeat you wish to avenge."

The trial lasted until October 6, when the prisoners were sentenced: the Prince to perpetual imprisonment in a fortress; Montholon, Lombard, Conneau, and De Persigny to five years' imprisonment; one was deported; others were sent to gaol for fifteen, ten, five, and two years.

The Prince heard his fate unmoved. To the greffier he remarked spiritedly: "Sir, they said formerly that the word 'impossible' was not French; to-day the same may be said of the word 'perpetual.'"

During the trial the Prince sat in a fauteuil, guarded by two soldiers with fixed bayonets. He was a trim, alert-looking figure, in frock-coat and high black stock, wearing to and fro a tall hat.

His six years' isolation at Ham—a huge fortress, with a moat—converted Louis Napoleon into a littérateur of almost the first rank. His industry was excessive. Reams of paper were covered with his straggling, careless writing, chiefly on military subjects. His foster-sister, Mme. Cornu, gave him valuable assistance by forwarding books which otherwise he would probably have been unable to obtain, looking after his proof-sheets, writing to his publishers, and sending him extracts from volumes for which she ransacked libraries. When, in his stonemason's or bricklayer's long blouse, cap, and canvas trousers, carrying a plank and smoking a pipe, he made his escape, "Badinguet" was the father of at least two children, boys, for whose maintenance and education he made adequate provision.[30]

On May 27, 1846, Louis Napoleon reached London, and put up at the Brunswick Hotel, where his name was entered as Comte d'Arenenberg. He is said to have astonished Lady Blessington and the friends who were dining with her by appearing at Gore House the same evening. He wrote to the French Ambassador (M. de Saint-Hilaire, who had been a friend of Queen Hortense) informing him that he had escaped from Ham solely to revisit his old father, and that he had no intention of making any more "attempts" against the French Government, his previous efforts having resulted so disastrously to himself. The Prince's widowed father, the Comte de Saint-Leu, ex-King Louis of Holland, was residing at Florence, and Louis Napoleon vainly applied to the Austrian Ambassador in London and to the Grand Duke Leopold for permission to visit his father, who passed away in the following July.

All that the Comte de Saint-Leu possessed he left to his only surviving son, Louis Napoleon—his palace at Florence, his landed property at Civita Nuova, his money, and all his relics of Napoleon I. By his father's death the Prince became a comparatively wealthy man. D'Ambès asserts that he had to his credit at Barings 150,000 francs (£6,000), and at Farquhar's 3,000,000 francs (£120,000). We are led to believe that the Prince was unmercifully "bled" on all sides, and that he was soon deluged with begging letters from France, Switzerland, and Poland. "He spends a great deal. He already owns several houses in London, and has bought a house in Berkeley Street for Miss Howard."

---

[30] The mother was Alexandrine Vergeot, a maker of sabots, who helped the prison-porter's wife to keep the canteen tidy. She married Louis Napoleon's foster-brother, and died poor at Paris in 1886.

CHAPTER IV

COURTSHIP AND ENGAGEMENT

WHEN Prince Louis Napoleon was rather over twenty-six he wrote to his father, the Comte de Saint-Leu:[31]

ARENENBERG,
June 5, 1834.

MY DEAR PAPA,

Since I wrote to you, the death of Mlle. de P.'s father has somewhat changed my marriage plans, for until now I did not know any of the ladies whose names had been placed before me. I had given attention only to the conventionalities, not to the affections, which can only display themselves when one sees people personally. Besides, the advantages I saw in the alliance which I desired to contract no longer exist, and should I persist in my matrimonial views, the best thing I can do is to cast my eyes upon Mlle. de Padoue. You will give me much pleasure by replying to me on this point, and giving me your advice, although I am in no hurry to marry.

I enclose you a copy of a law just passed by the Government, which has evidently been enacted against us, for it cuts short all the claims that my family may have respecting the debts owing to it by the French Government. In these circumstances, I believe that, if it is intended to press the claim, there is only one way of doing it—by commencing an action against the Government. It is unfortunate that we did not hear earlier of this law, which was passed without any noise, so that we might not be enabled to take any steps in reference to it.

I have received a letter from Charlotte, and am going to answer it.

As I have not been very well for the last month, I am going very shortly to take the waters at Baden, near Zurich, for a month.

With sincere attachment,
Your loving and respectful son,
NAPOLÉON-LOUIS B.

---

[31] King of Holland, 1806-1810.

It was not until the following year, 1835, that the question of the Prince's marriage was publicly mooted. He was then living with his mother in Switzerland, at the villa of Arenenberg. It was erroneously reported that the Prince was about to marry Queen Doña Maria of Portugal. Not sorry, perhaps, to attract attention by denying in the Press the report of a marriage which he knew was impossible, the Prince wrote the following letter to a provincial paper:

SIR,

Various journals publish that I am leaving for Portugal in the character of a pretender to the hand of Queen Doña Maria. Flattered as I am at the thought of an alliance with a young, beautiful, and virtuous Sovereign, the widow of a cousin who was dear to me, it is my duty to deny this rumour. I may add that, despite the interest I feel in a nation which has conquered its liberty, I should certainly refuse to share the throne of Portugal, if, by chance, it were offered to me.

LOUIS NAPOLÉON.

The historian will search in vain should he attempt to identify the other ladies "whose names had been placed before" the Prince.

The next heard of is the young Englishwoman, Miss Emily Rowles, of Camden Place, Chislehurst, the home in later years of the Emperor and Empress and their son. Miss Rowles indignantly terminated the engagement—which had been definitively arranged—when she heard of the relations which existed between the Prince and Miss Howard.

When he was residing in London (1847) the Prince aspired to the hand of Lady Clementina Villiers, daughter of Lord and Lady Jersey. Lady Jersey, however, disliked the suitor, and the affair was nipped in the bud. The Prince had asked Lord Malmesbury if he had any chance of success with the young lady, and was not encouraged by the reply, which appears to have been in the nature of a gentle snub.

Miss Burdett-Coutts was not to be won by an adventurous French Prince, although he was the nephew of Napoleon I.

Turn and turn about the Prince made advances to—

1. The daughter of the Prince de Wasa, husband of a daughter of the Grand Duchess of Baden (née Stéphanie Louise Adrienne de Beauharnais).

2. Princess Adelaide of Hohenzollern, niece of Queen Victoria's consort, and sister of that Prince Leopold whose selection by Prim to occupy the vacant throne of Spain, in 1870, led up to the war.

3. A daughter of the Prince de Wagram, who "did not please him," and who married Prince Joachim Murat.

4. The Infante Marie Christine, a daughter of Don François de Paule, and sister of the consort of Queen Isabelle II.

Doubtless he had an affection for his cousin, Princesse Mathilde, and felt a pang when the news reached him, at Ham, of her marriage with the Russian Prince, Anatole Demidoff. Neither as President of the Republic nor as Emperor of the French would the royal houses of Europe have anything to do with the son of Queen Hortense.

Mlle. Eugénie de Montijo, Comtesse de Téba? She was unheard of as yet.

There was never any question in the minds of those who were ever so little behind the scenes that Napoleon III. so completely "lost his head" over "the beautiful Spaniard" that he seriously proposed to her without knowing whither his impetuosity was carrying him. That marriage was far from the Emperor's intentions originally is highly probable. When, however, he saw there was nothing for it but to make the young lady his Empress, he allowed himself to be led with scarcely a word of remonstrance and only the faintest of objections. His Majesty had to deal with an experienced woman of the world in Mme. de Montijo, and with a clever one in the person of Mlle. Eugénie de Montijo. It was a question of "marriage or no marriage," and the ladies gained the day. The flirtation was remarkably strong while it lasted, and the Emperor made himself the laughing-stock and butt of most of his monde, whose ridicule, however, could not divert His Majesty from pursuing his campaign with infatuated ardour.

Numberless stories are told of this diverting love-chase. Every year, in October, there was a great gathering of guests at Compiègne. On one of these occasions a société d'élite sat round a table playing cards while waiting for tea. It was noticed that Mlle. de Montijo sat on the Emperor's right, and, the wives of some of the Ministers being present, the circumstance was regarded as a sign of the times. The game was vingt-et-un, and Mlle. de Montijo, who did not seem to be very expert, consulted her neighbour on the left when she was in doubt what to do. Presently, after looking at her cards, she showed them to the Emperor, letting her eyes play the part of an inquirer. Napoleon III. replied, "Keep them; you have a very good hand." "No," she remarked, "they're not good enough; I want all or nothing!" and she asked for more cards, whereupon the dealer tossed her what proved to be an ace. Of course she won, and she took up the stake with a smile which was interpreted by those present as the triumph of the will over fortune.

The courting was nearly all done at Compiègne, and Mlle. de Montijo got herself much talked about by her beauty, her grace, and her coquetry with the Emperor, who, on his side, was driven almost frantic by the malicious pleasantries of his uncle, King Jérôme, who, with the wickedest smile, never omitted to ask the Emperor the first thing every morning how matters were going. The attitude of the ladies of the Court towards the woman whom they regarded as a usurper will be best understood by what follows. One night, as they were going into dinner at Compiègne, Mlle. de Montijo, conducted by Colonel de Toulongeon, was walking immediately behind Mme. Fortoul, wife of the Minister of that name. Quite by accident the first-mentioned couple took precedence of Mme. Fortoul, who said to her escort, in a tone which all could hear, "Why did you let that woman pass before us?"

Mlle. de Montijo heard the remark, and almost fainted. Her blue eyes filled with tears, she ate nothing for dinner, and replied to all the Emperor's observations with a profound melancholy. After dinner the Emperor went up to her and said:

"Are you unwell, mademoiselle?"

"No, sire. Why do you ask?"

"Because I noticed that you ate nothing, and I suppose that——"

"No sire; I repeat, I am not suffering; but here, in this very room—here, chez vous, I have been insulted in the most flagrant manner, and I think it my duty to tell your Majesty that I intend to leave Compiègne this very evening."

The Emperor begged her to explain, and the young lady told him, as well as she could through her tears, what had happened.

"Mademoiselle," said the Emperor, "promise me that you will not leave Compiègne, and I promise you, in turn, that to-morrow nobody will dare to insult you." And the next day came the Emperor's offer of marriage.

The Emperor's intention to take to himself a wife was announced on January 22, 1853, by a speech from the throne, in the course of which His Majesty said the union which he was about to contract was not in accordance with political tradition; but that was an advantage. "She who is the object of my choice is of high birth. French by heart, by education, by remembrance of the blood which her father shed for the cause of the Empire, she has, as a Spaniard, the advantage of not having in France a family upon whom it would be necessary to bestow honours and dignities. Endowed with all the qualities of the soul, she will be an ornament to the throne, even as in the hour of danger she will become one of its courageous supports. Catholic and pious, she will address to Heaven the same prayers that I myself offer for the happiness of France. Gracious and good, she will, I firmly hope, revive, in the same position, the virtues of the Empress Joséphine. Then, gentlemen, I say to France, 'I have preferred a woman that I love and respect to an unknown woman, whose alliance might have had advantages mixed with sacrifices.' Presently, at Notre Dame, I shall present the Empress to the people and to the army. The confidence which they have in me will cause them to give their sympathies to her whom I have chosen; and you, gentlemen, when you have learnt to know her, will be convinced that this time again I have been inspired by Providence."

Thus did Napoleon III. reverse the policy of his uncle, who divorced and abandoned a woman who was loved to espouse a daughter of the Cæsars; the former renounced the possibility of a royal marriage in order to wed a woman whom he loved. The Court of the Tuileries was greatly divided on the subject of the Emperor's marriage. King Jérôme, Drouyn de Lhuys (Minister of Foreign Affairs), and Persigny (Minister of the Interior) were, with others, in favour of a dynastic alliance; Morny, Fould, and the military party (nicknamed "the clan of the amoureux"), at the head of whom were Edgar Ney, Toulongeon, etc., were for the marriage with the fair daughter of the Montijos. The Emperor had, however, made up his mind, and, despite his hesitating, uncertain character, which presently accentuated itself still more, he resisted all the pressure put upon him by his family. In vain did Princesse Mathilde throw herself, theatrically, at his feet, beseeching him to abandon a marriage which could only lower his prestige; Cæsar was immovable. Drouyn de Lhuys felt so strongly about the marriage that he asked the Emperor's permission to resign his portfolio; but he must have changed his mind when he went to do homage to Mlle. de Montijo. "I congratulate you," she said; "I thank you for the advice which you have given to the Emperor relative to his marriage. Your advice was similar to mine."

"The Emperor has betrayed me, then," said the Minister.

"No; it is not betraying you to render homage to your sincerity, and to tell me the opinion of a devoted servant—one who has expressed my own sentiments. Like you, I have represented to the Emperor that he ought to consider the interests of his throne; but I have not had to be his judge, and to decide whether he is right or wrong."

De Morny told one of his colleagues that the Emperor, having once got an idea into his head, could not be disabused of it. More than one of his courtiers said: "He is mad, and this marriage is an act of the grossest stupidity."

If the Emperor believed in his star, so did Mlle. de Montijo place an implicit reliance upon hers. A gipsy fortune-teller once told her that she would be a Queen. She might have made a good—nay, a splendid—marriage long before she set her cap at the Emperor. The Duc d'Ossuna was madly in love with her, and wished to make her his Duchess. The Duc de Sesto proposed to her, but she declared she would only marry a Frenchman.

The Emperor's private friends were more difficult than the Ministers to argue with, and he had many a mauvais quart d'heure with Mme. Drouyn de Lhuys, Mme. Fortoul,[32] and Mme. de St. Arnaud, the latter the wife of the celebrated Marshal who fought with us in the Crimea. These grandes dames sneered at the fair interloper, as they considered Eugénie de Montijo. When they were at Compiègne they did all in their power to snub her and make her look small. To such a point, indeed, did they carry their persecution that the victim complained to the Emperor, who, observing that all the ladies in question were close by, broke a branch off a tree, and, twisting it into a crown, put it on Eugénie's head, with the remark (which all had the satisfaction of hearing), "Take this until I give you the other!"

Judging by those who are, or were, in a position to know, it would seem that the Empress was somewhat coquettish. Her Imperial Majesty, however, never publicly compromised herself, as the ex-Queen Isabella of Spain is credited with having done. She was flirty, that was all: the sort of woman that "Gyp" has sketched in "Autour du Mariage"; perhaps "Gyp" got her idea of Paulette d'Alaly from the former fair ruler of the Tuileries. "You know," said the Emperor to one of his Ministers who had complained of the Empress's attitude towards him—"you know the Empress is very hasty, but, au fond, she likes you very much." She was not, however, hypocritical, but may be compared to a child who has got tired of a toy and cries for another. She became possessed of all manner of fancies, and was

---

[32] This lady died in 1910.

exceedingly romantic, while remaining perfectly mistress of herself.

"It is a delicate question," writes one of her biographers, "and I approach it with the greatest circumspection; but was the Empress the passionnée she was said to be, and was she faithful to the Emperor? Merely to ask the question was to misunderstand the Empress. Had she any love intrigues? Was she always the woman who is said to have confessed to the Emperor before marriage, 'J'ai aimée, mais je suis restée Mademoiselle de Montijo'? The answer to this is—'No; the Empress had no weaknesses. Yes; the Empress always remained the slave of her marital duties.'" There were, doubtless, times when it seemed as if she thought of somebody of more consequence than her imperial consort; but her leanings in this direction appear to have been platonic—the griserie to have been of very slight duration. "It was with her as with a fire of straw, which burnt and burnt, making one think and fear that it was going to destroy everything. Then the individual who flattered himself with having set light to it was surprised at the flame which had illuminated and warmed him, and turned away, his only consolation being the parody of a celebrated sonnet. The Empress was one of those women who like to be made (platonic) love to. If she flirted, it was without real peril to her honour and sans rien céder de son intimité." When she was a prominent figure in the salon of the Comtesse de Laborde, it is told of her that she was "très libre d'allures." Eugénie de Montijo tutoyait people very freely, and when she ascended the throne she made any lady who had been a friend in former days "thou" and "thee" her as of yore.

Much may be forgiven the Empress in consideration of her bringing up. From the first she knew what opinion the Emperor really entertained of her—how he saw in her a beautiful woman whom he had marked down as a pretty plaything, the toy of a week, a month, or mayhap a year. She quickly undeceived him, and brought him to his senses almost ere he had taken leave of them. It must not be forgotten that she was thrown among those who composed the gayest Court in Europe. Money was of no more value in the Paris of the "sixties" than it is to-day in the neighbourhood of Monte Carlo, where a sovereign is thought less of than a fourpenny-piece in London. That was the time when champagne baths were the vogue, and beauty was worth ten times the market value of respectability. Those were the days when adventurers flocked to Paris as to a promised land, when the Emperor's favourites—the De Mornys, the De Persignys, et hoc genus omne—got concessions for every "enterprise" that fertile brains could devise, and when to be "in the swim" was to be in the way of making your fortune.

At the reveillon du jour de l'an at the Tuileries—December-January, 1853—the Emperor, in accordance with French custom, kissed all the ladies on the cheek. He approached Mlle. de Montijo with the same agreeable object; but she drew back, and, curtseying, said to the astonished Sovereign, "Sire, only my husband shall ever kiss me." This rebuff would have chilled most men, but the Emperor took it very good-humouredly, although such a display of excessive modesty was a new experience for him. Among those who had tried to put Mlle. de Montijo on her guard against the Emperor's compromising attentions was the Duchesse de Bassano. "Take care," said this lady; "you are preparing either regret or remorse for yourself. But do not forget that I warned you." A few days later the engagement was known, and Mlle. de Montijo was able to write to the Duchesse: "I marry Louis *without* regret and *without* remorse."

Towards the close of 1849—when the poor man whom she had seen under arrest, after the Boulogne fiasco, was in the second year of his Presidency—a Spanish gipsy told Mlle. de Montijo that she would marry an Emperor. The señorita knew very well that at the moment there was not one marriageable Emperor in existence, and she asked the gitana if she did not mean a King or a Prince. "No," was the reply, "I mean an Emperor—an Emperor of a great country." "Then it must be Souloque," said the Comte de Breda, then a French attaché, "for there is no other Emperor in the matrimonial market, and he would not be particular as to the number of his wives."

The proposed marriage was very obnoxious to some of the Emperor's Ministers; but when they began to remonstrate, His Majesty cut them short with that abruptness which characterized him when his wishes were opposed. "Gentlemen, there is nothing more to say. My marriage with Mlle. de Montijo is an arranged affair. I am resolved upon it."

The discomfited Ministers withdrew, but they did not cease to protest. There were people whose anger led them to say unpleasant things about both mother and daughter. The former, they asserted, held a very free-and-easy salon at her hôtel in the Place Vendôme. People gathered there after the opera, and the "goings-on" were of the liveliest. "Adventures" of the young lady in former years were fabricated, and openly discussed. People who stuck at nothing asserted that she had had a "past."

One of the numerous malcontents was M. Thiers, who appears to have had a sardonic kind of humour. "There is nothing to fear from people who are only tipsy," he murmured; "but they are to be dreaded when they get quite drunk." The French appreciate this description of wit, and the saying "went the rounds."

Prince Napoleon, for reasons, and his sister, Princesse Mathilde, for none, bitterly inveighed against what they regarded as sheer lunacy on the Emperor's part. The Prince, who, as long as there was no legitimate son of the Emperor in existence, stood next in the succession, had some sort of excuse for denouncing his cousin's marriage with "a mere femme du monde," who had nothing but her good looks to recommend her. Princesse Mathilde, who had contracted a most unhappy alliance with Prince Anatole Demidoff, but had been long freed from her tyrant, made theatrical appeals to the Emperor to abandon his intention. What was to be done with a man whose infatuation made him cover with kisses Nieuwerkerke's little bust of Mlle. de Montijo?

M. Vieil-Castel, a Rochefort born out of his time, marvelled what the Emperor would do when an Empress was at the head of a Court numbering among the officials so many men whose lives were the reverse of edifying. "Perhaps a day would come when Mlle. de Montijo would see herself allegorically depicted as a Hercules cleansing the Augean stables."

The Emperor, however, was supported by a few, among whom was the celebrated Lamartine. Another of the friendly minority declared that His Majesty was doing the right thing in marrying a lady whom he loved, and refusing to bargain for "some scrofulous German Princess with feet as large as a man's."

Before the projected marriage was officially announced, Princesse Mathilde gave a ball. Among the guests were the Emperor, the Duc de Morny, the Comtesse de Montijo, and her daughter. The Marquise de Contades wrote, in later years, of this entertainment: "The Emperor, as usual, paid the greatest attention to Mlle. de Montijo. For more than an hour she and the Emperor were engaged in a confidential chat, which no one had the audacity to interrupt. Mlle. de Montijo bears herself easily and gracefully. *She and her mother* both hope *for a marriage, and all their diplomacy is directed to securing it.* Everybody courts Mlle. de Montijo, curries favour with her, and seeks her intervention with the Emperor on their behalf. Ministers make much of her. She goes to all the fêtes. She is the actual rising sun."

Mlle. de Montijo, Comtesse de Téba, in November and December, 1852, and in the following month, monopolized attention in Paris. When she appeared in her box at the opera (Mauget tells us) people had no ears for the music, but they had eyes to see the young lady's peerless loveliness and graceful bearing. Nothing else mattered. She looked the Empress. The courrieristes of the papers followed her about; nothing escaped their lynx eyes. In newspaper argot, she made splendid "copy."

"Yesterday and to-day the Comtesse de Téba, accompanied by her mother, the Comtesse de Montijo, visited several shops on the boulevards and in the Rue Vivienne. The future Empress, being recognized by the crowd, was most sympathetically greeted. The hearts of all were conciliated by her simple yet distinguished manners, and by the alms which she bestowed upon several poor women whom she encountered during her stroll."

Sharp-tongued ladies like the Marquise de Taisey-Chatenoy (but this amiable person is not of much account) had an abundance of cutting things to say of Mlle. de Montijo when she had won the imperial crown. For example: "The Empress has a great taste for jeux d'esprit—I do not know why, for it is not by excess of brilliancy in this direction that she shines." And M. Irénée Mauget[33] is even more unflattering: "Of changeable disposition, she lacked judgment and reason. She was excessively nervous. Very impulsive, she acted under the influence of good or bad moods, and slighted and wounded many people by her unjust anger, regretting afterwards the pain she had caused. She was not untruthful.... Her sudden elevation, although not unforeseen, dazzled her—stunned her somewhat. Not having been born to occupy a throne, the transition was too brusque. She lacked proportion, and wanted to appear too much the Empress. She continued to be very much attached and very faithful to some of those who had been her intimates in early days, but she was capricious to most of the others, giving and withholding her favours with disconcerting fickleness. She was not loved like the Emperor. When she appeared in public she acknowledged with inimitable grace the salutations she received, and the French, very gallant, were won by this charm.... Had she been solidly educated she would have been capable of exercising the absolute

[33] "L'Impératrice Eugénie." Paris: Société des Publications Littéraires Illustrées. 1909.

power which she coveted."

M. Mauget apparently shares M. Rochefort's unfavourable opinion of the Comtesse de Montijo, who, simultaneously with her daughter's advancement in life, was said to have become miserly. "She made purchases right and left, and sent the bills to her daughter, sometimes to the Emperor. But Napoleon, always strongly épris of Eugénie, often shut his eyes at his mother-in-law's demands and revelled in the delights of the honeymoon. Was it the same with Eugénie? We may be permitted to doubt it. What she loved especially in her husband was the Emperor."

The Madrid journals waxed enthusiastic over the engagement—*e.g.*, the *España* (January 26, 1853):

> It is a Spanish woman who is going to impart to the throne of a great nation the lustre of her grace. The Comtesse de Téba, who was the ornament of our aristocracy, is about to assume the purple of the Cæsars, and share the destiny of him who is at once the heir of the man of the century and the conqueror of anarchy.... The lustre of a throne, however brilliant, will not eclipse the lustre of Marie Eugénie's eyes, and the fortune which is crowning her with all its gifts will not alter the noble serenity of her heart. For the glory of our country we express the wish, and have the firm expectation, that the former pearl of Castilian aristocracy will be the best of French women.

The Duchesse de Dino wrote:

> NICE,
> *January 21, 1853.*
>
> Letters received here from Paris always turn upon the same subject—the marriage of Louis Napoleon. I read in the newspapers the surprising speech which he made to the Senate and the Constituted Bodies [announcing his marriage].
>
> The sister of Mme. de Montijo married Lesseps, formerly a Consul. There is a little relationship toute gentille! Eugénie has chosen as her witnesses the Duc d'Ossuna and the Marquis de Bedmar, who have promised to lead her to the altar. They wanted to marry the son of Jérôme[34] to Mlle. de Wagram, but he recoiled in view of the Clary relationship, which he deemed beneath his dignity. That is flattering to the King of Sweden! What tohu-bohu all this is!
>
> NICE,
> *January 22, 1853.*
>
> It is decidedly a *love* marriage which Louis Napoleon is making. They tell me that Mlle. de Montijo, who was educated at a

[34] King of Westphalia, grandfather of Prince Victor and General Prince Louis Napoleon.

Paris pension, is very beautiful, and of high birth *on her father's side*. Her mother is the daughter of an English Consul, which explains the English kind of beauty — not at all Spanish — of the new *Empress*; for it is not a question of morganatic forms; so, *point de princesse*. I am charmed. But what a responsibility, at the age and with the health of the *sposo*, to have a young wife, beautiful and Southern! And that in the Bonaparte entourage and in the atmosphere which envelopes it.

Here are some other details, which I have gleaned from my letters from Paris, which are full of nothing but the marriage.

Mlle. de Montijo's age is from twenty-five to twenty-seven; of great beauty, with *auburn* hair, which she gets from her Irish mother; she has a bold look. It is said that, as they were playing cache-cache in the saturnalia of Compiègne, the Emperor discovered her concealed behind the curtain of a room, where, believing he was alone with her, he tried to embrace her, and that she pushed him away, saying, "Not before I am Empress." Another person who was similarly concealed professes to have heard these words.

Legitimists and Orleanists are charmed with this matrimonal affair and with all that it promises.

Nice [after the marriage].

The Empress is very beautiful. They say her only imperfection is that she looks much taller when seated than she actually is when standing up. She says that, in sacrificing her freedom and her youth, she gave more than she received; but *she lets herself be adored*. The ladies have a down-on-the-ground look, but decent. The decorations of Notre Dame were splendid, but the Cardinals did not make much of an appearance; in fact, excepting M. de Bonald, not one of them is of good family.

On returning [from the cathedral to the Palace] the imperial carriage, which was surmounted by a large crown, was passing under the archway of the Pavillon de l'Horloge when the horses stopped, unable to proceed. The surprised coachman whipped them, and then the obstacle to their progress fell: it was that crown, which was too high to pass under the arch, and, when it fell, was broken to atoms. *Ominous!*

Nice,
February 6, 1853.

Mme. d'Avenas writes to my daughter that two days before her marriage the Empress Eugénie went to [the convent of] the Sacré-Cœur, Paris, in which she had passed some years of her infancy—Mme. d'Avenas happened to be there also, and thought the Empress charming, natural, and simple—wanting to see once more all the souvenirs of her youth, even to the lay-sister who used to wash her. This visit has had a good effect in the pious world.

Another correspondent wrote to the Duchesse de Dino's son (February 15), telling him of the flood of sonnets, pamphlets, and riddles which inundated the Empress's salons. "As to me," this unknown Parisian said, "the Empress made a conquest of me at Notre Dame—not by her beauty, but by her dignity and her pious, thoughtful bearing."

The Maréchale d'Albuféra gave the Duchesse a specimen of the jokes made about the Empress. The Maréchale, after noting that "the Empress has blue eyes, and paints her eyebrows and eyelashes black," asked, "Do you know why the Empress Eugénie is the best horsewoman in France? Because she leapt over the barrière du Trône! This is one of the jokes with which we amuse ourselves here."

The Duchesse, as a talented diplomatist, noted: "The Empress, *until now*, decides nothing for herself. She submits everything to the Emperor, even as to the dress which she ought to wear."

On December 7, 1860, the Duchesse wrote:

> The Empress's annoyance with Fould arose from two causes. When the Duc d'Albe came to see him about the funeral of his wife [the Empress's sister] Fould replied, "That is a matter for the pompes funèbres."
>
> The Empress wanted to sell some of her diamonds for "Peter's Pence." Fould heard of her intention, and told the Emperor of it.[35]

The foreign Powers did not display particular alacrity in "recognizing" Napoleon III. There seemed to be much curiosity anent the genealogy of the Emperor's future bride, and an elaborate statement was issued by the Heralds' College at Paris, informing all whom it might concern that the lady who was about to become Empress of the French belonged "to the House of Guzman, whose origin dates back to the earliest times of the Spanish Monarchy," several historians asserting that the Guzmans were the issue of royal blood. "All the branches of this family have played a distinguished part in history. Amongst them were the Dukes of Medina, Las Torres, Medina-Sidonia, and Olivares; the Counts of Montijo, of Téba (or Téva), and of Villaverde; the Marquis de Ardales, the Marquis de la Algera, etc., grandees of Spain. The Duchesse de Téba, Comtesse de Montijo, descends from this last branch. This is not the first time this family has been called to ascend the throne, for in 1633 a daughter of the eighth Duke of Medina-Sidonia married the King of Portugal, Dom Juan IV. of Braganza. The Counts of Montijo have the same arms as the Dukes of Medina-Sidonia; they are near relations, and bear the same name, which is De Guzman."

---

[35] "Souvenirs de la Duchesse de Dino" (*Chronique*, tome iv.). Paris: Plon.

CHAPTER V

CÆSAR'S WIFE

THE Empress, to say it for the thousandth time, was incomparably beautiful, "divine," and, like most pretty women—although a Sovereign, and perhaps because she was a Sovereign—liked people to occupy themselves about her, liked to be courted. "Although romantic, her physical sense did not seek emotions which are foreign to those which the most elementary virtue imposes upon a woman. Her heart was in no wise desirous of sensations such as those which agitate tender and sentimental women." She was neither "tender" nor "sentimental." She loved the Emperor. When they were apart, her thoughts were always with him. Her letters prove it. Once, on her fête-day, she wrote: "This year again I have passed to-day far from the Emperor. This makes the day sadder; but I hope to rejoin him very soon."

A phrase uttered by the Empress provoked some harsh criticism at the time, and has been, even to this day, quoted against her. It was ungraciously and unjustly assumed that she had special ideas on virtue. But there is really nothing in her remark to justify the implication that she took advantage of that moral freedom which she sometimes apparently seemed disposed to favour.

It was at the Tuileries that, in the early years of the reign, she was credited with saying:

> One cannot guard young girls too closely, cannot keep them too far from danger and evil. I constantly watch over them and their surroundings. As to married women, that is another matter, and I admit that I am indifferent about them. Their virtues and their weaknesses are to me perfectly equal: that is their business. They can look after themselves. And, besides, have they not their husbands to protect and watch over them?

Brought up in a milieu quite foreign to any Court (that of Spain always excepted), the Empress, as Sovereign, sometimes lacked that overpowering gravity which women destined to reign are taught from the cradle. She believed sincerely, and without arrière pensée, that it was open to her to enjoy life as she found it. She saw no harm in causing the hearts of men to beat with sentiments which really only flattered her. She was curious to read the souls of others; and the adulation bestowed upon her interested and moved her as a powerful romance would have done. In a word, she was the popular idol. She knew that she was adored, and, receiving all this homage in a perfectly passive manner, felt that she was surrounding herself by friends and devoted admirers, whose sole object was to serve her and to love her. Besides, she was very fond of discussion and argument, and consequently sought the society of men capable, by their esprit, of entertaining her.

Fully aware that a person cannot charm and fascinate people without taking some little trouble over it, the Empress, before talking to a politician, a savant, an author, or an artist of any kind, "got up" her subjects, and made up her mind as to what she must say in order to take the man captive. Moreover, she was as careful to conquer him by the attractions of her person as by those of her conversation; and when she had captured him, when she felt assured that he belonged to her—"when," in her own phrase, "she found his homage agreeable and amusing," when she knew that she had stirred his heart, then, and only then, she checked the pretty poem or the half-finished sketch, and wrote with her own fair hand at the bottom of the page which she had read the one word "Fin!" All this was, no doubt, imprudent, and not in conformity with the gravity which ought to have been hers: it may even have been cruel; but what pretty (and virtuous) woman will rise to blame the Empress? What pretty (and virtuous) woman will dare to say that she has never acted in the same way in the drawing-rooms which she frequents? And what man, not entirely virtuous, but amoureux, has not been the victim of similar feminine perfidies? "Le péché veniel des unes, les bourgeoises; deviendrait-il le péché mortel des autres, les reines?" Shall we be wrong in answering the question in the negative?

From the outset the Empress displayed no little fickleness, now lavishing attentions upon those who pleased her, then suddenly dismissing them with a word or a gesture, and henceforth ignoring them. She appeared to act upon uncontrollable impulses, the most glaring temperamental defect in her otherwise generous nature. It was one of the "defects of her qualities," calling less for censure than for record in an impartial narrative. With all this, however, the Empress was loyal and susceptible of great devotion to her friends, and one sought without finding anything approaching egotism or vaingloriousness in her many inconsistencies. When she gave her hand to a woman or a man she was perfectly sincere, and when she sealed a friendship, or an attachment, with some signal mark of her approbation, she did so in all good faith and in all honour. The Emperor deplored, and with reason, the waywardness displayed by his consort in the choice of her friends, and had often to allay the bitter enmities and discontent which she heedlessly, and perhaps unconsciously, aroused.

The cynical saying of François I., "Souvent femme varie," might have been applied to the Empress, who was as fickle in her sensations as in her sentiments. She was a Spaniard, and to that fact may be attributed her somewhat eccentric manner. Her character was truly remarkable; she took all sorts of fancies into her head: was very romantic even while remaining practical, prosaic, and mistress of herself. In her romantic disposition the Empress, strange to say, found a certain strength, as letters written by her in the first year of her marriage confirm. One of these epistles may be cited in proof of this view of her character.

The Empress, much pressed by Mme. de M., one of the leading members of the Legitimist party, to obtain for her husband a diplomatic post, did not rest until she had gratified the applicant's wishes. It should not be forgotten that the Emperor always cherished the idea of rallying to his dynasty the notabilities of the Faubourg St. Germain, and showed every courtesy to those Legitimists who attended the Court of the Tuileries. It is doubtful if the Empress seconded his efforts in this direction, but in the matter alluded to she certainly laid herself out to do a kindly action.

"Mme. de M.," wrote the Empress to the Emperor, "wants the vacancy at The Hague for her husband, and I much wish him to have it." She added, as one who was worried by repeated applications of this kind: "Comme ça on me laisserait tranquille!"

A week afterwards the Empress wrote: "I saw Mme. de M. on Sunday, and she seemed perfectly satisfied."

Writing immediately afterwards about another lady—also one of the Royalist group—for whom she had done something, Her Majesty said: "As to Mme. de C., up to now she hasn't uttered a word of thanks to me. If you should see her—especially if you should see her husband—say that he does not owe his post entirely to his personal merits. As to gratitude, I have my own opinion about that; and, as I never expect any, I am never disappointed."

These letters reveal a melancholy philosophy, throwing much light upon the Emperor's entourage, and showing that, if the Sovereigns did their utmost to conciliate members of all parties, they were too often rewarded only with ingratitude by those on whom they had bestowed favours, or to whom they had accorded high positions in the public service.

That the Empress, strong in her own virtue, should have been grievously pained, and sometimes exasperated, by her inflammatory consort's peccadilloes is not very surprising. That there were "scenes" was but natural. It was, then, all the more to her credit that in public she invariably showed the Emperor the greatest deference; even in her own apartments, if he appeared, as he sometimes did, when the Empress was entertaining friends, she would rise directly he entered the room, and make him a profound reverence. At one time, too, she sought to amuse the Emperor in a variety of ways, and when one or other of her suite mustered up sufficient courage to repeat to her the rumours and the cancans of the hour, Her Majesty would remark: "Really, they blame us for amusing ourselves at the Tuileries! Surely the very least I can do is to give some distraction to the poor Emperor (who is ennuyé all day by politics), and show him some pretty women!"

It need hardly be said that the observation, coupled with what the Empress had previously said touching the conjugal fidelity of women generally, did not tend to diminish the reputation for légèreté which she had acquired even before her accession to the throne. This frivolity, although perhaps it was more apparent than real, was made the most of by certain ladies, and particularly by the Princesse de Metternich.

That there were evil counsellors among his consort's bosom friends none knew better than the Emperor, who said to her:

You admit to your most intimate friendship a heap of people who do not wish either of us any good, and who are no better than spies. You tell them a thousand things without thinking of what you are saying. Nigra [he was the Italian Ambassador], Metternich, and the rest only "spoon" you to get your secrets out of you! You may take it as certain that every word you say to them, or in their hearing, finds its way to Turin or Vienna. You place too much reliance in them, and in return for your confidence they are for ever doing their best to "pump" you.

Did not events prove that the Emperor was right?

Quite early in the reign the Empress became a dissatisfied and disappointed woman. Many untoward circumstances combined to produce, with welcome intervals, a disorganization of the family life at the Tuileries, or wherever the Court happened to be. There were, too, those famous charades, remarkable for the lavish display of feminine charms, and resulting in much hostile criticism at second-hand. This entertainment was referred to by the Empress in a letter written by her to the Emperor (July 13, 1860):

I thank you for your welcome letter. I am much better now than I was a few days ago. When I left Fontainebleau I felt ill both in mind and body, having been feverish, and suffering from an irritation of the chest which compelled me on two successive days to go to bed soon after I was up. The weather and the calm of St. Cloud have worked wonders for me, and you will find me in good health and delighted to see you.

Your philosophic reflections are very beautiful; the thing is to put them in practice. I am very weak against that malice which is not based upon *hatred*. When, by chance, I find in my way people endeavouring to make mischief out of nothing, and tearing reputations to tatters for lack of something better to do, I feel inexpressibly sad, because I say to myself: "One must be very wicked to find pleasure in vexing and injuring those with whom one shakes hands, for not only do the blows show, but defiance takes the place of all other sentiments, and, as the anonymous is masked by friendship, we distrust people without knowing why." These are the reasons why you found me so sad lately at Fontainebleau.

That innocent charade, unveiled by the papers, was described in a manner which shows it to have been supplied by somebody who was present at the performance, and who got it published either out of malice or to satisfy people's curiosity. It must have been published by a friend, or, at least, by a guest, and this is one of those things to which I cannot get accustomed. I shall always be strong against my enemies; I cannot say I shall ever be so against my friends.

If those who seek to deprive us of the little time that we have for enjoying the air and for liberty knew how precious this time is to those who are condemned to the preoccupations of the present and fears for the future, they would leave us this oasis, where we try to forget that we must march, always march, with the passions of some and the fears of others.

I have written you this long letter to explain to you that the little tear in the corner of my eye has not even dropped. My eight pages are sprinkled with orthographical blunders, which give originality to my letter, and prove that when I write to you I forget myself.

Does not this letter show the Empress at her best?

Mlle. de Montijo, wrote M. de Mazade in the *Revue des Deux Mondes* shortly after her engagement, "impressed one by a sort of virile grace, which might easily have made her a heroine of romance, and before assuming the imperial diadem she proudly wore that crown of hair whose colour a Venetian painter would have loved."

The relations which existed between the Emperor and Empress used to be discussed in the most unreserved fashion, not only in Paris clubs and salons, but in many London circles. All manner of stories were told about their Majesties. Some strong sidelights are thrown upon the lives of the imperial couple by Mme. Carette, in her entertaining "Souvenirs." If that estimable woman be accurate (and as she was "reader" to the Empress for several years, she should be, and, I have been recently informed, is, a competent witness), the trouble began some eight years after the marriage, by which time "the Empress had known more than one sadness."

"The Emperor," says Mme. Carette, whose resemblance to the Empress seems to have been very marked, "led away by his old habits of pleasure, by the easy manners of some of those by whom he was surrounded, was not invariably mindful of his consort's feelings as Sovereign and wife. The Empress, in all the splendour of her youth and beauty, had made acquaintance with the subtle poison which corrupts all which is most delicate in woman's heart. After distractions, some of which had a regrettable notoriety, the Emperor, who, like many men, attached no importance to his fleeting liaisons, appeared to be always surprised that he had wounded his wife's feelings at a time when she occupied the largest place in his life. Sisterly friendship had supported the Empress in these trying experiences. The Duchesse d'Albe, all sweetness and tenderness, consoled her sister, whose ardent nature increased her sufferings tenfold. She helped the Empress to reconcile herself to her hours of trouble and bitterness and to find strength to pardon [the Emperor]. When the Duchesse d'Albe died, the Empress felt for the first time the loneliness which grandeur brings with it. She remained alone with her grief, with nothing to distract her, having no courage to fulfil her worldly duties. Her health suffered greatly, and the doctors urged the Emperor to persuade her to travel in order to remove the painful strain which she was enduring. The Empress accordingly left on a visit to Scotland, where she remained a few weeks.[36] She returned to Paris much improved in health, ready to take up the duties of her position, but she had been irremediably touched by her melancholy situation. From that time dated a profound change in her tastes, as well as in her habits. Her youthfulness seemed to have vanished, and under the charming features of the woman ripened by sorrow appeared the Sovereign whom one had not hitherto seen."

When Napoleon III. was writing his "Life of Cæsar," and casting ambitious glances at a chair in the Academy, a poet wrote a few verses on the Emperor's work, referring to him as the "greatest Cæsar of these later years." In return for this compliment the Emperor sent his panegyrist a diamond ring and an invitation to call at the Tuileries. The Emperor received him very graciously, and, after some casual talk, asked him if he were married. "No, sire," was the reply. "Why don't you marry? Would you marry a lady who is young, beautiful, of ardent disposition, and with a handsome dowry, if you met such a one who was willing to have you?" The young man began to wonder if he was in, not the Palace of the Tuileries, of the glories of which he had heard and read so much, but in Aladdin's cave. But, though dazed at the prospect, he speedily recovered himself, and replied: "Yes, sire, I should be only too happy." "Well, then," said the Emperor, "come here to-morrow night at ten o'clock, and I will present you to her."

At the appointed time the poet, still rather fancying that he was dreaming, entered the Palace, and was immediately ushered into the Emperor's cabinet. Napoleon III. was in morning dress; he donned a large cloak and a hat which concealed his identity, and led the poet to a side door. A carriage was waiting, and in it they were driven to a bijou villa which stood in spacious grounds in a retired part of Paris.

"My dear Marie," said the Emperor to the beautiful woman, scarcely more than a girl just out of her teens, "allow me to present my friend, Monsieur — —, who comes as a suitor for your hand." With this the Emperor retired, and was seen no more!

The poet found the lady quite willing to accept his wooing, and, knowing that the imperial favour depended upon his discretion, did not make any inquiries as to madame's history. A few weeks later they were quietly married, and the husband found that his bride's dowry was the handsome sum of £100,000. He was never again invited to the Tuileries, nor did he ever have another interview with the Emperor. To his surprise, one morning he received an appointment in the Diplomatic Service in a distant country. Needless to say, he accepted the post, and resided, with his wife, at the scene of his labours until his death more than a quarter of a century ago. His widow returned to Paris and married a Russian noble. When the news of the poet-diplomatist's death reached Paris, General Fleury, who knew the faiblesses of Napoleon III. better than most men, pleasantly remarked: "Ah! he was a lucky fellow to get such a wife; but it was hard luck for the Emperor to have to pay such a price to get rid of so charming an encumbrance!"

Mlle. de Montijo had not been an Empress many weeks before her greatness

[36] The ever-recurring infidelities of her consort prompted the long-suffering Empress to absent herself from France for a while, and to confide her troubles to Queen Victoria.

and the luxe by which she was surrounded began to be distasteful. "She had never loved the Emperor. Her heart remained faithful to the Marquis d'Alcanises, her former fiancé. The Marquise de Bedmar, one of Her Majesty's Spanish friends, told me that the Empress said to her, on the eve of the wedding: 'If Alcanises came to fetch me, I would go away with him!' But Alcanises never came, and, some years later, when he was the Duc de Sesto, married the widow of the Duc de Morny."[37]

The strict etiquette which the Emperor insisted should be observed weighed upon the lady who had hitherto revelled in complete independence, while she was exasperated at the surveillance of the Palace ladies, even the domestics. This irritation disappeared as if by magic after she and her consort had visited Queen Victoria and the Prince Consort, and seen how things were done at the model English Court. How bored she was she showed very plainly in a letter written to one of the friends of the old days, begging to be "thou'd" as in former times: "Je suis seule dans mon palais, et très chagrinée des bouderies [sulkiness] que je sens autour de moi."

A collection of what M. Mauget describes as "Notes of a Member of the Imperial Police" provides curious reading:

March 8, 1853.

The Comtesse de Montijo is still residing in Paris, and it is said that her influence is by no means so trifling as some have believed it to be. At the last soirée M. Fould[38] was very assiduous in his attentions to her. That is not surprising when one recalls the intrigante of the salon at Madrid.

March 24, 1853.

Mme. de Montijo has left [Paris] on very bad terms with the august occupants of the Tuileries.

The *Journal d'Indre-et-Loire* reports the arrival at Tours of the Comtesse de Montijo, *accompanied by M. Mérimée.*

Everybody knows the amount of scandal talked at Paris concerning the former relations of the author of "Colomba" and the Comtesse de Montijo.

The same people who discuss the Comtesse also talk a great deal about the Empress. People maliciously pretend to pity her. They say she lives in a state of constraint which afflicts her all the more because it is such a great contrast to the freedom she enjoyed before her unexpected elevation. It is said that letters addressed to her are first taken to the Emperor, who, when replies are sent, himself dictates the answers, without the Empress being informed either that anyone has written to her, or that someone has answered the letters in her name. This manner of acting could not last long without her becoming aware of it, and she has exhib-

[37] Mme. de Ferronays.
[38] A prominent Minister of the period.

ited the greatest irritation. Very lively scenes between the Emperor and his wife have taken place. Those who know her imperious character say they would not be surprised if the Empress, abandoning all her grandeurs, fled to Belgium or to England.

March 25, 1853.

It is asserted that if the Empress's mother left Paris several days ago it was because she had received a positive order to do so from the Emperor, who had been informed of the scandalous conduct, past and present, of his mother-in-law. The Empress is said to have been greatly annoyed at the compulsory departure of her mother. There had been a women's quarrel; Princesse Mathilde said recently: "If the Emperor had wanted an Impératrice mère, he would have sought one elsewhere."

April 1.

The Empress's condition is the subject of much sympathy. To profound ennui has succeeded an intense melancholy.

April 5.

People continue to describe the Empress as being tired of everything. She cannot forget the complete freedom she enjoyed before her marriage. Sometimes she allows herself to play childish tricks upon the Emperor. The other day, when they were walking together in the garden, the Emperor stooped to examine some plants. The Empress thought it amusing to push him from behind, so that he fell on all fours.

April 20.

It is believed that the Empress is enceinte.

May 5.

The Duchesse d'Albe is coming to Paris. It is stated that the Comtesse de Montijo wished to accompany her, but, by a special order, the Emperor has forbidden her to do so.

May 25.

Yesterday the Emperor went out without the Empress. The Empress is still ailing, and people continue to talk about it. Her sufferings are more mental than physical. She cannot accustom herself to the etiquette imposed upon her by the Emperor. He is suspicious and severe to excess. At the least infraction by the Empress of the rules imposed upon her she is reminded of it with a frigidity which, to her, is worse than harshness.

When the Emperor sees that some lady has the particular confidence of the Empress, he hastens to get rid of her. This is what happened to Mme. Aguado. This dame d'honneur is greatly beloved by the Empress, and the two often talk in Spanish. The Emperor does not know that language, so he gave Mme. Aguado her congé. The Empress's supplications had no effect upon the Emperor. This has deeply wounded her. It is said to have been one of the causes of the fausses couches.

May 28.

The Empress always occasions much talk. The following was said yesterday à propos of the announcements published by the *Moniteur* concerning Her Majesty's privileges:

The Empress is of a stubborn, scoffing disposition, which adapts itself with difficulty to all the fictions of her imperial existence. Some are privileged to arouse her spirit of fun. She laughed heartily when she was informed of M. de Persigny's report and the imperial decree regulating her privileges, and it was with a gaiety ill according with the event that she signed the documents. As she scribbled her name she turned towards the Emperor with the remark: "You see, sire, that I somewhat imitate your Corps Législatif—I sign blindly."

In the years that were before Chislehurst the name "Empress Eugénie" signified the most radiant incarnation of beauty under which a woman could appear in order to dazzle, to touch and captivate, assemblies of men; it signified generosity of heart, inexhaustible charity, virtue, modest serenity in bearing the weight of fortune's favours, an elevated intelligence open to the comprehension of all great things, a free and tolerant mind, a sweet and pitying piety. It was no secret that she was pleased by heroic deeds, but, as Providence had not as yet afflicted her with the heaviest trials which the human heart can bear, she was not thoroughly known. To-day the same name signifies patriotism even unto sacrifice, chivalrous abnegation, courage, disinterestedness unexampled in history, dignity supreme in misfortune, resignation to unhappiness, and never-failing patience in the woes and duties of exile.

Lord Kitchener.

The Hon. Charlotte Knollys.   The King of Denmark.   King Edward.

Queen Alexandra.   The Empress.   Princess Beatrice of Coburg.

THE EMPRESS EUGÉNIE ON BOARD THE ROYAL YACHT, AUGUST, 1902, AT THE REVIEW OF THE FLEET BY KING EDWARD.

From a Photograph by J. Russell & Sons, Baker Street, London,
Photographers to H.M. the King.

Specially prepared by Messrs. Russell for this work (1911).

This double character of her destiny has stamped upon the physiognomy and the person of the Empress a pathetic expression which strikes those who have not seen her often of late years. It is with a tender and sympathetic respect that one contemplates the widow of Napoleon III. and mother of the Prince Imperial, enveloped in sombre vestments, but, in the winter of her days, more beautiful than ever, if the supreme expression of beauty is that of the ideal. She evokes in our imagination the picture of Marie Stuart at Holyrood or on the banks of Lochleven. The look of melancholy, which has become a second nature, cannot efface the sweetness and charm which will be always hers. It is her tranquil and touching majesty which reveals the woman beneath the Sovereign, the tenderness of the heart under the height of the rank; but there is, besides, the victorious prestige conferred upon her by misfortune heroically borne. That power of attraction which would have made Napoleon I. say of her as he said of Joséphine, "I win the battles, she wins the hearts," is now shown afresh by the emotion which is aroused as we gaze upon her venerable figure.

"Dans toute grande chose il s'est toujours rencontré une femme," said Lamartine; and there will be found in history certain epochs—the most brilliant ones—which are incarnated for posterity in a feminine personality. The Empress represents, in the most fascinating guise, the greatness of one or other of those epochs—the noble impulses, the generous inspirations, the heroisms, the radiant dawns, and the grandiose twilights. Such women impress their personality upon their contemporaries by their witchery, for they are beautiful even to idealism. In their souls they are still more perfect; they achieve conquest by their suffering, for, in order that they may be quite complete in all things, misfortune touches their brow with its black wing. And behold them become, for all men to remember, the eternal radiance, the eternal compassion, of history, of poetry, of legend.

In the sixteenth century such a personality as is here depicted was called Marie Stuart; in the seventeenth, Henrietta Maria, daughter of Henri Quatre, and wife of Charles I.; in the eighteenth, Marie Antoinette. With an incontestable moral superiority over all these, the Empress Marie-Eugénie lengthens this list by the purity of her name, and will remain the touching symbol of that part of the history of France known as the Second Empire.

Writing one day to Napoleon III., the Empress said: "My life is finished, but I live again in my son, and I believe I shall find the truest happiness in that which comes into my heart from his." Never was the maternal sentiment more beautifully expressed than in those pathetic words. Into the heart of this mother entered many joys and ineffable happiness. Who, looking upon that son of Cæsar, whose visage had all the sweetness of his mother's united to the virility of his father's, could fail to have believed that he, too, would be the hero of a new and great chapter of history? Who was not tempted to apply to him the phrase of Virgil: "Tu Marcellus eris"? They had no presentiment of the invasion, the defeats, the captivity, the vanishing of the father, the tragedy in the mealie-fields.

In the broad ways of the once beleaguered city there reappears ever and anon the silhouette of the woman who aforetime filled it with her grace, her splendid beauty, her charity, and her solicitude.

Her letters to the Emperor before their marriage displayed so much more literary skill than Mlle. Eugénie de Montijo was supposed to possess that ill-natured people asserted they were written by that attached friend of the Montijos, Prosper Mérimée. This is to charitably suppose that Napoleon III. invited his friends to peruse the letters addressed to him by "the beautiful Spaniard" during the period of his ardent wooing—a course which would have been entirely foreign to his loyal nature. The Emperor probably destroyed his fiancée's letters; if not, they must be among the mass of papers preserved at Farnborough Hill, to remain unpublished until the expiration of fifty years after the Empress's death.

From her own chaplet of memories I cull these few blossoms:

Neither the mother nor the child is responsible for the faults of the father.

We should practise a policy of ideas, not of expedients.

Is it not too absurd to say that on September 4 (1870) I was afraid? What woman, what Sovereign, seeing her husband betrayed by fate, a prisoner; her son wandering about, perhaps dead; her country invaded and devastated; her crown lost—who would have thought at such a moment of her personal security, and who would not have preferred death a hundred times to so many sorrows?

I have an absolute confidence in the power of truth. I summon with my whole strength all that can hasten its coming. It will appear—it appears already. Calumnies arise from time to time, like the unhealthy vegetation of the tropics; but the sun kills the one, the light of truth destroys the others, and their ephemeral and evil life leaves no traces.

I cannot die. And God, in His clemency, will give me a hundred years of life.

We must not destroy the legends which the peoples weave round their Sovereigns.

I am left alone, the sole remnant of a shipwreck, which proves how fragile and vain are the grandeurs of this world.

I have lived; I have been. I wish to be nothing, not even a memory. I am the Past. I live, but am no more; a shadow, a phantom, a walking sorrow.... I have renounced the future. I live in my youth, in my past. And all the rest is shade, obscure shade. I am like these trees, voyez-vous. They also, like me, live on the memory of their past beauty. But they look forward to the spring-time. I do not—I have nothing more to expect. My sad winter even has come to an end.

Pray and weep with me. My sister is dead.

It is sad that after so many sorrows they will not let me have that calm which I need so much.

I firmly believe that they that are gone are happier than we. (In a telegram to Monsignor Goddard on the death of his sister.)

(She had been asked at Chislehurst why, although so many had offered to share her misfortunes, she had accepted the devotion of only one or two persons. And she answered:)

Quand on est au milieu de la tempête, et qu'avec soi on traine la foudre, il ne faut pas laisser les autres vous rejoindre. (When you are in the midst of the storm, and dragging the thunder in your wake, you must not let others be exposed to it.)

In leaving to others the honour of the defence of France in 1870, I obeyed a sentiment of personal abnegation. I did not wish to divide the country when the enemy might at any moment have entered by the breach opened to it by our internal dissensions.

I seek peace and forgetfulness.

I know how to get rid of them [General Fleury and M. Emile Ollivier], and to deliver the Emperor from them.

Doctors try to cure the body before the soul; but that is impossible.

Your philosophical reflections are very beautiful; the thing is to put them in practice.

One must be very wicked to wound the feelings of those who extend their hands in friendship.

The Empress had a protégée whose relatives were anxious that she should marry a Duke, and they entreated Her Majesty to induce the young lady to accept the suitor. This the Empress declined to do. "Greatness is purchased too dearly," she said, "and so I will not persuade Mlle. — — to enter into this alliance."

There are etymological purists who have asserted that Her Majesty's French is not absolutely flawless; but this is a reproach to which other august personages are subject. That the Empress's native Spanish colours her pronunciation of certain French words, she herself would probably be the first to admit. Similarly, the Emperor's German education accounted for his amusing mispronunciation of some French words. Did he not, for example, invariably address his consort as "Ugenie"? And is not Bismarck credited with having once said to him, with well-concealed sarcasm: "I have never heard French spoken as your Majesty speaks it"? In the opinion of that master of phrases, a Sovereign's education was complete if he knew French thoroughly and could ride well. Napoleon III. had a perfect seat on horseback—so good, indeed, that it was said of him that he only looked a real Emperor when he was mounted; and none but Bismarck would have ventured to criticize his pronunciation.

CHAPTER VI
APOGEE OF THE SECOND EMPIRE

The Empress has to her credit the creation of Biarritz, which developed from a little Basque village into the French Brighton, and became a seat of the imperial Court. The Villa Eugénie was a square, unadorned building, standing on a slope leading to the sea, with a glorious lookout over the waters of the Bay of Biscay. Felix Whitehurst, who was at Biarritz in 1867, the palmy year of the Empire, noted the curious fact that the fee-simple of the bit of waste land on which the imperial villa was built was acquired by the Emperor for £12; and that just beyond the valley, to the east, there was a model farm, worked by "Louis Napoleon, proprietor, rentier, and Emperor."[39]

The Court led a primitive life in what, a few years previously, had been no more than an insignificant little sardine fishing village, unknown to the great world even by name. The first thing the *Daily Telegraph's* sparkling Paris correspondent saw on his arrival was a compact crowd following the Emperor and Empress, who were strolling up the High Street. His Majesty wore a low two-inch-crowned white hat with a broad brim. It was not Biarritz, but St. Jean-de-Luz, which was "very nearly the scene of a catastrophe which would have plunged all Europe into mourning," as a result of the Empress (who was a good sailor and also a good swimmer) cruising in a small steamer in a very heavy sea. The Empress and the Prince Imperial had to get into a small boat to land. The boat struck on a rock, nearly capsized, and began to fill. The Empress was up to her waist in water, and the little Prince (then only eleven) almost out of his depth. The pilot lost his head, jumped into the water, and was drowned. The Sovereign and her son (according to other chroniclers) were carried through the boiling surf on the backs of sailors. How the Emperor learnt of the mishap has not been told; but he arrived at St. Jean-de-Luz, eight miles from Biarritz, "as fast as horses could bring him." There was mild scolding all round, but the soft-hearted Emperor was too thankful at finding his loved ones in safety to use harsh language to anybody.

Among the visitors at Villa Eugénie at that time was Baron Goltz, then Prussian Ambassador to France; and Mr. Whitehurst notes that "the great cloudy German Question" was even then "the incubus of Europe."

It was in the autumn of 1867 that Lord Lyons became H.B.M. Ambassador to France. Mr. George Sheffield, who enjoyed exceptional popularity for many years, was His Excellency's Private Secretary, and Mr. Falconer Atlee the Keeper of the

---

[39] The Emperor's description in the local records.

Archives and Consul. Other members of the ambassadorial staff were the Hon. Julian Fane (another favourite in social and diplomatic circles), Mr. Adams, Mr. Clay Ker-Seymour, and Mr. Hildyard. All through 1867 "the Emperor was in the best possible health."

At the beginning of 1867 the "tout Paris" was talking about the conversion of the Duc de Morny's widow (a Troubetzkoï) to Catholicism, previous to her marriage with the Duc de Sesto, who, it was said, had been violently épris of Mlle. Eugénie de Montijo, and who died in 1910. At the "Italian" concert given at the Tuileries in March "the Emperor and Empress went over to speak to all the artistes, the Empress talking to Mme. Adelina Patti during most of the interval."

The one house in Paris where "everybody" met at this period appears to have been the Austrian Embassy; naturally so, for did not "the Metternichs" dominate everybody, the Sovereigns included, malgré eux? In that same "Exhibition" year Mme. Conneau was the "star" at one of Princesse Mathilde's "great" receptions. The charming wife of the Emperor's doctor was regarded in Paris as "the finest amateur singer in Europe"; their son was the constant companion of the Prince Imperial. At the opera Patti was singing in Verdi's "Joan of Arc," and Prince Napoleon was selling his works of art at the Hôtel des Ventes.

All the élite of the British world of sport went over to see the race for the Grand Prix in 1868, and the Emperor, the Empress, and the Prince Imperial applauded the gagnant, The Earl, owned by the "plunging" Marquis of Hastings. The winner was led in, amidst great excitement, by Mr. Padwick, a notoriety of the period, who is not forgotten by a few veterans like Mr. Chaplin and Lord Coventry. The Prince Imperial wore his hat on one side, and the Empress made him put it straight. "Perhaps," says Mr. Whitehurst, "the Empress thought wearing it on one side was too much like Lord Hastings."

Lord Lyons (a bachelor) was not credited with overmuch hospitality during his tenure of the Paris Embassy, but in the June of 1868 he surprised people by giving dinners two or three times a week.

At one of the State balls at the Tuileries in "Lord Hastings' year" an Englishman was heard to remark at the top of his voice: "I say, this is d— —d bad wine! Not so good as Pinard's!"[40] Whitehurst was a very minute recorder of events. He observed among the guests—4,000 or 5,000—"Mrs. Moulton, a great American beauty, and a fine musician; and the Comtesse de Fernandina, glittering in a sort of silver cloud." Also that "Napoleon III. was with his relative, the Duchess of Hamilton, née Princesse de Bade. They stopped to speak to Mme. De Arcos,[41] Irish, but married to a Spaniard. In the corner was the ne plus ultra of Paris fashion." And there were to be seen Mmes. de Gallifet, de Pourtalès, and de Sagan, and Princesse de Metternich, who "sat in judgment on Paris society," and "out of whose mouths came the dreaded sentence."

---

[40] M. Pinard was a prominent Minister, who died in 1910.

[41] Mme. De Arcos and her sister, Mrs. Vaughan, reside in London (1911). The first-named lady represented the Empress Eugénie at the funeral of Queen Victoria.

The Emperor Alexander II.

The King of Prussia.

The Emperor of Austria.

Ismail Pasha, Khedive of Egypt.

Leopold II.

**GUESTS OF THE EMPEROR AND EMPRESS OF THE FRENCH
IN THE "GREAT YEAR," 1867.**

*Portraits of the period by Franck. Reproduced from "Les Souverains à Paris,"
by Adrien Marx. Paris: E. Dentu, 1868.*

The military review in the Bois de Boulogne on June 6 transcended in glitter and colour all other spectacles witnessed in Paris since the elevation of the Prince-President to the imperial throne. "Grand succès! Enthousiasme énorme!" Thoughtless people, attracted to the Bois merely by curiosity, shed tears. Adrien Marx himself, "with his own eyes," saw these impressionable folk overcome by their emotion. One must have had "a heart with the famous 'triple envelope of brass' not to have felt feverish and overwhelmed by the deepest national sentiment at such a scene. Quel coup d'œil!"

This parade of 60,000 troops was in honour of the Emperor Alexander II. and King William of Prussia. They were in the imperial tribune, by the side of the Empress Eugénie, "in all the radiance of her beauty." There, too, was the Prince Imperial, aged eleven, regarding the crowd, drunk with joy, with his look of former days—that look at once sweet and naïf. Behind the Empress were the imperial and royal Princesses and all the Palace ladies. Other tribunes were reserved for all the dignitaries, illustrious persons, and the grandes dames that Paris could boast. The general wear for the ladies was light-hued taffetas, garnished with white guipures. This, for the moment, was the "livrée de la femme distinguée."

The success of the day was made by the artillery of the guard. The other plaudits were for the chasseurs, zouaves, guides, and cuirassiers. Marshal Canrobert was in command, and he was "much moved," reminding some of the chroniclers of "dramatic authors on the night of a première." Was he not also presenting to the public ("and what a public!") an important piece? Not a piece "à femmes," but a piece "à soixante mille hommes."

After inspecting the massed troops, the Sovereigns and their brilliant staff rode into the centre of the parade-ground and faced the tribunes. Then came the great movement of the day. Thirty thousand cavalry, ranged in one line, galloped at breakneck speed to within five yards of their Majesties, halted, and shouted in unison, "Vive l'Empereur!" cleaving the air with their gleaming sabres.

With the King of Prussia were the Crown Prince, Count von Bismarck, General Baron von Moltke, Major-General Count von Goltz, and many personages less known to fame. The Tsar was accompanied by the Tsarevitch (the late Emperor Alexander III.); another of his sons, the Grand Duke Vladimir; Prince Basil Dolgorouki, Count Adlerberg, Count Schouvaloff (in later years Ambassador in London), the French Generals Lebœuf and Fave, and Baron de Bourgoing.[42]

After a day's interval came the "bal des Souverains" at the Hôtel de Ville. Thanks to the magnificent Haussmann, this entertainment eclipsed the raoût offered in 1855 to Queen Victoria. The 10,000 invités agreed that such a spectacle was not to be witnessed twice in a century. "The féeries of the Hosteins and the Marc-Fourniers, with their surprises, their silks, their spangles, their velvets, their gold, their electricity, and their mise-en-scène, will henceforward leave us cold, dissatisfied, and eclipsed. Place yourself before a candle after you have looked at the sun!"

---

[42] His son, the present Baron, one of the doughtiest of Bonapartists, after the war married the celebrated actress, Mme. Reichenberg, who assisted at a charitable fête in 1911.

By three o'clock in the morning many of the ladies, exhausted, sat, or otherwise reposed, on the great stairs, waiting for their carriages, some of which, ordered for 2 a.m., could not be got until seven. When the sweepers, with their brooms, came in to "tidy up," they found the carpets hidden by masses of faded flowers and crushed imitation pearls, mingled with which were scraps of lace, tulle, and muslin. This fête cost the municipality £36,000, and the opposition papers lashed themselves into a state of frenzy at the waste of public money.

More magnificent even than the entertainment at the Hôtel de Ville was the Tuileries ball on June 10. M. Marx candidly confessed that "only the pen which wrote the 'Arabian Nights' could have adequately described the spectacle." Had he attempted the task, he would have been repeating himself; besides, he had exhausted all his finest phrases, and his stock of adjectives had given out. At the Hôtel de Ville it was a crowd; at the Tuileries there were only 600 guests, and everything "went upon wheels." The success of the fêtes to the foreign Sovereigns at the Tuileries was asserted to be due to the "high solicitude" and the "incessant surveillance" displayed by the Empress, then in her forty-first year, and determined that the imperial and royal guests should take away with them the most favourable impression and the pleasantest recollection of the Court of the "parvenu" Emperor and the lady who was ungraciously spoken of by her detractors as "the Spanish woman."

When the King of Prussia and the Crown Prince visited the imperial stables in 1867, they found 360 horses and 150 carriages. The royal couple were greeted by General Henry and Comte Davilliers, Grand Écuyer and Premier Écuyer, surrounded by an army of piqueurs, coachmen, postilions, grooms, estafettes, and others of the personnel, all wearing their State liveries. The horse-boxes were in carved oak; the name of each animal might be read in a medallion at the head of its stall, and surmounted by an imperial crown. Everything was on the grand scale: the straw beds claimed admiration; on the bituminous floor were modelled eagles with outspread wings; the chains and other garniture of the boxes and mangers were of brass and steel, and "shone like carbuncles." The light fell obliquely on the satin coats of the horses, and on the troughs and fountains.

As the Prussian Sovereign and his only son (the consort of our Princess Royal) passed through the imperial écuries, they saw, standing stiffly and solemnly, piqueurs, postilions, and coachmen, in their buckskin breeches, patent-leather boots, embroidered coats and waistcoats. The green overcoats gleamed with gold braid. King and Prince admired the coachmen, with their plumed tricornes, powdered hair, and "respectable corpulence," as the celebrated chroniqueur, Adrien Marx, described it. "I believe," he said, "their grave air and their imposing appearance vanished when they descended from their seats; but there is nothing in that. When they are on their feet they maintain a special attitude, the majesty and chic of which are observable in their prominent 'corporations.' Buffon said: 'Le style, c'est l'homme;' he might have added: 'Le ventre, c'est le cocher.'"

The Emperor had twelve saddle-horses: Walter Scott, Buckingham, Hero, Roncevaux, Alesia, Merveille, Carlo, Marathon, Marignan, Perceval, Stentor, and Marco. "Walter Scott" in particular captivated King William; he found another object for admiration in the gala carriage, all gold without and satin lining within, which had not been brought out since the Exhibition of 1855. Alongside was a tiny carriage, splendidly decorated, belonging to the Prince Imperial. In the sellerie was a gorgeous saddle with blue velvet fringe and silver monograms on either side; this was preserved as a historic souvenir: it had been used by the Emperor when he was Prince-President of the Republic. His riding-school was remarkable in many ways—*e.g.*, its eight enormous sculptured pillars supporting the Salle des États, in which 10,000 people used to pack themselves to witness the opening of the Chambers, and its gently-sloping staircase with double banisters. Up and down this wonderful structure the horses walked unaffrightedly. The centre was ornamented with flowers, and a fountain discharged its waters through the jaws of two bronze dogs lying on marble pedestals. King William would not leave until he had formally called upon the Fleurys (who had a suite of rooms in the Cour Caulaincourt), and had complimented the charming wife of the Grand Écuyer in that amiable fashion which made him so popular at the imperial Court. The King gave the "Black Eagle" to the Marquis de Morestier, Marshal Canrobert, and Marshal Regnault de Saint-Jean d'Angely; but it was remembered that he did not decorate any of the personnel of the Prussian Embassy.

At the apogee of the Empire!

Imperialism appears to be firmly rooted. Paris is the social centre of the civilized world. The "petit Prince" has already become the popular idol. Amongst the gay throng in front of Tortoni's, the modish café-restaurant of the period, may be seen some of the makers of the Empire. The tall, handsome man—so like the Emperor—is the Comte de Morny, presently to be created Duke. The half-brother of Napoleon III. is talking, in his eager, airy fashion, to Prince de Metternich, the Austrian Ambassador of those days, husband of Princesse Pauline.

The renowned publicist, Émile de Girardin, hat in hand, is telling the ladies in a carriage the last bit of boulevard gossip, the newest mot, the freshest scandal. There is the burly figure of Aurélien Scholl, one of the cleverest of the chroniqueurs and tellers of diverting stories; and close by is the enterprising Comte de Nieuwerkerke, of whom Princesse Mathilde made so much. Seated at one of the little tables is the great Auber, in the full flush of his fame—a grave-faced, white-haired man of huge frame and enormous head, the kindly friend and encourager of all the young composers of his time. Théophile Gautier is here, too, and Arsène Houssaye, who, like Scholl, has always a witty story to tell.

A notable group is composed of the Marquis de Massa, the author of so many bagatelles which enlivened the imperial Court at Compiègne, General the Marquis de Galiffet, and the Duc de Grammont-Caderousse.

The Turf has its representatives in Charles Lafitte ("Major Fridolin"), the banker, and the Comte de Lagrange; and in a corner, under the awning of Tortoni's, is Isabelle, the flower-girl, of whom the Emperor and Empress now and then buy a cluster of roses or violets.

The immortal Meyerbeer, and, at the opposite pole, the equally immortal Jacques Offenbach; Victorien Sardou, the brothers E. and J. de Goncourt; the littérateur Jules Sandeau, the playwright Octave Feuillet, the actresses Déjazet and Augustine Brohan, sister of the incomparable Madeleine—all are here on the perron of Tortoni's in the golden days of the Empire.

We will assist (in 1868) at the "Sortie de l'Opéra," the old house in the Rue Le Peletier. "Hamlet" has been given for the first time, with Christine Nilsson as Ophelia. Here are that extraordinary Duke of Brunswick (whose eccentric will was in dispute for so many years), the Prince de Sagan, Prince Murat, Marshal Canrobert, Emile Ollivier, Henri Rochefort, Baron Haussmann (who made Paris what it is), Léon Gambetta, Paul Déroulède, the Duc de Mouchy (whose marriage with Princesse Anna Murat was arranged by Napoleon III.), Comte Edmond de Pourtalès, M. Thiers, M. Mirès (the financier), Prince Joseph Poniatowski, the Vicomte d'Harcourt (once French Ambassador to our Court), the Duc de Bisaccia (later Duc de Doudeauville), the Marquis de Caux (Mme. Patti's first husband, leader of the Empress's cotillons), Chevalier Nigra (the Italian Ambassador), Baron Alphonse de Rothschild, the Duc de FitzJames, Comte Walewski, the Duc de Crussol, Comte Paul Demidoff, M. de Villemessant (founder of the *Figaro*), and innumerable others—all people with histories.

The King of Holland (father of "Citron") condescended to "beat the asphalte" not seldom, and to mingle with the gay throng at Tortoni's, the Café Anglais, the Maison d'Or, and the other modish resorts. He married, firstly, Princess Sophia of Würtemburg, whose mother was Queen Catherine of Würtemburg, wife of King Jérôme. The Queen of Holland was consequently cousin-german of "Plon-Plon" and his sister Princesse Mathilde. The King was most lavish to his numerous favourites, but his wife was kept so short of money that when she went abroad—on a visit to France, for instance—she was accompanied only by an elderly lady as badly off as her royal mistress. The Queen was the friend of the Emperor and Empress. William III. would squander thousands on the Paris actresses and opera-singers, and refuse his wife sufficient guilders to buy a new dress; her cherry-coloured silk gown became legendary, for she endeavoured to impart a new aspect to it by substituting black lace for white, and vice versâ.

The monarch was much criticized for his intrigue with Mme. Musard, whose husband gave popular concerts during the brightest days of the Second Empire on the site of what is now the "Jardin de Paris." Mme. Musard was as well known by the boulevardiers and flâneurs as the Empress herself, and more talked about, while the complacent husband was accorded the customary amount of chaff. When congratulated on the improvement in his finances, Musard, with self-satisfied air, replied that it had pleased Providence to remove from this sublunary sphere a wealthy relative, who had left him a nice little sum. Unfortunately, Musard had quite forgotten to keep up his pleasant deception by putting a mourning band on his hat, so that the explanation of his good fortune was received with a general wink. But presently the pony-chaise which Musard had started shortly after his wife's acquaintance with the King of Holland gave place to a phaeton and a pair of horses, worth 800 guineas, while madame's magnificent turn-out made the great ladies green with envy. The former head-groom of a milord anglais had charge of the stables; everything was done in perfect style. There was a house in town and a château, whose grounds and flower-gardens ran down to the Seine.

To find a parallel to so much magnificence one had to recall the days of Louis Quatorze and Mme. de Montespan, of Louis Quinze and the Du Barry. Paris society was greatly intriguée to know the precise locality of the Pactolus from whence so much gold flowed, but it remained in blissful ignorance for many a month. While his legitimate spouse was vegetating in watery Holland, this King who dragged his ermine robes through the mire with such complete indifference to what the Mrs. Grundys of Paris and The Hague might say was receiving the lady at a charming cottage in a secluded spot, suggestive of Rosamund's bower. The excellent chef d'orchestre used to accompany his wife to the frontier, give her a marital embrace, and then return to his beloved Paris pour s'amuser. Not the least curious and instructive part of the story is the fact that the subjects of this monarch who took for his model no less a god than Eros looked on with amused complacence, and only the Queen suffered. There was another lady whom William of Holland held in the highest admiration—Mlle. Abingdon, "of the Paris theatres"; she, however, did not appreciate His Majesty to the extent that she might have done, and one day, when the King wanted her to read to him by the hour, she said she would "call her mother, who was a much better reader than herself." Mme. Musard died at the age of forty, blind and insane; but the roi galant lived to marry a charming young wife, the sister of H.R.H. the Duchess of Albany.

In the autumn of 1857 Mr. Allsop arrived in Paris. He spoke French perfectly; his Italian was singularly pure; he surprised people by declaring that he was an Englishman—Mr. Allsop. When he "descended" at a highly respectable hotel it was observed that among his luggage was a small box, rather heavy. The servants were to take it very carefully to his room; they were on no account to shake it or drop it. (Mr. Allsop had not allowed this precious box to be handled by the railway porters. He had placed it in the rack over his head, and he carried it to the cab upon his arrival at the Northern Station.) Presently Mr. Allsop's groom arrived at the hotel, and with the groom a horse, which the owner rode daily in the Bois. Mr. Allsop remained at the hotel a short time, then left it for an appartement.

Mr. Allsop, although a studious, grave man, mingled in the gay life of the capital. One night he went to a masked ball at the Opéra. Two ladies—femmes du monde—prompted by curiosity to see what this sort of thing was like, had gone to the theatre, somewhat imprudently, unescorted. They watched the scene from their box for a while; then, finding it "slow," left the loge, and were about to make a tour of the great salle, when they became the subjects of much "chaff," humorous and good-tempered, but sadly lacking in refinement. At an embarrassing moment two men—gentlemen—intervened, and so grateful were the ladies, that after a moment's hesitation—for form's sake—they accepted the strangers' invitation to sup at a neighbouring restaurant. That the two men had not known each other previously was additionally piquant. The names of the quartette were divulged at the supper-table: Mr. Allsop, M. Poplu (fashionable journalist), Mme. de Guersac, Mme. de Lubernay.

The ladies, and even M. Poplu, did not quite know what to make of Mr. Allsop. That he was a gentleman they felt certain. There was a great charm about his conversation. His manners were refined, and the ladies—Mme. de Guersac in particular—admitted that he had "a way" with him well calculated to win favour with women of sentiment. When the talk was led by M. Poplu in the direction of the Tuileries and its august occupants, Mr. Allsop was much interested, just as any other intelligent and travelled Englishman would have been. M. Poplu was very sarcastic and epigrammatic at the expense of the Emperor. Mme. de Guersac allowed it to be understood that her knowledge of the imperial couple was not derived from books, from the chroniques, or from salon gossip. Mr. Allsop and M. Poplu realized that this beautiful woman was "on terms" with "the pale Emperor," as they had begun to call him.

A result of this very gay supper-party after the Opéra ball was that Mme. de Guersac and Mr. Allsop became great friends, and that the latter learnt many facts—mingled, perhaps, with not a little fiction—concerning life at the Tuileries. The winter weeks passed very pleasantly for these two congenial spirits, thanks partly to M. de Guersac being somewhere abroad. On January 13 Mme. de Guersac casually told Mr. Allsop that on the next evening the Sovereigns were going to the Opéra. It was an event—a performance for the benefit of M. Massol,[43] and Ristori was appearing. Mr. Allsop remarked that the news had not been given in any of the journals which he had read. Mme. de Guersac rejoined that it was a titbit of information which she had given him.

The news leaked out on the following day, and long before eight o'clock the thoroughfares near the Opéra were thronged. Just as the carriage containing the Emperor and Empress approached the entrance to the theatre an explosion threw the crowd into a panic; it was followed by another, and by a third. Three bombs had been thrown, and they had wrought havoc. A hundred and fifty people were more or less seriously injured. The imperial carriage was partly smashed; one of the horses was killed outright, and another was apparently lifeless. The Emperor escaped with a very slight scratch on one eye. The Empress's dress was spotted with blood. The coachman and three footmen were badly maimed. One of the twelve Lancers of the Guard forming the escort was killed; all the other troopers suffered from the explosions.

> The door on the right-hand side of the imperial carriage opened, and the crowd saw a gentleman in evening dress get out. He seemed to be in some pain; he looked rather frightened; his face was as white as wax. His features were convulsed, the eyes those of a man waking from a nightmare, wondering if his nocturnal visions were real or imaginary; while his hat, almost crushed out of shape, and on the back of his head, gave him a ridiculous appearance. This mixture of two different characters imprinted on his physiognomy made him look like a tragical clown, affected by a sincere chagrin and ready to shed real tears. It was Pierrot haunted by a spectre; it was His Imperial Majesty Napoleon III., Emperor of the French.
>
> But the Emperor, courageous and cool, subdued his emotion.

[43] A well-known artiste.

He had always been calm in moments of danger, and now he did not raise a cry of alarm, nor utter imprecations, nor hasten his movements. The bystanders nearest to him scarcely noticed a slight feverishness in the gesture which he made in taking the Empress's hand, and the tremor in his voice when he said to her soothingly: "Come, Eugénie, get out of the carriage."

She alighted comparatively quickly. She, too, was livid. The diadem which encircled her golden hair was all awry, looking as if it had been struck by someone's fist. "Ah, mon Dieu, it is horrible! What has happened, Louis?"

"This blood upon thee!" the Emperor exclaimed. "Art thou injured?"

A long red stream trickled down her pink dress and over her white gloves.

"No, I don't feel anything," she answered. "It is not my blood; it must be the General's."[44]

The Emperor led his wife into the vestibule of the theatre, and here the Sovereigns questioned each other with that sincerity which even mutual incompatibility never completely banishes—sincerity which, in hours of danger, springs from some unknown source.

"Why dost thou rub thy eye, Louis?" said the Empress. Then, closely examining his face, she noticed a slight scratch on the Emperor's left eye. Reassured, she said: "It is nothing. But it might have blinded thee. God has protected thee. Fortunately, before we came out I offered a prayer to my patron saint and one to St. Christopher."

The Emperor thought the protection accorded them by the saints would have been still more complete had the catastrophe been prevented, but he said nothing; and having satisfied himself that the Empress was unhurt, he assisted her to make the slight readjustments of her toilette which were necessary to enable them to appear in the imperial box without any visible indications of the terrible ordeal they had undergone.[45]

Mr. Allsop was among the thousands who witnessed the explosions in the Rue Le Peletier. He was also among the victims. He entered a pharmacy, was duly attended to, returned to his lodgings, and went to bed. He had his own reasons for determining to leave Paris for England the next day. Full of this intention, he was endeavouring to get to sleep when he was disturbed by a loud knocking at the door. Then his room was invaded by the police, who unceremoniously hustled

[44] General Roguet, who was sitting outside, had been badly injured in the neck, and bled profusely.

[45] Derived from "Amours tragiques de Napoléon III.," by Gaston Stiegler. Dedicated to M. Adrien Hébrard, rédacteur-en-chief of *Le Temps*.

him into a waiting cab. And one head that rolled into the basket was the head of Orsini, alias Allsop.[46]

To the Republicans the Emperor remained in 1863 (the first year of the "adventure" in Mexico) the "Sire de Framboisy." They resolved never to come to terms with him. The Sire de Framboisy was the hero of an inept song, to which the stupidity of the police in 1859 had given a semblance of actuality. The Sire de [or Lord of] Framboisy, on his return to Paris from the wars, misses his wife. He searches for, and ultimately finds, his errant spouse in doubtful company at a bal de barrière. He addresses her:

"Corbleu, madame, que faites-vous ici?"

and she replies:

"J'y danse le cancan avec tous mes amis."

When the Emperor returned to St. Cloud after the Italian campaign some of the street "loafers" took to humming these two lines; the Censeur was shocked, and ordered this "couplet à clef" to be cut out—a step which had the natural result of increasing the popularity of the song.

The year 1860 (says M. James de Chambrier in his brilliant collection of studies, "Entre l'Apogée et le Déclin") finished under the double aureole of the "political successes and military glories acquired for the Second Empire as much by the personal action of Napoleon III. as by the endurance and entrain of his armies." The Syrian expedition had liberated the Christians of the Lebanon. Lord John Russell[47] had occupied himself less with the security of the Christians from Turkish attacks than with the Emperor's aims in Syria, and perhaps in Egypt. The Porte gradually became more reasonable, and on June 9, 1861, signed the Act by which the Lebanon, reorganized, had for its administrator a Christian Governor. Six weeks later French and English were again fighting side by side in China. By the end of October the war was over, and the news of the success of Palikao[48] was "received with just pride at the Tuileries."

In November and December, 1860, the Empress was in Scotland—the result of "scenes" with her consort at the Tuileries. She returned to Paris in time to receive the usual New Year congratulations (January 1, 1861), but her emotion overcame her as she stood by the side of the Emperor in the salon, where the members of the Diplomatic Body and of the Household had gathered to greet the Sovereigns.

---

[46] For what is known as "the Orsini attempt" to murder the Emperor and Empress on January 14, 1858, Orsini and Pierri were executed. Gomez and Count Rudio were sent to the galleys for life, the latter having been reprieved at the last moment. Rudio escaped from his prison, and died in California in 1910, aged seventy-seven.

[47] Then Prime Minister.

[48] Palikao (Montauban) was War Minister, under the Empress's Regency, at the downfall of the Empire.

CHAPTER VII

TWO EMPRESSES

To the château of Bouchout, hard by Laecken, the thoughts of the châtelaine of Farnborough Hill must often have wandered. The beautiful avenue of Meysse, which links the royal estates of Bouchout and Laeken, was a favourite walk of the late King Leopold, for it leads to his sister's house. The Empress Eugénie has, indeed, reason to bear well in mind this Belgian Princess—Charlotte, Empress of Mexico—whose widowhood is of older date than that of the Emperor Napoleon's consort, even as her story is still more pitifully tragic. The imperial crown of Mexico, which Napoleon III. placed on the heads of the Archduke Maximilian Ferdinand Joseph and the sister of Leopold II., cost the Emperor of Austria's ambitious brother his life and the Belgian Princess her reason. The Empress Eugénie must not, then, absorb all our pity; some of it should be bestowed upon the demented occupant of Bouchout, aunt of Prince Napoleon's consort, Princesse Clémentine.

Seven years before the disruption of the Empire the throne of Mexico was offered to Maximilian by Napoleon III., who guaranteed to leave in the country for three years an army of occupation, 25,000 strong, commanded part of the time by Marshal Bazaine. This engagement Napoleon fulfilled to the letter; then the French troops were withdrawn. Maximilian was in dire extremity, and in 1867 the Empress Charlotte journeyed to Paris to implore help. In her absence the Mexicans executed the man who had been foisted upon them as their "Emperor."[49]

The Empress Charlotte sailed for Europe full of hope. When she landed at Brest she looked round to see who had come to receive her on the part of the French Emperor. No one was visible. This was her first disappointment. Her suite sought to console her. There must have been a mistake. The official reception would be in Paris. Court carriages would be awaiting her at the railway-station. One of the Emperor's chamberlains would certainly be there to greet her—perhaps the Emperor himself. "Perhaps not," she murmured.

As it had been at Brest, so it was at Paris. No one at the station to receive her, no imperial carriage, no bowing court chamberlain to pay her homage and offer her the traditional bouquet, not even a strip of red carpet on the grey asphalte. Yet she was a King's daughter, a Kaiser's sister-in-law, and an Empress in Mexico.

Charlotte was taken to the Grand Hotel in a "carriage"—either a cab called "off the rank," or the hotel 'bus. Miss Howard or Mlle. Bellanger would have fared

---

[49] The idea of Napoleon III. appears to have been to secure what he called "the American equilibrium" by founding in Mexico "a regenerating Empire."

better.

The Empress Charlotte shut herself up alone in her room, refused to see any-one, and would not touch the food which was placed before her. One of the ladies of her small suite said: "Her Majesty has evidently had a great shock. She has never looked as she now looks since the death of her father, King Leopold. She is like a dead woman."

The next day passed without any indication from the Court that an Empress had arrived. On the third day an imperial chamberlain brought an invitation to lunch with their Majesties at St. Cloud. Charlotte disdainfully declined it, and bade the official say she would drive to St. Cloud during the afternoon.

She had been weeping all the morning, foreseeing that her petition for help would be addressed to "deaf ears and a callous heart." In the carriage she worked herself into such a frenzy that her companion, the Comtesse del Bario, was on the point of telling the coachman to return to the Grand. However, they drove on, and entered the courtyard of the château. Stiffening herself, Maximilian's wife walked up the great staircase and, with a firm step, her cheeks burning, entered a salon. Napoleon was there, waiting for her. He looked preoccupied and annoyed, and twirled his moustache. By his side were the Empress Eugénie and the Prince Imperial. There were the usual greetings, official smiles, and presentations. Eti-quette being thus satisfied, the Emperor entered his cabinet, followed by the two Empresses. The doors were closed, and Charlotte's suite resigned themselves to a long wait in an adjoining room.

Presently came a faint sound of talking, then it became louder, betokening an animated discussion, and then a silence. Charlotte's friends looked at one another anxiously, as they heard the raucous voice of their imperial mistress: "How can I ever have forgotten who I am and who you are! I ought to have remembered that the blood of the Bourbons flows through my veins, and not have disgraced my race by humiliating myself before a Bonaparte and negotiating with an adventurer!"

There was a sound as of someone falling — then dead silence. The door opened. Napoleon III., very pale, stood on the threshold. Glancing at the Comtesse del Bario, he said, "Venez donc, je vous prie."

In the imperial cabinet the Comtesse saw her mistress, stretched out on a couch, apparently lifeless. The Empress Eugénie, weeping, had unfastened Char-lotte's corsage, taken off the sufferer's boots and stockings, and was kneeling by the icy body, rubbing Charlotte's feet with eau-de-Cologne. Slowly recovering consciousness, Charlotte, seeing the Comtesse, held out her hand, saying trem-blingly, "Manuelita, don't leave me."

The Emperor, looking bewildered, hovered round the prostrate form on the couch, strode up and down the room, left the apartment, and came back again. He had "lost his head." He called for a doctor; then ordered a messenger to go as quickly as possible and bring Dr. Semeleder, the Empress Charlotte's doctor, from the Grand Hotel. Meanwhile the Empress Eugénie, in words interrupted by sobs, told the Comtesse what had brought about the attack — the Emperor's refusal to grant Charlotte's request, her prayers, her entreaties, her tears, her threats, and her wild ejaculations. Whilst speaking soothingly, the Empress Eugénie had prepared a glass of eau sucrée, and tried to make Charlotte drink it. But the Mexican Sovereign pushed it from her with a furious gesture, shrieking, "Assassins! Go away, and take your poisoned drink with you!"

A torrent of tears followed this outburst. Throwing herself into the arms of the Comtesse, Charlotte entreated her not to abandon her to "this race of Borgias, who wanted to rid themselves of her by making her drink a poisonous drug."

The Emperor, who had been overcome by this agonizing scene, now returned, bringing with him Dr. Semeleder, whose first words were to ask the Emperor and the Empress Eugénie to leave him alone with Charlotte. The carriage was brought, and the sufferer was taken back to the Grand. As she was borne past them to the landau the terrified courtiers pretended not to have seen or heard anything. Tears were in all eyes, even in the Emperor's. Charlotte was insane from that moment, and has never recovered, although she is said to have lucid intervals.

This tragic episode remained a secret for a long time.

The next day's papers stated that the Emperor and the Empress Eugénie had received a visit from the Empress Charlotte at St. Cloud. "The interview was of a very cordial nature, and lasted two hours."

*   *   *   *   *

If the Empress Eugénie's thoughts dwell sometimes on the fates of the occupant of the château of Bouchout, who will go to her grave happily unconscious of her husband's execution, she has many a joyous souvenir to gladden her declining years. I will recall only one—that relating to her first meeting with Queen Victoria, at Windsor Castle, in 1855.

In later years, recording this event, the Queen described the Emperor Napoleon's consort, then only between thirty and thirty-one, and "in full beauty," as "the very gentle, graceful, and evidently very nervous Empress." It was on that occasion that, at a "full Chapter," the Order of the Garter was conferred upon Napoleon III., with whom, on the previous night, the Queen had danced a quadrille. "How strange," wrote the Queen, "to think that I, the grand-daughter of George III., should dance with the Emperor Napoleon, nephew of England's greatest enemy, now my nearest and most intimate ally, in the Waterloo Room, and this ally only six years ago living in this country an exile, poor and unthought of!"

Strange was the picture, for since Prince Louis Napoleon had occupied those modest chambers in King Street, St. James's (now "Napoleon House"), and had been one of the ornaments of the Gore House réunions, chance had raised him to the proud position which he occupied until the disaster at Sedan overwhelmed the Empire and consigned him to captivity. His investiture with the much prized Order was marked by all the dignified and grandiose ceremony which made Queen's Victoria's Court the world's envy. The Queen looked magnificent in her purple velvet mantle, crimson velvet hood, and "collar" of the Order. By her side was her illustrious consort, that Prince Albert who, six years later, was to be taken from her at a moment when the nation had learnt to recognize his noble qualities.

The Knights Companions present who answered to their names as they were called out in sonorous tones by Sir Charles George Young, then Garter King of Arms, were the Marquis of Exeter, Duke of Richmond, Marquis of Lansdowne, Duke of Buckingham, Marquis of Salisbury, Duke of Cleveland, Earl de Grey, Marquis of Abercorn, Marquis of Hertford, Duke of Bedford, Earl of Clarendon, Earl Spencer, Earl Fitzwilliam, Duke of Northumberland, Earl of Ellesmere, and the Earl of Aberdeen. All these noble knights have passed away. King Edward VII., who had witnessed the imposing ceremony, long survived them.

Thanks to the "Court Circular" of the period, the scene of April 18, 1855, can be reconstituted. The Emperor Napoleon was conducted from his apartments to the Throne Room by the Prince Consort and the Duke of Cambridge, and took a seat in the Chair of State on the Queen's right. The Empress Eugénie witnessed the ceremony, surrounded by the Prince of Wales and the other members of the Royal Family. At the fitting moment the Queen, assisted by Prince Albert, buckled the Garter on the Emperor's left leg, the Chancellor of the Order (the Bishop of Oxford; the "Prelate" being the Bishop of Winchester) pronouncing the admonition. Then the Queen put the ribbon, with the "George," over the Emperor's left shoulder, and the Chancellor pronounced a second admonition. Next the Queen gave the accolade, and Napoleon III. received the congratulations of all the Knights Companions present.

The stately function was over. "As we were going along to the Emperor's apartments," wrote the Queen, "he said, 'I heartily thank your Majesty. It is one bond the more. I have given my oath of fidelity to your Majesty, and I will keep it carefully.'" A little later in the day the Emperor said to the Queen, "It is a great event for me, and I hope I may be able to prove my gratitude to your Majesty and to your country." And to a friend he observed, "Enfin je suis gentilhomme!" The "parvenu," as he had styled himself, was making headway, thanks to Queen Victoria.

No need to dwell upon the return visit paid by the Queen and the Prince Consort in the summer of the same year. The English Sovereign and her consort entertained the Emperor and Empress of the French for the second time in 1857. The scene was the Isle of Wight. Although it was a private, "an even most sequestered," visit, it was said that "matters of high import to the welfare of both nations" were discussed at Osborne, and that "more than one rock which threatened shipwreck to the cordial understanding between the two countries was removed." The suite accompanying the French Sovereigns was limited to the Princesse d'Essling, Comte and Comtesse Walewski, General Rollin, and General Fleury, whose son, Comte Serge, was in England, lecturing (and this is worthy of note) on the Empress Eugénie, in the summer of 1908. The imperial yacht, *Reine Hortense*, reached the island at half-past eight in the morning (August 6), and the Queen and the Prince Consort, accompanied by Prince Alfred, the Princess Royal, and Princess Alice, went down to the pier to welcome the imperial pair. Lords Palmerston and Clarendon enlivened the royal party at the dinner-table that evening. Of all these the solitary survivor is the Empress.

The Empress Eugénie must often recall those quiet, happy days which she and her consort passed at Osborne—the excursion to Carisbrook Castle, the drive to Cowes to witness the conclusion of the race for the cup, the visit, on the Sunday, to the Catholic Church at Newport, and the gay scene on the Solent as the *Reine Hortense* threaded her way between the yachts and warships. Nor can the imperial lady have forgotten that while she and her husband were the Queen's guests three Italians—Tibaldi, Bartolotti, and Grilli—were being tried in Paris for an attempt on the life of the Emperor. Possibly, too, she may remember that so anxious had the Emperor been, on the morning of their arrival, to get a good view of Osborne that he betook himself to the bridge of his yacht, slipped on the ladder, and rolled to the deck. "As we are proceeding to the conquest of England," he said, smiling, "I ought to have waited until landing before falling." These were true words spoken in jest, for throughout his reign he never lost sight of one object—the political conquest of England. And here one recalls what the Emperor is asserted to have said on his arrival, with the Empress, at Windsor Castle in 1855: "In seeing again the country in which I lived when I was poor, and which I left to make my fortune, I am reminded of the story of the man who, as a boy, arrived in Paris in wooden shoes, and when he became rich went for a day to his native village and slept in the hovel which had sheltered him in his boyhood."

CHAPTER VIII
THE TUILERIES

The "great" balls at the Tuileries were given before Lent; the "little" balls, otherwise known as the Empress's "Mondays," after Easter. At the larger of these entertainments all the men were in uniform. The Emperor, the Generals, and the officers of the household wore white cashmere breeches, silk socks of the same colour, and pumps with buckles. Civilians were in Court dress, with embroidered collars and cuffs, and swords; the crush hat (clâque) was carried under the arm. One person only wore buckskin breeches and high riding-boots of varnished leather: this was the écuyer on duty.

At the "Mondays" the guests were restricted to those who had been previously "presented"; they were selected in rotation from a list—this was the "séries." Court functionaries and a few of their Majesties' most intimate friends were invited to all the "Mondays." The regulation garb for men on these occasions was either "shorts," or very tight-fitting trousers, and black tail-coats. The Emperor and the officers of the household were in evening dress, the coat being of a dark blue cloth, with velvet collar, the lapels lined with white satin, and gilt buttons bearing a crowned eagle.

Each ball was preceded by a family dinner, the guests being Prince Napoleon and his wife, Princesse Clothilde; Princesse Mathilde, the Murat Princes and Princesses, Prince Charles and Princesse Christine Bonaparte, the Marquis and the Marquise de Roccagiovine, and Comte and Comtesse Primoli.

About ten o'clock the Emperor and Empress entered the salon of the First Consul. Here the guests had previously assembled, here new presentations were made by the First Chamberlain, Comte Bacciochi, and their Majesties made the tour of the room, saying a few words to all before the dancing began. The Empress, who seldom danced, took up her position in an adjoining salon, whither she was generally followed by diplomatists like Lord Cowley (H.B.M. Ambassador), Prince de Metternich, and Chevalier Nigra, and by intimate friends like Prosper Mérimée, Édouard Delessert, Onésime Aguado, and a few others.

During the dancing the Emperor chatted for an hour or so with his Ministers; then, reappearing in the ballroom, chose a partner, and himself led a "boulangère," or formed a set of the "lancers," preferring either of these to quadrilles, which he found lacking in "go." Then came the cotillon, led by Princesse Anna Murat and the volatile Marquis de Caux (both unmarried at the time, and both in high favour with the Sovereigns), who took up their position in chaises volantes in front of the fireplace. In the cotillon forty couples took part, including on one occasion (the Marquis de Massa noted) Mlles. de Heeckeren, de Seebach, de Bassano, Harvey, de Errazu, Magnan, Haussmann, Hamelin, and Bouvet, whose cavaliers were MM. Davilliers, Castelbajac, Poniatowski, d'Espeuilles, Duperré, du Bourg, Clermont-Tonnerre, des Varannes (all of whom were either écuyers or officiers d'ordonnance), Arthur de Cossé-Brissac (the Empress's Chamberlain), etc. The cotillons at the Tuileries were very simple affairs, the presents distributed being merely flowers and coloured rosettes. The guests supped standing at a buffet, and by one o'clock the ball was over.

At one of the first of the grand balls given at the Tuileries before the marriage the Emperor danced in the quadrille of honour with Lady Cowley, wife of the British Ambassador. "He danced another quadrille with Mlle. de Montijo, who," Baron Imbert de Saint-Amand has told us, "was assuredly the most beautiful of all the women present. Her resplendent beauty and extreme elegance excited general admiration.... How she would have shuddered could she have foreseen the state in which she would find this supper-room in 1870, at the beginning of the fatal war! Then she would instal an ambulance there. Instead of women loaded with jewels, there would be sisters of charity with their white cornettes."

At one of the "small" dances, or, as they were called, "Mondays," at the Tuileries—entertainments which always took place before Lent—after the author of "Colomba"[50] had regaled the chosen few who had been invited to join the "circle" with some tales drawn from the chroniques chevaleresques of ancient Spain, the Empress volunteered to tell a little story of herself when she was still Mlle. de Montijo. The scene was Estramadura. She was riding a richly-caparisoned mule, and, with her little party, stopped for a few minutes at an auberge, in front of which, taking a rest, was a man, shod in espradilles—

Plus délabré que Job, et plus fier que Bragance

—one of those lithe mountaineers, with flashing eyes, the type of Victor Hugo's Don César de Bazan and Hernani. The young lady was parched, and asked for a vaso de agua. Struck by her beauty, the mountaineer resolved that none but himself should have the honour of serving the fair traveller, and, snatching from the landlord's hands the jug of fresh water and the glass, he filled the latter and offered it to Mlle. de Montijo, but not until he had knelt a moment in homage. "Muchas gratias," said the future Empress, returning to the gallant caballero the glass, in which some water still remained. Raising the glass to his lips, he slowly drained it, keeping his gaze fixed upon the lady all the while, and finally breaking the glass into fragments, in order that no one else should ever use it!

Of the score or more of those who have essayed to depict the imperial vie intime during the first years of the reign—from the marriage in January, 1853, to the "attempt" by Orsini in January, 1858—none has surpassed M. Gaston Stiegler.[51]

It is early morning, and the Emperor's toilette is being completed by his faithful valet, Charles Thélin. The carpet is littered with opened telegrams and news-

[50] Prosper Mérimée.
[51] "Amours Tragiques de Napoléon III." Par Gaston Stiegler. Paris: Albin Michel.

papers. His Majesty is tired, and rubs his dull eyes, while Thélin waxes the large fair moustache which covers the master's mouth, and draws it into two fine points. After his sparse locks have been artistically combed and brushed, "washes" and pomades applied, and the pale cheeks brightened with rouge—after everything has been done as scrupulously as the most elegant petite maîtresse could have desired—Napoleon III. rises and puts on the severely cut frock-coat in which he is almost invariably seen, save when he is in uniform or hunting or shooting garb. His faithful companion, his meerschaum pipe, beautifully coloured, smiles upon him from a little table. He lights it, and joins his secretary (M. Mocquard) and Dr. Conneau, both blindly devoted to him. These morning moments were generally the best parts of his day. Mocquard and Conneau were the friends of his youth, the friends of his mother, who, on her death-bed, made the doctor promise never to leave her son.[52]

"Has your Majesty slept well?" asks Conneau.

"Not badly, thank you; but not enough, my good friend," came from the thick voice, which did not harmonize with his air of natural distinction.

"Yes, yes; I know. You returned late—always too late. It is telling upon you."

The Emperor took this scolding every morning very amiably. The solicitude for his health pleased him.

"Youth will have its fling," said Mocquard, smiling.

"You chaff, Mocquard," replied the doctor. "I am uneasy until I know the Emperor is here, in this château, with the doors locked, under the eyes of the sentinels."

"I chaff faute de mieux, mon cher. I am entirely of your opinion. But morality—that is not in my line. We knew nothing about it in my time. You have taken charge of it, and it could not be in better hands."

"Well, well," said Conneau; "let us leave him to kill himself—or to get killed!" And, growling, he put on his glasses, opened a large book which he had just received, and plunged into its pages as if he had had enough of the conversation.

"Charles," said the Emperor, "tell Félix to send the Prince down and inquire after the Empress."

Smoking his pipe, he paced up and down, his head sunk in his shoulders, balancing his massive body on his short, little legs, which seemed not to have been made to bear him. He stopped before the mantelpiece; the blazing fire absorbed his whole attention. He seemed to see in the red and blue sparks the reflection of the tricks played upon him by that fortune of which he was himself the most remarkable example, and he asked himself how long those petits follets would last. Suddenly a huge log broke into halves, littering the hearth. The beautiful flames were extinguished, and in their stead came a disagreeable volume of smoke. He grasped the tongs, carefully picked up the pieces of half-burnt wood, and, while amusing himself in this patriarchal manner, asked:

[52] Dr. Conneau was with the Emperor at Sedan, at Wilhelmshöhe, and at Chislehurst until the end came in January, 1873.

"What are you reading, Conneau?"

"I am not reading, Sire."

"And this great book?"

"It is a Bible, which I bought yesterday."

"Ah, yes, for your collection," said the Emperor laughingly. "What language is it?"

"Hebrew, Sire."

"Nonsense, Conneau! You don't know Hebrew, and you are not the man to go into ecstasies over a Bible, even a French one. Well?"

"It is a magnificent edition, published at Venice in 1551—printed by Giustinani."

"Well?"

"Sire, do I laugh at you when, at Champlieu, or elsewhere—in some camp of Cæsar or other—you pick up old tiles, Roman or pretended Roman; antique things without form or colour, broken vases which have been used for Heaven knows what purpose? However, you put them carefully in glass cases or in the museums, and you like people to look at them. Everybody has his own hobby."

"Oh, my poor potteries!" sighed the Emperor. "How they abuse you!"

He laid down the tongs, and, after rolling a cigarette, took up a fragment of an amphora which had been found during the excavation of a Merovingian tomb near Soissons. It was a common-looking piece of clay, without a vestige of decoration. But he held it up to the light, and examined it with all the tenderness of a connoisseur, while Conneau, with loving hands, turned the leaves of his beautiful Bible, in which some amateur had intercalated several rudely-executed pictures.

Less than three years after the imperial nuptials a very distinguished Englishwoman was the guest of their Majesties. Her son, Lord Ronald Sutherland Gower, wrote:

> In October, 1855, my mother[53] took me over to Paris for the first time. We visited the Tuileries and Versailles. During one of our expeditions to some gallery or exhibition the Empress recognized my mother, although she only knew her from her likeness to her portrait by Winterhalter, the lithographs of which were in the printsellers' windows, and immediately invited her to dine at St. Cloud, where the Court then was. My mother had known the Emperor slightly, for on a previous visit [of the Duchess] to Paris he had called on her at Meurice's Hotel. Although charmed by the beauty and grace of the Empress, my mother had little liking for the imperial Court of France or its master.

In the great year 1867 Lord Ronald, like thousands of English people, went to Paris for the Exhibition. "It was the apogee of the Second Empire—of the Empire

---

[53] The Duchess of Sutherland.

that smelt half of gunpowder and half of patchouli. Maximilian's death was not then known at the Tuileries. Napoleon III. was then host to all the Sovereigns of the Continent, and yet within three short years all was in the dust."

Later (in January, 1868) he was invited to a ball at the Tuileries:

> It was a hard winter, and all the gay world was skating in the Bois de Boulogne. There were Mme. de Metternich, plain, with the exception of fine, roguish eyes, and always beautifully dressed, and Mme. de Galliffet, with whose looks I was disappointed. Thanks to some French friends—the Boyers—I saw a ball at the Tuileries without the trouble of a presentation to their Imperial Majesties. As a sight the ball was interesting, unlike any other Court ball that I have seen. Perhaps the most striking sight was the double file of Cent Gardes, in their gorgeous pale blue and silver uniforms, lining the State entrance and staircase and standing sentry at the doors. After passing the Salon de Diane and struggling through a crowd principally composed of officers, I got a good place in front of the daïs, on which the Emperor and Empress were seated. The Empress was all in white, and looked strikingly handsome. The Emperor did not appear to advantage in his white silk tights and stockings, and seemed tired and bored. During, and between, the dances he walked across the open space in front of the daïs and conversed with some of the officers and diplomatists. He was a long time in conversation with a fat General, who I was told was Lebœuf. The supper was admirably managed. Piles of truffes en serviette abounded, and here there was less of a crowd than at Buckingham Palace.

The Duchess of Sutherland was Mistress of the Robes to Queen Victoria when the Empress paid Her Majesty a visit at Windsor.[54] Lord Ronald, then at Eton, was sent for by his mother, who was in attendance on the Queen. He says:

> I had a glimpse of the Empress as she passed through a corridor in the castle, and was greatly struck by her beauty. She had shortly before lost her sister, the Duchesse d'Albe, and was in deep mourning for her. An odd idea had taken her fancy—to build on the site of her sister's house in Paris, which, after the Duchesse's death, she had razed to the ground, a similar building in every respect to Stafford House, and she had visited that house and sent architects over to take its dimensions. But the plan fell through; perhaps it was thought to be too considerable a scheme for realization.

When the Duchess of Sutherland was in Germany in 1864, accompanied by Lord Ronald, the then Crown Princess (afterwards the Empress Frederick) invited her to dine at Potsdam, and the Duchess observed that in the royal lady's sitting-room the furniture was covered with Gobelin tapestry, the gift of the Empress

[54] There had been serious misunderstandings between the Emperor and Empress, and the latter came to London for a few days, staying at Claridge's, en route to Scotland.

Eugénie.[55]

Among the diplomatists accredited to the Court of the Tuileries until his retirement in 1867 was Mr. John Bigelow, United States Minister, who has put on record this not very complimentary appreciation of the Emperor and Empress of the French:[56]

> That the lesson of Louis Napoleon's life and death might not be too soon lost to the memory of that portion of the world still in need of its instruction, his widow, whose picturesque career raises the Tales of the Thousand and One Nights almost to the dignity of history, though happily spared in a measure the fate of her unfortunate sister of Belgium [the Empress Charlotte], shares another fate scarcely less pitiable. Like Salathiel,[57] she still tarries, one of the most unhappy of mortals, an Empress without a country.

In the sous-sols of the Pavillon de Flore were the kitchens of the Tuileries.[58] This annexe of the Palace was constructed, from the modified plans of Visconti, by Lefuel, who was interrupted in his work by the war. He had, however, just time to finish the great staircase, which is decorated with a beautiful ceiling by Cabanel and four bas-reliefs by Eugène Guillaume.

In this immense and sumptuous temple—such as Brillat-Savarin and Grimod de la Reynière could not have dreamt of—all the meals required for the imperial family and the household were prepared by an army of cooks, male and female. We can see, in the magnificent nave, the goings and comings of the officiers de bouche, the patissiers, and the marmitons. At the entrance of each section was a large marble slab, inscribed, in gold letters, Vestiaire, Contrôle, Porcelainerie, Lavoir de l'Argenterie, Pâtisserie, Lavoir de la Cuisine, and so on. All the walls were oak panelled, finely carved.

On great tables the silver and porcelain vessels were ranged—thousands of pieces. The most marvellous sight of all—after the kitchens (all separate) for sauces, for grills, for soups, for pastry, and for stews—was the huge kitchen in which the roasting was done. This occupied the whole of the sous-sol of the "Flora" wing. Between two immense stoves, each having three compartments, each compartment capable of receiving two sheep and five or six dozen fowls, was the Brobdingnagian fireplace, of wrought iron and varnished tiles. Each stove measured nearly fourteen feet in width and about sixteen feet in height, and each had two solid, movable beams, from which hung spits. Of the latter there were twenty, with steel racks. Here whole oxen could be roasted. Above the fireplace was a gigantic central motor, with a clockwork arrangement, for turning the spits. It was a complicated piece of machinery, subdivided, and furnished with devices for turn-

[55] Napoleon III. made a somewhat similar present to the Prince of Wales (King Edward VII.).

[56] "Reminiscences," 3 vols., 1910. London: Unwin.

[57] "Salathiel," a romance, by George Croly, on the subject of the Wandering Jew.

[58] Until the autumn of 1910 the Flora Pavilion remained undisturbed. Then some changes were made for Government purposes in the rez-de-chaussée and the two floors, the kitchens being left intact, just as they were prior to 1870.

ing joints at various speeds. The fuel was naturally wood, with which only can meat be properly roasted. The logs used were more than twelve feet in length. The table on which the meat was cut before roasting was of dimensions which suggested to the more imaginative lookers-on a "village green"! The wine-cellars sloped downwards beyond the kitchens and their annexes under the pavilion of the Salle des États, which extended to the entrances to the Carrousel.[59]

Among the newspapers which found their way into the Tuileries, or wherever the Court happened to be—St. Cloud, Compiègne, or Fontainebleau—was a very curious, very audacious, and very amusing little sheet, published in London only during the season and the Parliamentary Session. It was called *The Owl*. Much of its most diverting matter (1864-1869) had reference to Napoleon III. and his Ministers. The most amazing diplomatic "despatches" were concocted, so closely resembling the real article that it was sometimes difficult even for experts to discriminate between the two. To prevent mistakes I must quote the words of the editor of *The Owl*, Mr. Algernon Borthwick:[60]

> The Owls were Evelyn Ashley, Lord Wharncliffe, Stuart Wortley, and myself. Others wrote for us later ... but we really started the paper. One night I had a brilliant idea. There had been pourparlers between the Government and the Emperor Napoleon III. on the subject of the reduction of armaments. He was, however, unwilling to take the initiative, and had said, in a private conversation with the English Ambassador, "Je ne veux pas encore être snubbé" ["I don't want to be snubbed again"]. I knew the Emperor's style in writing, and concocted a letter supposed to be written by His Majesty, and ending with the words, "Je ne veux pas encore être snubbé."... The *Moniteur* [the official journal] telegraphed that the letter was *not* written by the Emperor, but was an impertinent fabrication, and our fame was established.... During the Congress of Paris the delegates lost their tempers, and hot words were exchanged. *We* wrote a fictitious account of it, and said that they shied the ink at each other, and that during a lull in the proceedings Lord Clarendon[61] got up with a bored air and looked out of the window at an Italian organ-grinder. This last incident really took place, so the astonishment of those who had been present was great.

> Once all the Owls went to Paris, and spent the day in woods near the city. We sang songs, and crowned ourselves with ivy garlands, and finally climbed up in a huge old tree, into whose branches we were hauled up by ropes, ladies and all, singing ballads the while. The next night we were all invited to a great din-

[59] Nothing remains of the cellars but the walls. All the furniture, fittings, and utensils of the Tuileries kitchens have been preserved intact, and this sous-sol of the Flora Pavilion is now one of the curiosities of the Louvre.

[60] The late Lord Glenesk, in a conversation with Lady Dorothy Nevill shortly before his death.

[61] Uncle of Mrs. Borthwick (Lady Glenesk).

ner and ball at the Tuileries, and the contrast with our woodland revels was charming.

Early in June, 1865, M. Drouyn de Lhuys presented to the Empress Regent, in the name of the Paris Cricket Club—an English institution—a box containing a complete cricketing outfit for the Prince Imperial, then a little over nine. The Empress sent the following reply:

MONSIEUR,

La fondation d'un club du jeu de cricket ne peut qu'être utile au développement d'une bonne hygiène publique, si l'exercice de ce jeu répand autant que je le désire et que le font espérer les efforts de votre société. J'applaudi de grand cœur à cette fondation, et j'accepte avec plaisir l'appareil de jeu que vous voulez bien offrir au Prince Impérial....

(Signé) EUGÉNIE.

ÉCRIT AU PALAIS DES TUILERIES,
le 7 Juin, 1865.

CHAPTER IX

FONTAINEBLEAU

Napoleon III. had a great liking for Fontainebleau, the scene of his Uncle's abdication. It may well have been that he desired to banish from the place all that reminded him of the ill-fate of his family. It seemed to him pleasantly audacious to make this attempt at the outset of his reign—to instal the newborn sovereignty in the very place which had witnessed the shipwreck of the victor of Austerlitz. This act pleased the nation by its audacity; people saw in it an evidence of disdain for the evil horoscopes which already abounded. By this clever coup he cast ridicule on the predictions of immediate disaster with which the new reign had been greeted. He left people no time to think of anything but years of prosperity and glory. It was a bold way of taking possession, almost equal to an 18 Brumaire.

But the days of the First Emperor at Fontainebleau were not recalled merely by lugubrious legends—by the table on which the Act of Abdication was signed and the staircase of the farewells. Everywhere in the Palace he had left the mark of his glory. Here, as at the Tuileries, he had written his name under the signatures of the old Kings of France: the calligraphy differed, it is true, but it was equally bold and equally firm. Under the Restoration, as under the Monarchy of July, Fontainebleau was not perceptibly changed. The Nephew entered into possession of his inheritance after the lapse of forty years. The trees had grown, and the carp in the pond had whitened, but nothing else seemed to have changed; one might have expected to see the Great Emperor's red-coated little pages and the Mamelukes, or even, at the end of an alley, Marie Louise and the King of Rome. The adventurous and sceptical temperament of Napoleon III. was allied to sentimental reveries. His ideas forced themselves upon him, and greatly amused him. Not that he showed himself an artist in these things. There was nothing of the artist about him, but there was great simplicity, often to the point of emotion. Formed in the fashion of his time, he was quite capable of pushing grave resolutions to extremes without regret, although he would weep over a poor man's dog or the cross worn by a peasant soldier. Fontainebleau had for him an interest of this kind, and he hastened to it at the earliest moment. The military subjects painted by Raffez, Charlet, and Bellangé greatly amused and interested Napoleon III. To those artists he owed a considerable part of his political success. They had resuscitated the Bonapartist legend, and had made the Great Emperor the hero of an artistic and literary cycle comparable to Charlemagne.

At the Fontainebleau "chasses" Napoleon III. wore the extraordinary hunting-dress which had been devised for him; it was, in fact, a revival of the Louis

XV. costume. The ladies and their cavaliers were equally delighted with it. English "followers," whom the imperial couple heartily welcomed both at Fontainebleau and Compiègne, thought the costume picturesque, but theatrical. The green tunic was worn in remembrance of Napoleon I. The waistcoats were similar to those worn by the roués of the Regency, as seen in the pictures by Compte-Calix. The hat was the tricorne ("lampion"), which looked well on the head of a pretty woman, but did not accord with whiskers or waxed moustaches; yet it escaped criticism — was, indeed, generally admired. And it was in this curious garb that Napoleon III., flanked by the irresistible Marshal Magnan, the head of the Imperial Hunt, entered the château which the Uncle had left in his grey redingote. Over the door of a room at Fontainebleau there used to be a picture, by Schoppin, representing the killing of a stag in a pond in the forest. The Emperor is taking a gun from the hands of Edgar Ney; the Empress is preparing to cover her eyes with a pocket-handkerchief; and in the background is Marshal Magnan, who looks as if he were thinking of anything but the stag which the Emperor is about to shoot.

Under the new régime events advanced at a gallop; everything had to be done quickly; and, as political considerations had to be taken into account, the odd sight was witnessed of the titular director of the Imperial Hunt being no less a personage than a Marshal of France, a good soldier, an excellent Freemason, but unlearned in the art and science of venery. By the grace of the Marquis d'Aigle, a ready-made pack came into being at Fontainebleau, soon reinforced by English hounds, and La Trace, who had been the piqueur of Napoleon I. and of the Orleans Princes, was placed in charge. We see the newly-promoted taking lessons from the subalterns — Napoleon I. from the piqueurs of Condé, and Napoleon III. from his Uncle's piqueur. The worthy La Trace was the real autocrat of the hunt, instructing everybody who was willing to be taught, and prescribing what was and what was not "good form"; and under his gilded "lampion" Marshal Magnan was observed learning his lesson with comical intentness. What was of the first importance was that members of the imperial house should be made to appear thorough sportsmen.

An Empress was still lacking when, for the first time, Napoleon III. rode into the old and melancholy château in the midst of fanfares, soon to be followed by torchlight "curées" and gay "shoots." It was a strange monde, mostly composed of very "new" people, not devoid of naïveté, and vastly different from their predecessors. Then an Empress came, and Fontainebleau was an Elysium.

At Fontainebleau the Empress could indulge in dreams. Her apartments, which had been occupied by Marie Antoinette, looked into the oval courtyard. The cabinet de toilette was decorated by Rousseau, the eighteenth-century architect, in honour of the Queen, who had made of it an exquisite boudoir. Painted in green and gold, mellowed by time, the ceiling of this room was the work of Barthélemy, pupil of Boucher; the door-hangings represented the Muses. On the mahogany parquet were mosaiced the Queen's initials; Goutière's brasswork ornamented the fireplace. This boudoir was more in accord with the Empress's tastes than the bedroom, hung with large Lyons flowered damasks, with its gorgeous bed in the centre, recalling that of Louis XIV. at Versailles. Despite the fleurs-de-lis on the ceiling, and the winged cherubs round the daïs, and Rièsener's furniture, the Empress was oppressed by all this parade. How different were all these splendours from the cosy little room, lacquered with white, which she had hoped to get for her villégiature! She had dreamt of a tiny chamber with all its little nothings within reach; walls covered with souvenirs and medallions; flower-stands, low couches, bureaux no larger than gridirons, no lustres—everything small and homely. At Fontainebleau, in the midst of the woods, in the full sunlight, the Tuileries followed her, just as they had followed Marie Antoinette to Versailles. But the Queen could fly off, alone, to Trianon in her early happy days. That made all the difference.

Hence her desire to break the bonds of strict etiquette and to become "Ourenia" once again. ("Ourenia" was Eugénie de Montijo, Mlle. de Téba.) The plainest walking dress, a simple hat, stout boots, cane in hand. How much she would have liked to milk a cow and to make butter! But that would have provoked ill-natured talk in the capital, and songs about the Andalusian dairymaid. So she resigned herself to sleep in that vast tabernacle, with its gleaming lustre, its gold and its silk—like a doll in a giant's bed. She felt thankful that she had not, like Marie Antoinette at Versailles, to don her chemise under the gaze of her "ladies."

When the "good-nights" had been said, the Emperor, the Empress, and the Prince were preceded to their rooms by the stately "Suisses," and followed by the members of the Court. The guests, after the baise-main, deep curtsies, and low bows, found their way to their bedrooms without further, or with very little, ceremony. Octave Feuillet has told us what these Fontainebleau bedrooms were like: delightful beds, baths already prepared for the morning ablutions, and the apartments brilliantly lighted by great chandeliers. In some of the rooms little parties of friends gathered to talk over the day's events, finish stories which had been commenced in the salon, and breathe fervent hopes that the new Empire had "come to stay."

The Emperor slept in what had been the room of Napoleon I. High above the doors were Cupids, in grisailles, by Sauvage; lower down, cameos of the old times and Pompeian arabesques. Placed close to the wall, against an immense glass, was the bed, still decorated with the Uncle's "N" and the gilded frontals. Louis Philippe had restored the wood panelling with its carved figures, and had renewed the hangings; but the clock of Pope Pius VII. stood on the mantelpiece, the arm-chairs were those of the Great Emperor, and he had paced the mosaiced floor. When Napoleon III. left his bedroom for his study he wrote surrounded by relics of the First Empire: the bureau carved by Jacob, the chairs, the writing-desk—everything remained intact. One new thing there was—Nieuwerkerke's white marble bust of the Empress, showing her as she was at the time of her marriage. Even she, by no means easy to please in these matters of portraiture, was enthusiastic over this work, revealing a face of charming archness.

The special attraction at Fontainebleau was the forest, through which long drives in char-à-bancs were often taken. Sometimes the Empress improvised a dinner in the open air at the gorges of Apremont, and clambered over the rocks with an alacrity which proved very disconcerting to those of her suite who accompanied her on these excursions in the glaring sun. At other times the Empress arrived unexpectedly in the valley of the Sole, while the annual manœuvres of the cavalry brigade of the Imperial Guard were on. Then there would be a goûter for the officers of the two regiments engaged, the Empress herself doing the honours and putting all at their ease. One day (and I give the story on the authority of that popular personage, the late Marquis de Massa) she asked if someone would sing a military ditty, "un peu Gauloise, mais pas trop." A young officer of the Chasseurs, M. de Batsalle, was indicated as possessing a repertoire of this description. When called upon, however, he energetically pleaded to be excused, on the ground that the songs which he knew were not suitable for the Empress's ears.

"But," replied Her Majesty laughingly, "when you come to a word which you may think rather strong, you can substitute for it 'turlututu.'"

"But, Madame, the song contains— —"

"What? Tell us."

"There are scarcely any words in the song, Madame, except 'turlututus'!"

The trumpet-call "à cheval" fortunately relieved the officer from his embarrassment.

Even a cursory study of the characters of Napoleon III. and the Comtesse de Téba shows that they belonged to the school of "romantics." Æsthetics they assuredly were not. Romanticism as a cult had almost disappeared at the period of their marriage, but the "new" people (and both Sovereigns were very "new") were unaware of that. The Emperor favoured the "Beaux Dunois"[62] or the "Preux de Palestine," and in the spirit of romanticism he rebuilt Pierrefonds, the château which furnished the Empress with a travelling name which she continues to use. The Empress admired the eighteenth century, the perfumed histories (as Bouchot terms them) of Trianon or Versailles, and had a predilection for panniers, à la Belle Fermière. Hence her passion for a rural life, her love of Nature, the woods, and the fields. For the satisfaction of this craving Fontainebleau was an ideal spot— superior to Compiègne; there she could revel in royal chronicles and stories of "gallant" Courts. Fontainebleau had the dual qualities of Versailles and Trianon. There the Empress—never without her hours of melancholy—could be solitary or gay. There she was happiest.

But Fontainebleau had to be made to breathe of power—all must be luxurious—so that the Tuileries might be relegated almost to the back of the stage. All this was not to be done in a month. Even in 1860—five years after the marriage— the work was only beginning to be complete. The Sovereigns spent a week or two at Fontainebleau, and gave some visitor, like the Grand Duke Constantine, an opportunity of assisting at a hunt and a curée; but by degrees the Empress's longing for an annual stay there was satisfied. It was there more than anywhere else that she could remain undisturbed and uninterfered with in her own room, or walk or

---

[62] "Partant pour la Syrie," composed by Queen Hortense, became the French National Hymn under Napoleon III. It was founded upon the imaginary exploits of a soldier, Dunois, in Palestine and, translated, was a very popular song in England in the fifties and sixties.

drive out as she wished, free from all "obligations."

Upon the arrival of the Sovereigns at their summer residence, which for splendour was not surpassed by the most fastidious of their defunct predecessors, the place was all movement from daylight. The guard was in grande tenue. Officers swarmed in the courts. From their windows peered excitedly pretty women in light toilettes. Then bugles blew, drums rolled, and cannon thundered until the walls trembled. All this meant that the imperial train was at the station. The Emperor alighted from the waggon-salon (which was surmounted by an eagle with outspread wings), and gave his hand to the Empress. Their Majesties entered their daumont, preceded by Cent-Gardes, and followed by other carriages. It was a rush to the Palace. In front of the "Adieux" steps the daumont stopped, and the officers of the household greeted the Emperor and Empress, who had for each person a word and a smile. At the top of the steps they turned, saluted à la ronde, and crossed the threshold amidst cheers.

Fontainebleau signified Liberty Hall—and not only to the Empress. How different to the Tuileries, where the walls heard and saw everything! The men of the Military Household were as light-hearted and as full of fun as schoolboys on a half-holiday. The ladies told their little stories, of much the same pattern as those told by the courtiers of the Valois or of Louis XIV.

The keynote of the life here was struck at one of the first of these villégiatures. At the Emperor's request, M. Albéric Second wrote a humorous trifle—it was called a "saynète"—for the "Théâtre Impérial, Fontainebleau." And the Duc de Morny "scored" with a witty impromptu in his best style, he himself taking one of the two parts. In this bagatelle the audience saw a sedate provincial, come to Paris with the laudable object of talking seriously to the Emperor on State affairs, to the Empress about her charitable works, and to M. de Morny about his able diplomacy. "How you must have bored all three!" said the "compère" (De Morny). "You don't seem to know much about the ways of these people. The next time you come to Paris on such an important errand I advise you to talk to the Emperor about his 'Vie de César,' to the Empress about her crinolines, and to M. de Morny about his marvellous talent as a playwright!"

The Empress and the Emperor gave the signal for the laughter and applause which followed.

When the Emperor, wearing a light waistcoat, a short jacket, trousers more or less "pegtoppy," and a small black felt hat, was told that business awaited him, and that it was time for him to take his place on the throne, his face underwent a pitiful change. As a simple bourgeois he might have spent the whole day amusing himself; as Emperor he must go and seat himself in a chair higher than the others—not, perhaps, for very long, happily for himself and everybody else.

A marked difference between the imperial Court and that of the Kings of France was that at table at the former the conversation was general and almost without restriction. The Emperor, who usually spoke in a low tone, raised his voice at luncheon and at dinner, so that those whom he addressed could hear him, and had not to guess at some of his words. The Empress invariably spoke loudly, and on occasion—in moments of excitement, which were not seldom—even stridently.

During dinner the music of the Garde played softly. The "Beau Dunois" ("Partant pour la Syrie") was followed by one of the choruses from "Faust" or a prayer from "L'Africaine." To please the younger people songs were arranged as military marches—the "Bouton de Billou," "Le pied qui r'mue," or other minor works. The Emperor had no ear for music. At the Opera he would doze until aroused by a tap from the Empress's fan. Something from the "Grande Duchesse," or the duet of the "Deux Gendarmes" from "Madame Angot"—these were his favourites. At night, when he was going to his room, preceded by suisses, and followed by a group of silent personages, he would be heard humming:

> "Brigadier, répondit Pandore,
> Brigadier, vous avez raison."

To the Empress, as to many of her friends and attendants, the principal features of life at Fontainebleau were the carriage drives, the déjeuners on the grass in the forest, the excursions to neighbouring villages, and visits to the churches. When the Emperor attended these rural outings his carriage was drawn by six horses—two more than those of the other vehicles. As the imperial party left the château the drums beat "aux champs," the guard presented arms, and the cavalcade swept along to the music of the horses' bells. Neither black clouds, threatening rain, nor mists, nor a scorching sun prevented an excursion if it had been arranged. One day, after a pelting shower, the Empress waded through muddy paths until she had reached the top of a steep hill. The Chevalier Nigra (Italian Ambassador) and M. Octave Feuillet followed her as they best could through the slush, to the ruin of their silk hats (!) and thin boots. The Empress had not a dry thread on her; some of her garments were in rags; the dripping branches made walking a heavy business. When in time they got back to the carriages, the sun was shining, making the men's coats smoke like a chimney. Never had the Empress more enjoyed herself, never had she looked more beautiful. A quarter of an hour after her return to the château she was the first at table, laughing at the spectacle of the Ambassador and the author in their ruined hats, her cheeks still rosy from the long tramp in the sodden forest paths and up the slippery hillside. As, however, she insisted that she was late, she had wrapped in paper ten sous, the fine which all who were not punctual at dinner had to pay to General Lepic before daring to seat themselves at table. (This fine was a survival of the custom which had prevailed at the royal Courts. The Duchesse de Berry was so unpunctual that she was fined every day!)

In the early days of the Franco-Mexican campaign—after the defeat of the imperial forces in their hopeless attempt to capture Puebla—Count Bismarck was the guest of the Emperor and Empress at Fontainebleau. He had just been appointed Prussian Minister to France. No one could have had a warmer welcome than the diplomatist. Bismarck was well known to his host and hostess, who had received him in 1855, the year of the first Exhibition—the year also of the visit to France of Queen Victoria, the Prince Consort, the Princess Royal, and the Prince of Wales. Next he attended the conference held in Paris to settle the question of Neuchâtel. In 1857 Bismarck did not display any hostility to the Emperor Napoleon's wish for a rapprochement between France and Prussia. The Emperor had said to his Foreign Minister, Thouvenel: "These two neighbouring States (France and Prussia), placed by their intellectual culture and their institutions at the head of civilization, ought to mutually support each other."

Bismarck and the Emperor had a "political walk" through the grounds of Fontainebleau, then in their autumnal beauty (it was October, 1862). The Prussian Minister[63] had the art of making himself agreeable, and became a general favourite with the guests of the "séries," among whom he was the most striking figure. As the Emperor unbosomed himself to his guest, and smoked and talked with him, nothing could have been farther from his thoughts than that, eight years later, he would find in Bismarck (who had yet to earn his sobriquet, the "Man of Blood and Iron") his implacable enemy.

"The Emperor," said Bismarck later, "asked me abruptly if I believed the King was disposed to conclude an alliance with him. I replied: 'Circumstances alone can enable us to appreciate the necessity and the utility of alliances.'"

Bismarck had been almost the only man in his country who admired Napoleon III. He had even advised King Frederick William IV. to enter into an alliance with France. When he took over the Paris Legation he was received with much favour, not only by the Court, but by the official world; and the Foreign Minister (Thouvenel) wrote to the Duc de Gramont: "We are assured that Bismarck has the most friendly feeling for us." When King William succeeded Frederick William IV. he was not far from sharing Bismarck's views of the French Emperor. Those views underwent a change in 1863, the result of the intervention of Napoleon III. in the affairs of Poland—a step which did the Poles no good, and temporarily alienated the Tsar (Alexander II.) from Napoleon. Bismarck was not slow to see how he could utilize the Emperor's mistake, and henceforth dismissed from his mind all idea of a Franco-Prussian alliance.[64]

It was at a Ministerial Council held later at Fontainebleau that a dramatic incident occurred. The Emperor had asked his consort to be present, somewhat to the embarrassment of Thouvenel, whose duty it was to present a report recommending an early recognition of the new kingdom of Italy. This did not at all accord with the Empress's well-known views. Scarcely had the Foreign Minister concluded the reading of the report than she burst into tears and left the Council Chamber. There was a painful silence, broken by the Emperor saying to Marshal Vaillant: "Please follow Her Majesty and attend to her."

---

[63] Bismarck had been recalled from St. Petersburg to replace Comte Albert de Pourtalès at Paris.

[64] James de Chambrier.

CHAPTER X
COMPIÈGNE

The social history of the Second Empire was resumed in the Tuileries, St. Cloud, Fontainebleau, Biarritz, and Compiègne. The name of the latter lingered fondly on the lips of the fine fleur of English society between 1855 and the winter of 1869-70. It is well to remember that it was to Queen Victoria that we owed the entente cordiale. That, as time passed, the mutual understanding which she secured flickered, and gave place to bad blood after the "attempt" of Orsini, Pierri, Rudio, and Gomez, was no fault of Queen Victoria. But the bombs were designed by the master-mind in Belgium, and manufactured at Birmingham, and London was the scene of the "conspirations." It is true that the personal relations between the Sovereigns, which had been securely cemented in 1855 at Windsor, London, Osborne, and St. Cloud, remained unchanged, and naturally. Was not Queen Victoria the best friend the French Sovereigns possessed in Europe? What angered the French nation was the shelter given to the Italian assassins by England. Had it been otherwise, the tragedy of January 14, 1858, would have been more difficult—perhaps impossible—of achievement. Such was the French view, and not an unreasonable one.

But even the attempted murder of Napoleon III. and the Empress Eugénie did not, we may assume, cause English people who were honoured with invitations to Compiègne to think twice before accepting them. Those "Compiègnes"—how many souvenirs the mention of them evokes! Was it not at Compiègne that Mme. Fortoul's gross insult had as an immediate result the Emperor's belated "proposal" to Mlle. Eugénie de Montijo? Was it not there that the Prince and Princess of Wales were the principal figures in 1868, when any Cassandra who had ventured to predict the imminence of a "Sedan" would have been derided and scorned?[65]

The first of what came to be known as "the Compiègnes" dates from December 18, 1852, six weeks before the marriage, and the Comtesse de Montijo and her daughter were of the party. The Emperor of a fortnight had arrived at the château a few days previously amidst the roar of cannon; he had passed under triumphal arches and between rows of troops and the local firemen; his unmusical ears had been amused by the "tralalas" of the peasantry gathered from the countryside for miles around. With him came his cousins, Prince Jérôme Napoleon (not yet married to Princesse Clotilde, one of the survivors of to-day) and Princesse Mathilde (who had been long separated from her impossible husband, Prince Anatole Demidoff), Ambassadors and Imperial Ministers, and, of course, many ladies—Mme. Drouyn

---

[65] The Comtesse Edmond de Pourtalès (who happily survives in 1911) had, it is true, courageously uttered no vague warnings; but they fell on heedless ears.

de Lhuys, Mme. de Persigny, and Mme. de Contades, to mention a few.

THE EMPRESS EUGÉNIE IN SPANISH COSTUME.

THE EMPRESS EUGÉNIE IN CIRCASSIAN COSTUME.

Her Imperial Majesty represented these characters at costume balls given at the Palace of the Tuileries. The illustrations are from private photographs, and are reproduced by permission of the proprietors of *Femina*, the popular illustrated Paris paper, in which they originally appeared.

The Emperor knew what was expected of him. He had not been four years President without learning the métier. The festivities began with a ball on the 18th; on the 20th there was a great "meet," attended by two hundred ladies, all mounted, and in Louis XV. costume—"casaque à basques" and "chapeau mousquetaire." Of course, "the Montijos" were among the "dames chasseresses," and provoked criticism as well as admiration at the "meet" at the carrefour Bourbon and in the evening at the curée, by torchlight, in the court of the château. At this stag-hunt the first of the "boutons" made their appearance; these were favoured persons allowed by the Sovereign to wear the green uniform and three-cornered hat, which, to unæsthetic British "pursuers," smacked of the theatrical, just as scarlet coats may have seemed to Frenchmen who were occasionally seen in our shires.

The two "foreign ladies"—Mme. and Mlle. de Montijo—were ardent sportswomen. They rode boldly in the stag-hunts, and they appeared at the "shoots" with guns—delicately-made weapons—"jolis joujoux," M. Bouchot calls them. They tramped through the coverts alongside the Emperor; no other ladies shared this privilege. This alone was enough to set envious tongues wagging. Nobody admitted the possibility of what actually happened; nobody believed in an "engagement"; but many believed in "adventures" which never occurred. In reality there was played in the alleys and coverts of Compiègne a final act of diplomacy, in which Spain wasted less powder and shot than the spectators imagined.

Between December 18 and 25—that fateful week for the Emperor and Mlle. de Montijo—the Gymnase company performed the "Fils de Famille," and on Christmas Day came another big "meet" of the imperial hounds. The "foreign ladies" assisted at both these events, which preceded by a few days the news of the engagement. Every year thereafter the Court removed to Compiègne in November, and there the Festival of Ste. Eugénie was regularly celebrated on the 15th.

Compiègne was neither a Fontainebleau nor a St. Cloud; in some respects it was like the Tuileries. The Empress's "Compiègnes" were at once sans-gêne and dignified—an amalgam of town and country festivities; château life carried to an excess of luxuriousness; an intermediate existence between summer at Fontainebleau and winter at the Tuileries. In the country, amongst the vast woods, with relays of guests, the Empress was happy. In the day there was now a "meet," anon a "shoot"; at night there were raouts, dances, charades, theatrical performances. The invités, as a rule, remained four or five days; others, a week or so. On the Empress's fête-day (Ste. Eugénie) there was a family gathering. Towards the end of November snow or rain usually interfered with hunting and shooting.

Each of the "seriés" was composed of from sixty to eighty persons—social stars, actors and actresses, singers, authors, painters, journalists, and mere gens d'esprit. They left Paris by a special train at two o'clock, and it was often dark when they reached the château in the English chars-à-bancs. Amongst the guests of every variety were some who were not remarkable for social graces. Here and there were men who apparently did not find it easy to tie a white cravat properly; yet for these the sunniest smiles of the imperial host and hostess were reserved. Some of the guests were encumbered by baggage—huge boxes and trunks choked with uniforms and dresses. The sorting of these, under the superintendence of valets and suisses, provided amusement for those who watched the scene from the upper windows.

By a quarter-past seven the guests had to be correctly dressed—the men in tail-coats, short breeches, black silk stockings, and shoes with steel buckles—and in the large drawing-room awaiting the entry of the Sovereigns. Only the official personages had places allotted to them at table; the others sat where they pleased, or where they could. Dinners at Courts are said to be very much alike. But those at Compiègne had a spécialité; everything was superlatively good, and the music excellent. On the stuccoed columns of the dining-room were statues of Mme. Lætitia and Napoleon I. The plates were of Sèvres, the girandoles of silver, a surtout in biscuit (which faced the Emperor) was adorned with a hunting scene. The legion of servants wore coats with gold lace; their perruques were powdered, their stockings of pink silk. The head-servants—maîtres d'hôtels—wore plum-coloured tail-coats, embroidered with silver; each had a sword. The unseen orchestra played softly, so that conversation was undisturbed. In less than three-quarters of an hour the Emperor and Empress rose; the guests, passing through the salle des gardes, returned to the salons.

When professional actors and actresses appeared at Compiègne, the great salle de spectacle was more than usually crowded, for on these occasions the audience was composed, not only of the Sovereigns' guests, but of the officers of the garrison and many of the principal residents. The comédies de salon were represented in a gallery on the ground-floor of the Palace, where a temporary stage—technically known as a "fit-up"—was erected. These amateur performances were given for the exclusive benefit of the imperial couple's guests, the "house-party." On evenings when there was no acting there were "games" of various kinds, some of them very similar to those provided for children's gatherings; or there was an informal dance, to the strains of a piano-organ, "played" by the guests in turn, and sometimes by the Emperor himself.

It was in the little theatre on the ground-floor of the château that Octave Feuillet's piece, "Les Portraits de la Marquise," was originally produced. This was an event, for the Empress played the principal part, which was "specially written" for her. Here, too, was given M. Legouvé's spirituelle charade, the word being "anniversaire," and the occasion the Festival of Ste. Eugénie (November 15).

> In the autumn of 1865 (says the Marquis de Massa[66]) the little private theatre of the Palace of Compiègne was placed at my disposal for the production of a revue de circonstance, the principal scenes and the "cast" (comprising thirty characters!) having been approved of by the Empress after she had suggested a few alterations. The first volume of the Emperor's work, "Les Commentaires de César," had just been published, and this was the title of my revue. Of the ladies who appeared in the piece, the "star" was the Princesse de Metternich, with such charming satellites as the Comtesse Edmond de Pourtalès, the Marquise de Galliffet,

[66] "Souvenirs et Impressions." Paris: Calmann-Lévy.

the Baronne de Poïlly, and Mme. Bartholoni.[67] Baron Lambert (then "Lieutenant" of the Imperial Hunt) was the compère [the stage butt], Edmond Davilliers the manager, and Viollet-le-Duc [the eminent architect and antiquarian] the prompter. The "orchestra" was a piano, played by Prince de Metternich, who as an amateur accompanist was unexcelled. The dresses were designed by Marcelin and by Émile Perrin, director of the Opéra.

The prologue was a very simple one. The compère—a worthy tradesman arriving in Paris to witness an assault-at-arms on the Champ-de-Mars—was surprised to hear that the event was in honour of Julius Cæsar, who, having been recently exhumed, was going to review our modern legions and our centurions. As, however, the Roman General did not make his appearance, the military review was transformed into a theatrical revue, in which the events of the year were treated, with comments by the compère.

The scenes of actualité in the first act included a parody of a kicking mule, performing every evening at the Champs Elysées circus, the person who succeeded in mounting the animal receiving 100 francs. The requisite accessories had been lent to me by Jules Noriac, director of the Variétés, and the mule was represented by two of the Prince Imperial's young friends, Conneau and Pierre de Bourgoing, who ensconced themselves in the cardboard carcass, one in front, the other behind. As they found it difficult to see where they were going, Lambert, at the first rehearsals, was obliged to raise the animal's tail, and give them instructions by this most curious telephone. Princesse de Metternich took several characters, her best being the one called "La Chanson," containing some verses having a direct reference to the Empress, and alluding to her presence at the bedsides of the victims of the cholera epidemic at Amiens.

A recent cordial meeting of the French and English squadrons at Plymouth formed the subject of an allegorical scene in the second act. England was represented by Mme. Bartholoni, Imperial France by Mme. Edmond de Pourtalès. The first was accompanied by an old sailor and a soldier in scarlet uniform; the second by one of the corps of the "invalides," wearing the St. Helena medal, and a young soldier of the 90th Foot Regiment, who had been in the fighting at the taking of Puebla. In this scene the Prince Imperial appeared, in a grenadier's uniform, as the "Future" (l'Avenir).

"Les Commentaires de César" was so successful that it was performed the next night, when the Emperor complimented me, and gave me a copy of his book, inscribed "Souvenir du Commentateur de 'César' au commentateur de 'César.'" The Emperor

---

[67] Of the five ladies mentioned, two survive in 1911—Princesse de Metternich and Mme. E. de Pourtalès. Mme. Bartholoni died this year.

added: "But you must not let your profession of dramatic author interfere with your military duties." "Heaven forbid, Sire," I replied; and I proffered a request to be sent to Mexico (where war was then raging). "Well," said His Majesty, "I will think over it." A few days later my request was granted.

"Some may perhaps consider," said the Marquis, "that I have availed myself of 'reportage,' sprinkled with water blessed by the Court, but 'holy water' sprinkled sorrowfully over cinders, for what remains to-day to represent that Court of the Tuileries which was so splendid? Only some disinterested partisans, who, without conspiring, sometimes cross the frontier to salute the noble heir of the name of Napoleon. And elsewhere Pietri, the faithful and devoted secretary, and the Duchesse de Mouchy, a weeping niece—two waifs, tending with pious care, forty years after the shipwreck, an august widow, sacred by misfortune, after having worn a crown, and standing on the shore—a foreign shore—guarding two tombs."

At Compiègne, in the autumn of 1861, the talk was mainly of Mexico and its proposed Emperor. This "Idée Napoléonienne" was quite outside the intentions of the three Powers (France, England, and Spain) as expressed in the Convention signed on October 31, 1861, and the Emperor's idea was not suspected by the guests then at Compiègne. Among them were some of the Portuguese Princes. Consternation fell upon the Court when, in the midst of the festivities, news arrived, first of the sudden death of the Infant Don Fernando, then of the young King of Portugal, Dom Pedro V. The convenances had to be observed; there was an end of the programme of entertainments arranged for that particular "series."

After the regulation period of the Court "mourning" for the Infant and the King (poisoning had been darkly hinted at), fêtes were organized for the next batch of guests and the following "séries," and mingling with Princes of the Blood were many intellectual lights—Octave Feuillet and Prosper Mérimée (both quite at home at the château), Gounod and Meissonier, Camille Doucet and Paul de Musset (brother of Alfred, the poet), Jules Sandeau and Cabanel (the renowned painter). The Empress was in exceptionally high spirits, for she was aware of her consort's secret views concerning Mexico, and rejoiced at the coming struggle. Had not her beloved Spain been grossly insulted and its Ambassador expelled? Had not Juarez disregarded treaties and shown contempt for the two Vice-Consuls of France? The expedition would be at once an avenging and a civilizing army, which would make a country in which the flag of Castille had long floated respect order and the Catholic faith. Vain dreams!

THE EMPRESS EUGÉNIE AS
MARIE ANTOINETTE.

THE EMPRESS EUGÉNIE AS AN ODALISQUE
(TURKISH DANCING-GIRL).

Her Imperial Majesty represented these characters at costume balls given at the Palace of the Tuileries. The illustrations are from private photographs, and are reproduced by permission of the proprietors of Femina, the popular illustrated Paris paper, in which they originally appeared.

CHAPTER XI

THE FOREIGN LEGION;
AND SOME GREAT LADIES

A LEGION of foreigners awaited the establishment of the Second Empire to swoop down upon Paris and make it their happy hunting-ground. These invaders came from all countries; the majority, perhaps, from the South American Republics, the lands then flowing in milk and honey, as typified by gold and silver. They were called "Exotics," and Paris was swamped by "l'Exotisme." For countenancing these parasites, these nobodies, with their riches and their low moral code, three ladies were blamed—the Empress Eugénie, the Princesse de Metternich, and the Comtesse de Castiglione: a Spaniard, an Austrian, and an Italian.

In this vulgar crowd were Princes and Princesses, some, at least, of whom, had conferred these titles upon themselves; a few were of princely rank, but these were not the wealthiest. "Paradoxical as it may appear, Exoticism was Parisian in its essence."[68] The women were superb, "with lips amorously red and facile; the girls had wicked eyes and undulating forms; the faces of the men were sufficiently bronzed to give a suggestion of dramatic adventures aforetime. The Exotic ladies, with all the assurance of a ribald gang raiding a town, gave themselves great airs"; but their hauteur did not prevent them from opening their arms. Parisians at first held aloof from these besiegers, smelling disgustingly of money; but the revolt did not last long, and it was followed by new expressions of amiability. Brazilians, Armenians, and Turks—new and unknown meteors—came, and in a fit of remorse for their previous disdain Paris society flocked to the abodes of the new-comers, clamouring for champagne and sandwiches.

> The spiteful talk of society, and also a natural instinct, threw the Empress among this cosmopolitan society, which only asked to be officially received. The salons of the Tuileries overflowed with people who felt themselves all the more at their ease because nobody troubled about their antecedents or their morality.

> To the Empress Exoticism was like a palliative for the disdainful attitude of Royalist society, and it seemed as if she surrounded herself by these crazy people, who transformed the Palace into a sort of Babel, to revenge herself for the aloofness of the Royalists. Thus she was surrounded by a throng of women throwing glances all round, and sometimes their lips—women with hoydenish

---

[68] "L'Impératrice Eugénie." Par Pierre de Lano. Paris: Victor-Havard.

ways, eccentric tastes, feverish desires, amorous and tempting laughs, like an assembly of foreign and French Sultanas, whose nationality and difference of blood disappeared in the supreme object, pleasure. In the chroniques these women were qualified by the word "Cocodettes"; in history they are classified as "Femmes de l'Empire."

The latter have left a special reputation. They remain as the absolute representation of an epoch of voluptuous aspirations, of pleasures of the flesh, of feverish passions. The men were merely "supers."

The greater part of the responsibility fell upon the women. The sensualism which filtered through their bodies, the thrills of passion which animated their bosoms, captured men. In those days they loved readily and madly.

Young men, dominated by the intoxication of the flesh which stole into their brains, forgot the things of the heart; the "male" replaced the "man." They had not to look far for their ecstasies, when women concealed their souls to show their beautiful limbs. It was an orgy—a perfumed, coquettish, gracious orgy, all the more seductive because it was veiled, because it was full of caresses; élégance was everything.

Some of these women, overcome by a thirst for orgies and by the vertigo impelling them to seek the unknown, roamed the boulevards by night in quest of an adventure, or betook themselves to the Opéra masked balls, finishing their Odyssey in a cabinet particulier.... Roman history was fashionable under the Empire, and people played at being Romans.

Others, of a more poetical temperament—perhaps less ardent, certainly more sober outwardly—found pleasure in intrigues with clerics. Louis XV. abbés are not rare in Paris, and more than one priestly hand could write interesting memoirs. These men who live with Christ have a magnetic influence over some women. They do not understand the ordinary priest—the priest of the people. They want to find in their priest a man of fashion; he must have a perfumed stole, just as they demand, at the altar, a gold or an ivory crucifix to kiss. Were it of wood it would kill their unreasoning faith, and they would fly from it; a plain, severely-cut soutane would be a terrible blow to their senses.

There were certainly radiant and pure women who passed serenely through this cohue. Protected by their virtue—or, what is better, for virtue is relative, protected by some chaste dream, some wifely or motherly love—there were some who emerged immaculate from this whirlwind. Like those hastily-scribbled messages which shipwrecked sailors put in a bottle and confide to the waves, these women, after being shaken by the storm of passion which growled around them, returned to the hearth, to the conjugal bed, with all their grace and all their charm of female purity; and to the mad shouts of the mondains, to the sterile hymn of the fevered throng, they answered with the sweet and simple murmur of the song of songs of fruitful and infinite love.

But there is another side to the medal. In those Second Empire days it was not a case of the abject degradation of a society which, rotting, engulfs itself. All these men, all these women, these Don Juans and these Ninons de l'Enclos', had healthy blood in their veins, and fire under the skin. They bore themselves proudly. The men were brave; the women were beautiful—some intelligent. There were women who exercised a sovereign rule over the arts and politics. There were salons which had at their head some feminine aristocratic personality; others, swayed by some radiant bourgeoise beauty. With their slender fingers, bourgeoises or patricians, they led the grand farandole of the lazy. They sought out the poets, the artists, who work in the shade. A smile, a flower taken from a palpitating corsage, for a sketch; a kiss—more still, sometimes—for a sonnet. "With very little alteration, I would write this page, if it had to be rewritten, just as it is given here."[69]

Among these ladies, two especially—"Exotics"—are noted by M. de Lano as having preoccupied the Empress by their actions in various ways—the Princesse de Metternich and the Comtesse de Castiglione. The first of these was apparently the Empress's friend; the second openly hostile to her Majesty, posing to her face as her rival, at one time the Sovereign's successful rival. "On one side [that of the Austrian Princess] was an affection which, perhaps, still continues; on the other, a hatred which ended only in death."

Among the foreigners of distinction received at the Imperial Court in 1861-62 were the members of some leading Mexican families, who found in Paris a haven of refuge. The Empress, as a Spaniard, welcomed these visitors and condoled with them when the intended expedition was no longer a secret. They saw in her the liberator of their country. In the minds of the Sovereigns there was already the germ of an idea of offering Austria, in revenge for the loss of her Italian possessions, an Empire for one of her Archdukes.

Very reserved at the outset concerning an eventuality flattering to the House of Austria, but which might result in illusions, the Prince de Metternich studied the question during a visit to Vienna and discussed it with his Emperor, who appeared to be not unfavourable to the plans of Napoleon III. Metternich wrote to the Empress Eugénie expressing his enthusiasm for her personally, and on his return to France co-operated zealously in an expedition for which some have asserted the Empress was wholly responsible.

---

[69] M. Pierre de Lano.

From the year in which she first appeared in Paris as the wife of the Austrian Ambassador, Mme. de Metternich aroused criticism. "She gave us the impression," says M. de Lano, "of one who had set herself the task of publicly discrediting the imperial Court by her eccentricities, her lightness, and the equivocal style of dress which she made fashionable at the Tuileries. Her influence had not a favourable effect on the destinies and the undertakings of Napoleon III. and his consort; and if this were the place to inquire into the sincerity of the sentiments professed by the Prince and Princess for the Emperor and Empress, one might be disposed to ask if the Ambassador and his wife did not from the first enact a comedy—the comedy of friendship—the better to aid in the downfall of a man whom, au fond, they could not love."

Irreproachable as a wife, the Princess brought "trouble, and almost indecency," to the Court of the Tuileries. The Empress saw only with the Princess's eyes, and heard only with that lady's ears. The Court ought to have been able to reply to the raillery of foreign Courts by an absolute correctness; but the Princess made the Tuileries a sort of school-boy's playground. Mme. de Metternich took lessons of the café-concert singer, Thérèsa,[70] took her to the Tuileries, and gave "imitations" of her at the Palace, to the dismay of some, whom these displays saddened, and to the amusement of not a few feather-headed folk. Entirely owing to the influence of the Princess, Thérèsa was made acceptable to—at all events, was accepted by—some of the aristocrats of the old Faubourg, and one night, at a ball given by the Duchesse de Galliera, the Princess presented her café-concert friend to the Duchess's guests, who waxed indignant.

> As Thérèsa came forward to sing, a young lady, Mlle. de L——, rose, and, going up to the Duc d'H——, a very witty man, said: "Do you think, Monsieur le Duc, that the moment has come when a young girl should retire?" He smiled, and, pointing to Mgr. Chigi (the Papal Nuncio), who did not withdraw at the appearance of the comic singer, said: "Why should *you* retire, mademoiselle? Where the Nuncio is to be seen, I suppose a young lady is in no danger!"

When the incident was reported to Mme. de Metternich, she said: "Ah! these old heads upon young shoulders! It seems that I have rather upset them!" She not only coped with the suggestive "cancan," but one evening, in a charade, appeared as, and in the dress of, a cabman.

M. de Lano affirms that "these incohérences, these insane manifestations of a decadent society, pleased the Empress, who encouraged and authorized them with the unconsciousness of a pretty woman, intoxicated by unforeseen happiness and her unhoped-for royalty." The intimacy with the Empress, resulting from Mme. de Metternich's "originality"—which perhaps was studied and calculating—doubtless made her the clever collaboratrice of her husband in his ambassadorial labours, enabling her, it was said, to snatch precious secrets from one[71] who regarded her as a devoted friend. "This, apparently, is the explanation of those

[70] The "star" of the Alcazar—the Yvette Guilbert of the Second Empire period.
[71] The Empress.

checks so often sustained by the Emperor and his Ministers in their negotiations with foreign diplomatists."

Enemies abroad, intriguing ladies at the imperial palaces, an Emperor "using himself up" by his indiscriminate "affairs," an unsuspecting and too-good-natured Empress—what were all these but precursors of ultimate dynastic ruin?

It was the Princesse de Metternich who, after the Empress had been singing the praises of Marie Antoinette, said: "Je voudrais bien être votre Princesse de Lamballe"—a doubtful compliment, if all that has been recorded of that lady can be believed.

Princesse Pauline de Metternich is[72] the daughter of Comte Sandor, a Hungarian grand seigneur, and granddaughter of the celebrated President of the Congress of Vienna. In the sixties she was as much a Parisienne as a grande dame, and she had the courage of her opinions. Needless to say, she was severely criticized. She had her own method of answering her assailants, one of whom she sought out and thus addressed: "Sir, in what you have publicly printed about me you have absolutely lied, for you know that I am incapable of acting in the manner you have described."

She was one of Worth's principal clients, and not only superintended the making of her own robes at the great man's atelier (it would be profane to call it a "shop"), but gave him hints and advice. The late M. Aurélien Scholl, in one of his most mordant articles, audaciously asserted that the celebrated couturier of the Rue de la Paix—whom Scholl described as a "faune de la toilette"—had dared, when "trying on" one of the Princess's toilettes, to "lay his mercenary hands on the bust of this patrician." The Princess resented the expression, and Scholl, to allay her anger, wrote, and sent her, a poem of thirty-six lines, beginning:

> "Si je vous demandai, Madame la Princesse,
> Un pardon que le ciel n'a jamais refusé,
> Pourriez-vous me trouver seulement bien osé
> Après l'aveu loyal de ma grande détresse?
> Laissez plutôt tomber, ainsi qu'une déesse,
> De vos yeux si hautains un regard apaisé!"

The Marquis de Massa thinks this poetical apology "le plus galant du monde, as they say at the Comédie Française." The story goes—and it was repeated by the Marquis shortly before his death in October, 1910—that at the first performance of "Tannhäuser" at the Paris Opéra (March 14, 1861) the Princess was so exasperated at the derision with which the work was received that she broke her fan.[73] Let us hear Princesse de Metternich's own version of how Wagner's great work came to be represented in Paris in 1861:

> As I had been told on all sides that no work by Wagner would
> ever be performed in France, and least of all in Paris, I hesitated

---

[72] She still (1911) resides at Vienna, and is one of the rapidly-vanishing participants in the splendours of the Second Empire.

[73] This was a pardonable exaggeration. We know from the Princess's own lips that her fan was too valuable to be destroyed in a moment of anger.

before taking any steps to secure a representation of "Tannhäus-er." One day, however, an unexpected opportunity occurred of realizing my idea. At a ball at the Tuileries the Emperor honoured me with a somewhat long conversation. We talked about the Opéra, and I could not help expressing my regret that the réper-toire was so seldom varied, not extending beyond "Guillaume Tell," the "Huguenots," or the "Favorite."

"Why," I asked the Emperor, "is it not possible to perform in Paris new works such as are produced at the Austrian and German opera-houses?" And I said to myself, "Now or never is the moment to mention Wagner and 'Tannhäuser.'" I made up my mind to do so without delay. I said, "I have a great request to make to your Majesty."

"A request à propos of the Opéra!" exclaimed the Emperor, surprised.

"Yes, Sire, à propos of an opera which, above all others, I should like to see represented here. It would be the happiness of my life."

"And what is this marvellous opera?" asked the Emperor.

"It is by Richard Wagner, Sire, one of the greatest of living composers. It is called 'Tannhäuser'; it is done at Vienna, and, although it is not admired by everybody, connaisseurs regard it as a chef-d'œuvre."

"'Tannhäuser!' Richard Wagner!" said the Emperor, stroking his moustache in the well-known way. "I have never heard either of this opera or of the composer. And you think it is really a fine work?"

I replied affirmatively, whereupon the Emperor, turning towards the Grand Chamberlain, Comte Bacciochi, who super-intended the imperial theatres, said, in his simple fashion: "You hear, Bacciochi? Mme. la Princesse de Metternich is interested in an opera called 'Tannhäuser,' by one Richard Wagner; she would like to see it represented here. Have it produced."

That is how "Tannhäuser" came to be performed in Paris.

While preparations were being made for introducing the composer of "Tann-häuser" to the Parisians in 1861, Liszt happened to be staying in the French capital. The Emperor and the Empress Eugénie had heard that the Abbé was amongst them, and they expressed to Princesse de Metternich their desire to see and hear him. I was asked to bring him to the Tuileries, and Liszt received an invitation in due form. After dinner Liszt came in, and charmed everybody by his playing—notably of one of Schubert's waltzes. The next day the Emperor charged my husband to present the Cross of the Légion d'Honneur to Liszt, and to thank him on behalf of the Emperor and Empress for the delight he had given them.

On Sunday, March 12, 1861, the eve of the première, Wagner wrote to the great cantatrice, Marie Sass, whom he addressed "Mlle. Marie Sax":

> Ma très sainte Elisabeth!
>
> Ne savez-vous pas que l'on refuse même à la cour des places, puisqu'il n'y a plus?
>
> Croyez-moi, je suis déchiré de tous cotés et prêt à me jeter dans l'eau!
>
> Envoyez pourtant demain matin pour voir s'il y avez [*sic*] possibilité de vous procurer *une* place. Je ne parle pas de plus.
>
> Pardonnez et soyez bonne à votre très dévoué.
>
> RICHARD WAGNER.

This highly-born and highly-educated woman was, in the opinion of many, the evil genius of the imperial Court, while her husband took no pains to conceal the fact that he "adored" the Empress. A merry lady was Pauline de Metternich in those days, as this story will show. It was at Fontainebleau, and the pretty butterflies of the Court were dying of ennui, when Mme. de Metternich proposed that they should go for a walk in the neighbourhood with shortened skirts. The suggestion found general favour, with the Empress as well as with the ladies by whom she was surrounded. While the majority were arraying themselves in abbreviated drapery, it occurred to one of the suite that the spectacle of the Empress of the French rambling along the country roads in a frock barely covering her knees would be a rather pitiful one, and she ventured to remonstrate with Mme. de Metternich for proposing it.

The "fashionable monkey" was, as may be supposed, equal to the occasion, and, with much naïveté, replied: "What harm can there possibly be in the Empress dressing as we do, and going for a walk with us?"

"There may not be much harm in it, perhaps," observed the remonstrating lady; "but it strikes me that it is unsuitable for a Sovereign. *We* might venture out in short skirts, but not the Empress—decidedly not." She added: "And, besides, my dear Pauline, pray tell me this: Would you advise your own Sovereign, at Vienna, to dress herself up in such a style?"

"Oh," was Mme. de Metternich's answer, "that would be quite a different matter. I certainly should not advise the Empress Elisabeth to go out in short skirts; but you must remember that *my* Empress is a real Princess, a *real* Empress, while yours, ma chère, is Mlle. de Montijo!"

Some probably regarded this as clever; others may have deemed it impertinent, if not impudent, and doubtless among these latter was included the Empress Elisabeth, who often manifested her friendly feeling for her sister-Sovereign. Let us, however, be perfectly just and fair to the Austrian Ambassadress. She was admittedly more than a little méchante; but it should not be forgotten that she induced some of the most brilliant and beautiful women of the time to attend the Empress's Court, and that but for her the Palace might never have seen within its walls such grandes dames as the Princesse de Sagan, the Comtesse de Pourtalès, the Comtesse de Beaumont, Mme. de Canisy, e tutti quanti. If she was as "ugly as a monkey," she was at least, "spirituelle comme un démon et bonne comme un ange," the most radiant star of the constellation of pretty women which graced the Tuileries.

Thérèsa, who was dubbed, very irreverently, "the music-hall Patti," interpreted what later were styled "les chansons rosses," and Mme. de Metternich was blamed, not altogether unjustly, for having introduced into the salons a singer and reciter of impertinent "comic" effusions only to be heard in the cafés-concerts. By most people Thérèsa's ditties were regarded as highly diverting; others considered them "impossible," and calculated to lower the public taste.

Mme. de Metternich's presence in Paris certainly gave an impetus to the reviving fashionable movement. On all sides there were receptions and other entertainments, to the complete satisfaction of the tradespeople. Among the frequenters of the official salons were to be found many young men from the Government offices who were something more than good dancers. Many of them had a future; some attained success, and some came to the ground when their fortunes appeared to be brightest. One of these latter was young Soubeyran, who reached a high position under M. Achille Fould, Minister of Finance. He was a grandson of Savary, Duc de Rovigo, and experienced all the vicissitudes of fortune. Luckily he had a wife (daughter of the Marquis de Saint-Aulaire) who remained devoted to him in his darkest hours. Before he became almost the greatest financier during the reign of Napoleon III., Soubeyran (who, in many respects, was a man of the Albert Grant type, although, unlike the English speculator, he was "born") had joined the Crédit Foncier as Deputy-Governor, his chief being M. Frémy. The latter retired, and Soubeyran stepped into his shoes. Unfortunately for himself, Soubeyran embroiled the Crédit Foncier so deeply in the affairs of the Egyptian Debt that the Government removed him from his position, and ordered him to pay his successors 40,000,000 francs, although later it was recognized that Soubeyran's methods were highly beneficial to the country! Soubeyran, whose figure remains legendary in the world of la haute finance, was not, however, even then, completely "broke." He started afresh, founded two large banks, and lived in sumptuous style; then he involved himself in dealings in the Italian rente, and fell, never to rise again, dragging down with him all who had believed in his "star."

It was a moment in the reign when the Bourse and the great banks joined in a vast development of commercial undertakings, among them the magasins of the "Louvre," inaugurated in 1855, and viewed rather sceptically by some of the leading financiers, who did not rush to invest their capital in the huge drapery business of MM. Hériot and Chauchart.[74] They had been employés, without any other advantages but those accruing from exceptional intelligence and untiring industry, and they found their patrons among the tout Paris of the Second Empire. Of course, the success of Hériot and Chauchart led to imitators of their methods, and ere many years had elapsed there arose similar immense "stores" — "Lafay-

---

[74] M. Chauchart died in 1910, leaving an enormous fortune and a marvellous collection of works of art.

ette," "Dufayel," the "Printemps," and others. It was in the reign of Napoleon III. that the "Bon Marché" sprang up in what had been one of the quietest quarters of Paris.[75] The Emperor saw with supreme satisfaction the creation and rapid progress of these establishments, the success of which spelt ever-increasing national prosperity.

Of the "fast" set—composed of men of all ages—the most conspicuous was the Duc de Grammont-Caderousse.[76] A fair-complexioned man, of average height, with small moustache and reddish whiskers, small head, and an abnormally long neck, circled by a straight collar, his high cheek-bones, sunken face, slightly rouged, and cavernous voice, evidenced the existence of phthisis. There were few more brilliant talkers even among the men of letters whose society he affected—Aurélien Scholl, Théodore Barrière, d'Anatole de la Forge, Jules Noriac, and Alphonse Cayron, to name only a few. Despite the English cut of his clothes, he was a Frenchman to his finger-tips. Some of the achievements of the notable viveur whom the Duchesse de Persigny christened "le Duc Darling" may be summarized. He had much to do with the bringing-out of Hortense Schneider, the creator of the principal character in Offenbach's "La Grande Duchesse de Gérolstein." He jumped his horse over a dining-table covered with Sèvres—a freak which cost him a small fortune. "Rigolboche," the notorious dancer of the "cancan," won the considerable bet which he made with her that she would not, in broad daylight, cross the boulevard from the Café Anglais to the Maison Dorée in Nature's own garb. "He lit his cigar on La Marche steeplechase course with an English thousand-pound bank-note (which he had just won), because the rustling of the crisp paper grated on his nerves. He gave Cora Pearl[77] the famous silver bath-tub, filled it with magnums of champagne, and then got into it before the amazed company. A few hours before his death he gave a farewell supper-party, made his friends very drunk, and then, very quietly and without a struggle, expired before they had time to get sober. Had Caderousse been properly brought up he might have made a name for himself, but he frittered away his existence and died, as he had lived, like a clever clown. He had the best opinion of himself, or, when Paul Demidoff[78] once asked him to take the head of the table at a dinner-party, he would not have replied: 'The head of the table is wherever De Grammont-Caderousse sits.'"[79]

It was only when the Second Empire began to dazzle the world—the new as well as the old—that the foreign colony of Paris assumed importance. During the previous quarter of a century the société étrangère consisted mainly of rich bachelors, English and Russian, like the Marquis of Hertford, Lord Seymour, Prince Mentschikoff, and Comte Rostopchine. There were, however, a few distinguished ladies, the most notable being the two Russians—the Princesse de Lieven, who inspired Guizot, and Mme. Swetchine, the goddess of M. de Falloux. In those

---

[75] "Entre l'Apogée et le Déclin," par James de Chambrier. Paris: Fontremoing.

[76] Ludovic de Grammont (sometimes spelt with one "m"), Duc de Caderousse, died in 1865.

[77] The Irish Emma Crouch, whose father composed "Kathleen Mavourneen."

[78] Brother of Prince Anatole Demidoff, who married Princesse Mathilde, aunt of the Princes Victor and Louis Napoleon.

[79] "Sornette."

pre-Bonapartist days the Parisians also welcomed several Spanish families—the Aguados in particular—who soon became naturalized.

MRS. RONALDS.

One of their Majesties' guests at the Palace of the Tuileries.

A private photograph, lent for this work by Mrs. Ronalds.

With the advent of Napoleon III. and his consort came the first of the foreign contingent—Spaniards, naturally, drawn to Paris by the Empress, whose compatriots saw with real pleasure Mme. de Montijo's peerless daughter on the imperial throne and in the éclat of her marvellous good-fortune. In the salons now began to be seen a number of these fair foreigners—young women who, as De Morny gallantly said, "all had beautiful eyes, even the ugliest of them." Prominent among the most beautiful were the Empress's sister, the Duchesse d'Albe; the Duchesse de Frias, the Duchesse de Rivas, and Mme. Alfonso de Aldama (whose daughter married the Emperor's equerry, the Comte de Castelbajac). The Spanish division was later reinforced by Queen Isabella, who, physically, was the greatest woman in Europe, but not enjoying a monopoly of all the virtues; the Duchesse de la Torre and her two daughters, the Marquise de Guadalmina, and Mme. De Arcos (Spanish only by marriage—Irish by birth).

The young Spanish ladies left in Paris the happiest souvenirs. They were gay, laughter-loving, and très honnêtes, despite—or perhaps on account of—their Southern expansiveness. They got up parties and organized "tertulias," now with French gentlemen, and now with their compatriots of the epoch—MM. Alvarez de Toledo, the Marquis de Guadalcazar, Calderon, and jolly old Diego, the joy of Paris for more than thirty years.

The Italians rivalled the Spaniards by their beauty as well as by their entrain. There were the Comtesse de Castiglione, Princesse Belgiojoso, the Duchesse Riario-Storza, the Comtesse Marcello, the Duchesse de Bojano, to name only a few of the best known.

There were many reasons why the advent of the Second Empire coincided with the reign of the foreigner in Paris between 1853 and 1870. Firstly, the Faubourg Saint-Germain would have no intercourse with the new régime. The Empress, as we have seen, welcomed with open arms the Spanish aristocrats. Thus the ladies from beyond the mountains found themselves in the centre of the social whirlpool, and to this point naturally gravitated other of the foreign invaders. It was this attractive cosmopolitanism which inspired the amusing boutade of Meilhac and Halévy in their (and Offenbach's) "Vie Parisienne": "You are a foreigner—so am I. Then, as *compatriots*, let us," etc.

Another reason—and the principal one—was the facility for getting about by the multiplication of means of locomotion. If a new railway was to be inaugurated the Emperor was always ready to preside at the ceremony, and to make one of his telling speeches, abounding in happy phrases, and glorifying French genius and French enterprise. It was steam which acted as the great conductor of the foreigner to the Paris of the Second Empire—steam which linked France with, first, North, and then South, America. In 1852, when, until December, Louis Napoleon was only Prince-President, Paris did not contain a dozen American residents. The first American ladies seen in Paris salons when the new reign began were Miss Ridgway and Miss Moulton. Then came Mrs. Post and her daughters; Mrs. Moulton, whose daughter married Count Hatzfeldt; Mrs. Ronalds and her sister, Miss Josephine Carter, both beautiful; Mrs. Pilié, one of whose daughters became the Marquise de Chasseloup-Laubat; Mrs. Carroll, who found in the Comte de Kergorlay a husband for one of her daughters; Mrs. Davis, two of whose daughters married Frenchmen; Mrs. Payne, whose daughter became Mme. Ferdinand Bischoffsheim; Miss Beckwith; and Miss Polk, who married General Baron de Charette, the redoubtable leader of the Papal Zouaves.[80]

While Princesse de Metternich had a monopoly of notoriety, there were four ladies who enjoyed greater social triumphs than any others—a charming quartet, who shed lustre on the imperial Court, and were immune from the barbed shafts of the satirists, which is not to say that they escaped the attentions of the gossip-mongers. They were Jeanne de Tallyerand-Périgord, Princesse de Sagan; the Marquise de Galliffet, Princesse de Martignes; Mélanie, Comtesse de Pourtalès; and the Marquise de Canisy.[81] In the lives of each there is material for a chapter. Mme. de Sagan was dubbed in her monde "Canaillette"; Mme. de Galliffet, "Cochonette"; and Mme. de Pourtalès, "Chiffonette." The Junoesque Mme. de Canisy had no such enigmatical "fond-name." These ladies figure in the chronique as among what was known as the Prince of Wales's coterie, which included a few others who do not call for particular mention.

One of the most noted speculators of the epoch was Baron Seillière, father of the Princesse de Sagan. Her husband was the eldest son and heir of the Duc de Valençay; the great Talleyrand, Bishop of Autun, was of this family. If the Princess lacked beauty, she had exceptional intellectual gifts, and was prized for the staunchness of her friendships and her never-failing good nature. It was not her brilliant mental equipment that attracted the Prince; she had a very large dowry, or she might never have been presented by De Sagan with his hand, his heart (or what remained of it), and his title. The De Sagans' princely abode, in the Faubourg Saint-Germain, had belonged to an Englishman—Mr. Hope, the banker, whose London residence was converted into the Junior Athenæum Club, from whose upper rooms the Crystal Palace is visible.

The Princesse de Sagan used to assemble her relations and friends round her hospitable table every Sunday. Although she sprang from the wealthy middle class, Madame la Princesse, by her marriage, was immediately accorded a place in the forefront of the aristocracy, and she was one of the most notable figures at the Court of the Tuileries. One would have thought she had been born, if not in the actual purple, at all events very near it. They said of her that her husband, grand seigneur as he was to the finger-tips, developed her instincts, and that "she formed herself in his school."

The immense wealth which this fascinating woman brought her husband enabled them to outshine the great majority of even the richest members of the French aristocracy. Her magnificent toilettes were the envy of all the women—the De Sagans' horses and carriages excelled those of everybody else. The purple liveries, braided in gold, were singled out for special admiration by the crowd at Longchamp, where the Prince of Wales was seen fairly often. I have heard that the stables were not inferior to those of the Emperor. The luxe of the De Sagans' resi-

---

[80] It was this old soldier whose support was so anxiously sought by Napoleon III. after Sedan.

[81] Mme. (Edmond) de Pourtalès is (1911) the sole survivor of these four charmeuses.

dence was amazing. Very few, if any, royal palaces could show anything equal to it. There were said to be twelve hundred silver plates and dishes, and everything else was on a similarly regal scale.

A striking feature of the De Sagans' hotel was the principal staircase, suggestive of the grand escalier at the Royal Palace at Madrid. The marble steps, covered with rich Aubusson carpeting; the cushions on the balustrades; the beautifully-decorated salons on the first floor; the bibelots of every kind; the white-and-gold adornments of the apartments; the galerie des glaces, scarcely less beautiful than the mirrored corridors at Versailles; the immense dining-room in which a hundred guests were often entertained; the rez-de-chaussée reserved for the use of the family; the park-like garden stretching over an immense area of the Faubourg Saint-Germain—how often did not our Prince see and admire all these!

The Princess had been the spoilt child of her wealthy father, who indulged her every caprice and humoured her every whim. Her jewels were the world's talk at the time I am speaking of—and after. During one of her visits to London she made up her mind to appear at some great gathering in all her diamonds, and a telegram to Paris brought over one of the secretaries of her father (Baron Seillière) laden with the gems! Needless to describe the sensation which these bewildering stones, valued at many thousands of pounds, made in London.

Before very long the Prince and the Princess were living apart. Of the Prince and Baron Hirsch[82] this story is told by a friend of mine who was in the Bonapartist set during the reign.

The Prince de Sagan was offered by Baron Hirsch the liberal fee of £40,000 to go to Constantinople and conduct a business "deal." Needless to say, the Prince closed with the tempting offer at once. The news soon reached the ears of the Princess, for, as M. de Blowitz very wittily said, "In Paris the fish talk—in Berlin the parrots are dumb." Mme. de Sagan was furious, and, bursting in upon her husband at his bachelor's "diggings" near the Petit Club (his favourite cercle), angrily exclaimed: "Is what I have heard true, Boson?" "What, ma chère?" innocently inquired the dandy. "That you are going to sell your name—going to be the commission agent and tout of that Jew Hirsch for some speculation of his in Turkey? Is it true?" "Hélas, ma chère, it is only too true. As I have but little money, and can hardly make both ends meet on what you allow me, I am forced to take advantage of any opportunity which arises to add to my scanty store." "Oh, you are going to Turkey for the sake of the money which that Hirsch gives you?" "Of course; why else should I take the trouble of going all the way to Constantinople about this wretched railway business, dont je m'en fiche comme de l'année quarante?" (Which I care no more for than for the year forty.) "Well, then," continued the Princess, now somewhat mollified, "if you got the same amount as that which Hirsch offers you, you would give up all idea of going?" "Ma foi, oui," smiled the Prince. "Will you promise?" asked "Canaillette," suspiciously. "Yes, I will promise." "How much did Hirsch say he would give you?" "Oh, a bagatelle to you, but a large sum to me—a million francs." "Indeed! Well, I will send you a cheque for the million this afternoon, on condition that you give up this absurd, degrading

[82] The wealthy gentleman who adopted the Baron de Forest as his son.

trip to Turkey. Is it a bargain?" The Prince, much amused at his wife's earnestness, kissed her hand, thanked her, and accepted the terms. That afternoon De Sagan received Madame's promised cheque, and the next morning saw him with one for a similar amount in his pocket from Baron Hirsch on his way to Constantinople!

To Mme. de Sagan we owe this epigram: "A husband can only hope to be a hero in his wife's eyes for two months—the month before he is married, and the month after his death."

Frank Seillière, brother of the Princesse de Sagan, married Mlle. Diane de Galliffet, of whose mother, the Marquise (the wife of the famous General), a few words must now be said.

The Marquise de Galliffet was half English, her father, M. Lafitte, the banker ("Major Fridolin," of Turf celebrity), having married an English lady. The blonde Marquise was truly beautiful—"as beautiful as the Empress," some enthusiasts vowed; "blonde comme les blès," as my friend "Sornette" wrote of her "in the days that were earlier." "Her few faults," he asserted, "for all of which she was most bitterly punished, proceeded from her tenderness of heart. The beautiful and dainty Marquise could not find it in that sweet little cardiac arrangement which I suppose she called her heart to say 'No' to anybody who did not ask too audacious a favour, the result being that her generosity was abused."

The Marquise was in great favour with the Empress, and the Emperor spoke of her in the most rapturous, but perfectly respectful, terms. Her nickname, "Cochonette," to which she never objected, is said to have been conferred upon her because she was supposed to pay less attention to soap and water than she might have done. De Grammont-Caderousse (according to "Sornette," the all-knowing and ever-humorous) used to tell this story of Mme. de Galliffet:

> Her husband,[83] having reason to believe that his wife did not care over-much for soap and water, played upon her a practical joke in order to satisfy himself whether his suspicions were or were not well founded. One night, after they had returned from a ball at the Tuileries, he went into his wife's dressing room, and, lighting a cigarette, began to talk over the events at the Palace before retiring to his own rooms. He found Madame taking off her jewels and (like the Empress) throwing them about on the carpet, for her maids to pick up in the morning. After a brief talk, the Marquis kissed his wife's hand and retired for the night. On the following morning he came in again, and asked the Marquise to let him take a ruby bracelet to Boucheron's to be reset, as they had previously arranged he should do. The Marquise told one of her maids to bring the bracelet, but, after a long search in all the rooms, the jewel was not to be found. "You must have been robbed," said the Marquis; "but never mind—I must get you another like it."

---

[83] One of the heroes of the historical cavalry charge at Sedan.

THE COMTESSE EDMOND DE POURTALÈS.

The Author is indebted to the Comtesse for the loan of this beautiful portrait.

Le Jeune, L. Joliot Succr., Paris.

A week or so later he again entered his wife's room in the morning, and nonchalantly inquired if the ruby bracelet had been found. "No," replied the Marquise innocently, "of course not, or I should have told you." "Oh, 'Cochonette,'" laughingly exclaimed the hero of Puebla; then, taking her by the hand, he led her to the washing-stand, which closed with a lid to keep out the dust. Lifting the cover, he showed his bewildered spouse the bracelet lying in the basin, where he had put it on the night he had gone into her bedroom after the Tuileries ball! A week without a visit to the hand-basin was (said Caderousse) proved against the Marquise by this trick; for, had she lifted the cover, she would have found her missing bracelet.

The imperial couple would have readily admitted, had they been asked, that they had no better friend, and that France did not possess a more patriotic soul, than the Comtesse de Pourtalès (who was born Mélanie de Bussière), who was always most warmly welcomed by the Emperor and Empress at the Tuileries entertainments, at the chasses and theatricals at Compiègne, and wherever else their Majesties happened to be. In that beautiful house in the Rue Tronchet, a museum and gallery of art combined, were to be found many English who were in Paris in obedience to the imperial invitation, the Prince of Wales not seldom being among them. It was Mme. de Pourtalès who, upon her return to Paris from a visit to Berlin, warned the Emperor and Empress of the high state of efficiency of the German forces. But she only had her trouble for her pains. The self-satisfied Generals made light of her forebodings of evil. Only Colonel Stöffel listened to her sympathetically, for he, better than anybody, knew how right she was. Who does not remember the portrait of Mme. de Pourtalès, garbed à l'Alsacienne, which, when France was humbled to the dust, evoked emotion all over the world? Who can forget the practical help which she hastened to extend to the Empress after her flight from the Tuileries?

At the amateur theatricals at Compiègne none of the ladies outshone the Comtesse de Pourtalès. In the Marquis de Massa's Revue de l'année 1867 she represented the River Seine, magnificently dressed, of course. A phrase, sublime in its audacity, was put into her mouth, and was delivered with such charming naïveté that the little theatre resounded with peals of laughter. Prudhomme (Baron Lambert) exclaimed rapturously, "Mais, quel superbe costume vous avez, belle dame!" a compliment to which Mme. de Pourtalès had to reply, "Oh, j'en ai un beaucoup plus beau *par-dessous!*" (I have a much more beautiful one *underneath.*)

In the last years of the reign there figured at the Court of the Tuileries (and equally in the Royalist salons of the Faubourg Saint-Germain), among the pléiade of dazzling forms, the Baronne Alphonse de Rothschild.[84] The hôtel of the Baron and Baroness Alphonse in the Rue St. Florentin, which had been acquired from the heirs of the Prince de Talleyrand, was not only the rendezvous of the brilliant society of the Second Empire and of the intransigeante aristocracy of the ancien ré-

---

[84] Daughter of Baron Lionel, sister of Lord Rothschild, and widow of Baron Alphonse. She died on January 6, 1911.

gime, but frequently opened its doors to foreign Princes, who, with lesser mortals, were also entertained at the magnificent château of Ferrières (a landmark in 1870-71) and at the fairy-like home at Cannes. Like the other (Continental) Rothschilds, the Baron and Baroness Alphonse liked to be surrounded by the artistic element. In their Paris hôtel were to be seen the leading lights of literature, science, and art. Of course, the Baron and Baroness were what is called "keen" on every kind of sport, otherwise they would not have been Rothschilds. Alexandre Dumas fils, calling on the Baroness Alphonse one Monday afternoon, was met with the inquiry: "Well, Monsieur Dumas, were you at the races yesterday?" "At the races, Madame la Baronne! Oh no; I never go to them." "Never go to the races!" exclaimed the Baroness, surprised, if not horrified, at such an avowal; "then what on earth do you do with yourself on Sundays?"[85]

Mme. de Courtval was well known to the Court coterie, as any intimate friend of the Princesse de Sagan was bound to be. After dinner one night, at her villa at Deauville, she and her guests sat down at the whist-table. Presently there was a loud knocking and ringing at the door of the villa, and, to the dismay of the servants, a much-whiskered and moustached gentleman forced his way into the salon. Questioned as to his right to intrude upon the privacy of Mme. de Courtval and her guests—the Prince of Wales included—the stranger, in very aggressive tones, replied, "I have the honour to be the Mayor of Deauville!" and, unbuttoning his overcoat, he displayed to the stupefied party his scarf of office. He apologized for having to discharge a painful duty, and proceeded to say that the fair hostess, by permitting card-playing, had converted her villa into a tripot, or gaming-house, and had brought herself within the meshes of the law. The farce continued for some little time, to the great amusement of "the Prince" and Mme. de Sagan, who were the only members of the party in the secret. Then the whiskers of "M. le Maire" fell off, and revealed the features of a gentleman who was well known to the hostess and her friends. To complete the story, it must be added that the joke which had so perturbed Mme. de Courtval and most of her guests was due to the ingenuity of the Princesse de Sagan and—the Prince of Wales!

I pass from the recital of these frivolities to the Tragic Year. We shall see precisely how the Empress fulfilled the duties of the Regency, and hear the conversations of the Sovereigns.

---

[85] Needless to say, Sunday is the great race-day in Paris: the reason why "the Prince"—the King—of happy memory never witnessed the contest for the Grand Prix.

CHAPTER XII

THE SOVEREIGNS' WAR DESPATCHES

To the Comtesse de Montijo, Madrid.

St. Cloud,
July 28, 1870.

The Emperor and Louis have left. I am full of confidence as to the final issue. Everybody well.

Eugénie.

The Prince Imperial to his Mother.

Metz,
Same date.

We have had a magnificent reception at Metz, and all along the railway, Papa and I. We are quite well. Your affectionate and respectful son,

Louis Napoléon.

The Empress to the Prince Imperial.

St. Cloud,
Same date.

I hope thou art not over-fatigued, and that the emotions of the day will not make thee unwell. I am always thinking of thee. I am happy and proud to see thee sharing the fatigues and dangers of our brave troops.

Eugénie.

The Prince to his Mother.

Metz,
Same date.

Everything goes well. I am not tired. I have just been to see the camps. All the soldiers are delighted. I embrace you with all my heart. Your affectionate and respectful son,

Louis Napoléon.

On July 29 the Empress writes a long letter to the Emperor concerning the negotiations between France, Austria, and Italy. These appear to her to be proceeding favourably, having regard to a telegram received from Count Beust (Vienna), an analysis of which the Empress encloses in her letter; and to another telegram from the Marquis Visconti Venosta (from Turin), stating that the Roman Question[86] is about to be settled. The Empress, in her letter to her consort, congratulates herself upon having opposed the demands of the Emperor of Austria and his Minister (Beust), whose advice was that France should leave the Pope to his fate. The Emperor received this news very calmly, and on the following day replied by telegraph as under:

The Emperor to the Empress.

METZ,
July 30, 7.35 a.m.

Louis is very well. He slept sixteen hours straight off. I have received thy letter of the 29th and the copy of the other [letter]. The intention is good, but I want to see deeds. We embrace thee tenderly.

4 p.m.

I am very well, but fatigued by the heat. We embrace thee tenderly.

NAPOLÉON.

On the 31st Captain Guzman, one of the Emperor's orderly officers, takes to Metz news from the Empress. His sterling character has gained him Her Majesty's confidence, and she tells him to inform the Emperor that she wishes to visit Metz! Without an instant's delay the following telegram is despatched:

The Emperor to the Empress.

METZ,
July 31.

Despite my wish to see thee again, I think it will be best for you not to come. Besides, we shall possibly be leaving here to-morrow. We have just come from Mass. The Bishop was very agreeable. We embrace thee tenderly.

NAPOLÉON.

On July 31 and August 1 the Emperor contemplates an attack upon Saarlouis, but changes his mind, and all the plans which had been in the air end with the little affair at Saarbrücken[87] on August 2, which the Emperor describes to his wife by telegraph as soon as he returns to Metz.

The Emperor to the Empress, St. Cloud.

METZ,

---

[86] In other words, the question of protecting the Pope.
[87] The Prince Imperial's so-called "baptism of fire."

August 2, 3.55 p.m.

Louis has had his baptism of fire. His sang-froid was admirable. He was in no wise disconcerted, and seemed as if he were walking in the Bois de Boulogne. One of General Frossard's divisions captured the heights dominating the left bank of Saarbrücken. The Prussians made a feeble resistance. There was only rifle-fire and a cannonade. We were in the front line. But balls [shells] and bullets fell at our feet. Louis has a ball [bullet] which fell close to him. There were soldiers who wept at seeing him so cool. We embrace thee tenderly. I know the sort of language to use to Vimercati.[88]

NAPOLÉON.

This last phrase (says M. Germain Bapst) was important; it showed that the Empress, knowing that Count Vimercati was at Metz with a treaty, approved by the Emperor of Austria and the King of Italy, which Napoleon III. was to be asked to sign, had insisted that her consort should ignore it.

When the telegram reporting the engagement at Saarbrücken reached the Empress at St. Cloud she was walking in the park. Someone took the despatch to her. She read and re-read it aloud, very happy, and proud of her son. She hastened to the voltigeurs who were on guard and read it to them—then sent it, marked "private," to M. Émile Ollivier, President of the Council [since January 2]. M. Ollivier perhaps forgot that the despatch was marked "private"; at all events, he showed it to a "Gaulois" reporter, and it appeared in large print in that paper the next day. The Empress, upon seeing it, declared that its appearance in the journal was the result of an "indiscretion." Unfortunately, the telegram was not read by the public in the right light, and the little Prince was made the subject of ridicule.

Leaving the voltigeurs, the Empress went to her little study and wrote these telegrams:

The Empress to the Emperor.

August 2, 6.32 p.m.

I am very happy at the news you give me. It compensates me for my disquietude during so many days. You tell me nothing about yourself; but you well know how I have you both in my thoughts. Are you fatigued? I embrace you with all my heart.

The Empress to her Son.

Same date, 6.33 p.m.

I know thou hast conducted thyself well. I am proud and very happy. Thy telegram has greatly pleased me. Thy cousins [Mlles. d'Albe, the Empress's nieces] congratulate thee, as does everybody. I embrace thee with my whole soul.

---

[88] Count Vimercati, one of the Emperor of Austria's representatives.

Eugénie.

The day following the famous "baptism" was quiet. On the next day (the 4th) Marshal Canrobert's wife dined at St. Cloud, and she was still there when the Empress received the two telegrams, announcing the defeat at Weissemburg, sent by Marshal MacMahon to the Emperor, who transmitted them to the Empress without any alteration.

Marshal MacMahon to the Emperor.

1. Douay's division attacked by two divisions. Douay seriously wounded—obliged to retreat fighting—rallied near the Pigeonnier.

2. Three regiments of Douay's division—the General killed [this was in cipher]—enemy's forces considerable, at least two army corps [*i.e.*, 60,000 men]—one gun taken—position at rear of Froschweiler—I shall attack if necessary—to resume the offensive at least three more divisions are necessary.

The Empress to Marshal Lebœuf, Metz.

As soon as you get news from MacMahon—no matter at what time of night—have it ciphered by Pietri[89] and send it to me. I do not want to awaken the Emperor; that is why I telegraph direct.

Eugénie.

Half an hour after midnight Marshal Lebœuf telegraphed to the Empress to say he had no news.

MacMahon's dread telegrams were withheld from the public for more than twenty-four hours. They appeared in the papers on the 5th, after 3 p.m. This unexpected news produced great irritation in Paris. But the people's exaltation of spirit increased and their chauvinism was unbounded. The Parisians comforted themselves by saying: "It required 100,000 Prussians to defeat 8,000 French, and our troops were not beaten until they had inflicted greater losses on the enemy than the total number of French engaged." The boulevards rang with a hundred other similar stupidities on the 5th. "However, MacMahon will take his revenge to-morrow!"

But the bad news seriously perturbed Ministers. "If," they said, "the Crown Prince enters Alsace with 100,000 men he will attack MacMahon, who has only 35,000. That is grave indeed." The night wore on without any further news. At midday some idiot or other, or perhaps a speculator "for the rise"—nobody ever knew which—stuck up at the Bourse this telegram: "Great victory: 25,000 prisoners, including the Crown Prince." The Bourse became a Bedlam; the crowds on the boulevard yelled and danced and sang and wept. The "Marseillaise" was roared by men and shrieked by women and children. The grocers' shops were cleared out of Venetian lamps, for use in the evening. Flags passed from hand to hand; houses were decked with them; and still the crowds, maddened with joy, sang themselves

---

[89] M. Franceschini Pietri, the Emperor's Secretary.

hoarse, and still they danced and wept. Traffic was stopped, carriages and cabs blocked the way, people climbed into them, stood on seats, and kissed each other.

A brief hour, and it was known that no news had been received from the frontier. The Bourse "telegram" was a huge "joke," a diabolical "sell." Then the mob, split into sections, roared, "Down with the Ministry!" and sang "Des nouvelles, des nouvelles!" to the air of the "Lampions." And M. Chevandier de Valdrôme (Minister of the Interior) hastened to St. Cloud and reported to the Empress the day's events.

Her Majesty maintained her composure, although for hours her nerves had been unstrung by suspense. At her suggestion Ministers met at six o'clock, and discussed the expediency of sending M. Maurice Richard to the Emperor with an urgent request to His Majesty to arrange for a constant supply of information. During the discussion a telegram from the Emperor announced that Frossard's army corps was engaged—with what result was unknown.

Meanwhile there were wild "demonstrations" in front of some of the Ministries. All night the crowds remained on the boulevards. At midnight a thunderbolt fell. The Government received a copy of a telegram from the Empress announcing the double defeat at Forbach and Froschweiler. In forwarding this despatch the Empress ordered a meeting of Ministers, and announced that she was returning from St. Cloud to the Tuileries.

All this Saturday (August 6) the Empress was in a highly nervous condition. She could not be still, but walked in the park a few yards, then returned to her little room and wrote these telegrams:

The Empress to the Prince Imperial.

All at St. Cloud think of you. The hours are very long, but the idea of a better time supports our strength and our hopes.

EUGÉNIE.

The Empress to the Emperor.

The impression produced in Paris has increased patriotic feeling without shaking confidence. I have already received a reply respecting General Douay's widow. I expect to write to her by post.

EUGÉNIE.

The Emperor to the Empress.

METZ,
August 6, 3 p.m.

I have no news of MacMahon. This morning the reconnoitring parties on one side of the Sarre did not observe any movement by the enemy. I now hear that there has been an engagement near General Frossard's position. It is too distant for us to go there. As soon as I have any news I will send it to thee.

NAPOLÉON.

The Empress to the Emperor.

ST. CLOUD,
Same date.

We await your news with feverish impatience. All seems quiet for the moment. The Council will reassemble this evening. Do not worry yourself; I am sure Paris will not give us any trouble. Courage, dear friend! Everyone must do his duty where circumstances have placed him. I am calm and confident. Be the same yourself.

EUGÉNIE.

The Emperor to the Empress.

METZ,
Same date.

The result of General Frossard's engagement is still uncertain. I have good hopes.

NAPOLÉON.

Although over-excited by her emotions, the Empress displayed splendid energy all through this terrible crisis, which was to last a full month—until September 4.[90] She had not a moment's weakness; never abandoned her dignity. She set an example of constancy, dignity, and courage, while around her were many instances of weakness.

On the evening of August 6 the Duc and Duchesse de Montmorency and Prince de Metternich dined at St. Cloud with the Empress. After dinner the two former spent the remainder of the evening at Bougival, with the Princesse de Metternich, who had just been delivered of a girl. When the Prince got home he said to his wife and her guests: "The Empress is much exhausted. No news has reached her this evening. She is resting on her bed. I hope she will have a quiet night."

At midnight there is a dramatic scene at St. Cloud. Admiral Jurien de la Gravière, M. Brissac, and Prince Poniatowski are sitting up awaiting news. At twelve o'clock they are called to decode a cipher telegram from the Emperor. They read: "General Frossard in retreat." The Admiral goes to the Empress in her room to report this event. He finds her lying on the bed, fully dressed in a purple robe; she springs up from the bed, and goes to the salon, where Brissac reads the fateful words: "Marshal MacMahon has been beaten. Army in retreat [or "routed"]. Must expect the gravest events. We must retain our composure. Paris must be armed and a state of siege declared. All can be repaired. I have no news of MacMahon."

Even this violent shock in the middle of the night does not overwhelm the

---

[90] The day of her flight from the Tuileries.

Empress. "They must all have lost their heads!" is her only comment. She orders a copy of the Emperor's telegram to be sent to the Minister of the Interior, tells him to call a meeting of the Council, and says she is returning to the Tuileries immediately. She telegraphs to the Emperor asking him to send further details, as she cannot understand the last six words.

The Empress to Princesse Mathilde.

St. Cloud,
12.35 *midnight.*

I have bad news from the Emperor. The army is in retreat. I am returning to Paris, where I have called a meeting of Ministers.

Eugénie.

The Empress sends Prince Poniatowski to Bougival for the Prince de Metternich, whom she wishes to accompany her to Paris, as it is "the dead of night." At the Metternichs' house (Villa Staub) a white form appears at an open window, and demands excitedly, "What do you want?" The Prince dresses quickly, and the two men dash off to St. Cloud. Upon learning from Poniatowski what has happened, the Austrian Ambassador abruptly says, "This is all the worse, because now an alliance is impossible."

At the château a landau was ready, drawn by two Russian horses, black, with long manes and long tails. The Empress, in travelling dress, was waiting for Metternich. Admiral Jurien de la Gravière, Cossé-Brissac, and Poniatowski got into another carriage, and the party started for Paris at top speed. During this midnight drive not a soul was visible — not even a solitary drunkard.

When the Empress's carriage crossed the Avenue Marigny it stopped; Metternich alighted and walked to his Embassy, which he rented from Her Majesty, who owned the house.[91] Ten minutes later the Empress reached the Tuileries; General d'Autemarre and his aide-de-camp awaited her. There was an air of desolation throughout the Palace. The rooms through which the Empress passed were empty. The curtains had been taken from the windows. The furniture was covered by striped stuff. The chairs were ranged in rows close to the walls. The pictures, busts, garnitures of the fireplaces — all were swathed in cloths.

Ministers trooped in immediately, followed by Marshal Baraguay d'Hilliers, commanding the army of Paris; Trochu, General Chabaud-Latour, and a few others, summoned from their beds by the Empress's orders. The capital must be put in an immediate state of defence. The Emperor had said it, the Empress had said it, and now the Government said it. There was still an Ollivier Ministry; but its days were numbered.

It must have been verging on four o'clock, the daylight was streaming into the Palace, when another cipher telegram was brought to the Empress. In it the Emperor answered his wife's request for an explanation of the concluding words of the previous despatch — the last she was to receive at St. Cloud. From the new mes-

[91] Subsequently the late Baron de Hirsch purchased this hôtel, No. 1, Rue de l'Elysée, at the corner of the Avenue Gabriel.

sage all learnt that no telegram direct from Marshal MacMahon (announcing his defeat) had been received at Metz; that news had come, according to the Emperor, from "General de Laigle." What was meant was "Colonel Klein de Kleinenburg." But it did not occur to anyone at the Tuileries that there was no such person as "General de Laigle," and the message, blunder included, was sent off to the *Journal Officiel*, which published it at eleven o'clock, to the mystification of all Paris!

MISS JOSEPHINE CARTER (SISTER OF MRS. RONALDS).

She represented "America" at the famous fancy ball given by the Marquis and Marquise de Chasseloup-Laubat at the Ministère de la Marine, February 12, 1866.

A private photograph, lent for this work by Mrs. Ronalds.

In this despatch the Emperor said he was about to leave Metz and proceed to St. Avold, if, with the 3rd and 4th Corps (the Guard), he could assume "a vigorous offensive" with some success over the Prussians, who had suffered severely in the battle at Forbach (situated at a short distance from the high ground overlooking Saarbrücken which, only four days and a few hours before, had been the scene of the Prince's "baptism" and of the first "victory" of the French).

This early-morning Council at the Tuileries was opened by the Empress, whose freshness and vigour amazed everybody. A diversion was caused by General Trochu, who asked all round, "Have you read my book? I foresaw all that has happened!" Trochu's inane query at such a moment was met with looks of contempt and disgust. Ministers were now convinced that the defeats of the first week of the war meant the fall of the Empire and, with the awakening of Paris to the facts, their own overthrow.

Telegrams from the Emperor to the Empress flowed in, revealing the disorder prevailing at Metz. "Nothing is decided upon, it seems," said a Minister; "they are floundering about!"

Well, the country must be told of the disasters. But how? In this manner: With the help of a despatch from the Emperor and another from Marshal Lebœuf, the Ministers composed, and all signed, a pretended telegram, preceding it with a statement that they were concealing nothing, and dating the document "6 a.m., August 7."

The Ministers were talking in low tones, as if at a funeral, when a huge form appeared in the doorway—that of Haussmann, the maker of the new Paris. He had returned from a journey; walking along the Rue de Rivoli, he had noticed an unwonted movement in the Palace, had inquired, and had hastened to offer his services to the Empress. Her Majesty asked him to give his opinion, and he did so, clearly and emphatically. "A state of siege must be proclaimed immediately. If there were not sufficient troops in Paris, those still in Algeria and the regiments of marine infantry at the ports must be sent for." But at 1.30 that morning Admiral Rigault had ordered the marines to be in Paris within forty-eight hours. A proclamation announcing these measures must be issued immediately. Haussmann, asked by the Empress to draw it up, sat down at a corner of the table and penned the document currente calamo.

Before the Council dispersed, at 6 a.m., orders had been sent recalling to Paris all available land and sea forces. France had still men with heads on their shoulders, and an indomitable Empress-Regent. General Chabaud-Latour went straight from the Tuileries to the Rue St. Dominique (the bureau of the comité du génie), and told of the impression made upon him by the "admirable and simple" courage of the Empress, who had said, "Ne vous occupez pas de l'Empereur et de mon fils, mais uniquement du pays."

At 8 am. the Ministers were again at the Tuileries. During their short absence the blackest news had arrived. There was a general retreat on Châlons! The Empress read the telegrams without a break in her voice or a quiver of the lip.

Certain members of the Government wanted to make General Trochu Minister of War, vice General Dejean. A Minister proposed to the Empress the desirability of this change, on the ground that Trochu was an "orator" and very popular, while Dejean was a slowcoach. Getting wind of this intrigue, Dejean went to the Empress, who asked him to retain his post. M. Ollivier, who had approved of the Emperor's plan to retreat from Metz and concentrate the army at Châlons, now changed his mind and telegraphed to the Emperor to say that the Government did not like the idea, and to request permission to replace Dejean by Trochu.

The Empress to the Emperor.

PARIS,
August 7.

In your military operations do not consider the opinion of Paris. The important thing is not to act quickly, but properly. In three days we shall have here 29,000 good troops, besides the four regiments from Africa. With the National Guard it will be easy to increase this force to 40,000. We can easily defend ourselves should an army [the enemy] hold the country. The audacity which they are showing will be fatal to them, if we do not take our revenge too quickly.

EUGÉNIE.

The Empress rushed away from a Cabinet meeting to dictate some telegrams to the Emperor and to write others herself. She was still the moving spirit—restless, never giving way to fatigue, indefatigable. All her combative spirit, inherited from an illustrious ancestry, manifested itself. She was in her element. Her consort was reigning, but she was governing, and those around her—not all friends—could not withhold their admiration. Ministers thought the young Prince should be brought back to Paris. They were perturbed by the Emperor's bad health, and asked themselves if he was in a fit state to hold the supreme command of the army.

M. Ollivier to the Emperor.

The Council of Ministers and the Privy Council are unanimously of opinion that the Prince Imperial should return to Paris.

OLLIVIER.

The Empress added the words: "I do not think it my duty to oppose this." Then she sent the following telegram, in her special cipher:

The Empress to the Emperor.

For reasons which I cannot explain in this despatch I desire that Louis should remain with the army, and that the Emperor should promise that he [the Prince] should be sent back, but should keep him with the army....

EUGÉNIE.

The Government knew nothing of this subterfuge. The Empress's next step was to summon from Cherbourg Charles Duperré (then commanding the frigate

Taureau), in whom she had full confidence. He was to go to Metz and tell the Emperor what she could not telegraph to him.

Trochu bluntly told Ollivier he would not accept the headship of the War Office.

Hearing from the Emperor that the enemy was at no point pursuing the French, and that Frossard's army corps was concentrated at Puttelange, the Empress telegraphed:

> *The Empress to the Emperor.*
>
> *August 6.*
>
> I have received your despatch, and am quite satisfied with it. It is evident to me that we shall have a success, if we do not press forward.

> *The Empress's Second Telegram to her Consort.*
>
> *Same date.*
>
> Opinion in Paris increases against Marshal Lebœuf and General Frossard. They are accused of having brought about the defeats. Speak to Marshal Bazaine respecting future operations.

The Empress had not previously mentioned Bazaine's name. The Emperor telegraphed to her that at the moment only "very vague details" about the fighting had reached Metz. "It was said that there had been several cavalry charges." Such was the state of the French "intelligence" department—if it ever had more than a shadowy existence.

Paris was naturally indignant. "The Ministers ought to be arrested! They are to blame for all that has happened."

"Those who remember those days," says M. Germain Bapst, "can recall the terrible anguish which tortured all hearts." And, with admirable fairness to the Empress and the Emperor, he adds these significant words:

> Overwhelmed, deceived in our blind confidence—*for all, it must be said, had wished for the war*, believing in the invincibility of our army—we cursed the Ministers. Since Sadowa all the Deputies, the spokesmen of the country, had opposed those armaments which were declared by the Emperor, Marshal Niel, and M. Thiers to be indispensable. Those who became Ministers six months ago [the Ollivier Cabinet] reduced the contingent and declared loudly for disarmament. Now they are reproached for our defeats, and it is impossible for them to govern owing to their unpopularity. One sole authority remained in Paris—that of Marshal Baraguay d'Hilliers.

The Emperor to the Empress.

METZ,
August 7, 8.30 a.m.

To support us here it is necessary for Paris and France to make great patriotic efforts. Here we do not lose sang-froid or confidence, but we are sorely tried. After the Battle of Reichshoffen MacMahon retired, covering the road to Nancy. Frossard's corps has been determinedly attacked. Energetic measures are being taken to defend that corps. The Major-General is with the outposts.

While, that afternoon (August 7), the Empress was presiding at the Council, the Opposition Deputies demanded the immediate convocation of the Chambers. Jules Favre was at their head.

One of the best-informed Ambassadors perceived what was coming—what, in fact, did come less than a month later. He telegraphed to his Government these inspired words:

The Republican party is agitating. Should there be another check, the worst is to be feared—déchéance of the Emperor, proclamation of the Republic, and the rest.

The Emperor, on August 8, ordered the junction of the Lorraine army corps at Metz and the creation of a new army in Paris.

The Emperor to the Empress.

METZ,
August 8.

The retreat upon Châlons is dangerous. I can be more useful by remaining at Metz, with 100,000 well-organized men. Canrobert must return to Paris and be the kernel of a new army. Then there will be two great centres—Paris and Metz. Such is our opinion. Let the Council know. There is no news.

NAPOLÉON.

The Empress replied by trying to persuade the Emperor that Paris was quiet, and that there was "no fear of a revolution." She was preoccupied with the hope of concentrating, to face the enemy, the largest possible number of troops.

The Empress to the Emperor.

PARIS,
August 9.

Do not worry about Paris; I will answer for it. We are also trying to form an army here. Do not get rid of Canrobert. You have not too large a force. We have called upon Palikao to form an army here. Opinion points to him.

On August 7 and 8 M. Maurice Richard saw the Emperor at Metz. His Majesty was much cast down, absorbed in studying a map, and made no answer when spoken to. Sighing, and pressing his hand upon his left side, he said every now and then, "What a misfortune!" But no words of recrimination escaped him. His bent figure and slow movements gave M. Richard the impression of a man who was at his last gasp—whose illness made him unfit to command. General Lebrun, M. Davilliers, and M. Franceschini Pietri advised the Emperor to return to Paris and hand over the command to Marshal Bazaine. The Government shared that opinion. The Empress also advised the transfer of the command to Bazaine. Pietri telegraphed to her proposing the Emperor's return to Paris. Her Majesty's reply was telegraphed direct to the Emperor, and ran: "Have you thought of all the consequences of your return to Paris after two defeats?"

Faced by this pregnant question, the suffering Emperor gave way, as always, for he dreaded above all his wife's anger. One week of warfare had brought Napoleon III. to this piteous state. Bowed down by bodily pain, tortured by defeat following defeat, unable to "see daylight" in any direction, forbidden from returning to Paris, motiveless, powerless, the nominal head of disorganized forces, perhaps (fatalist that he was) even foreseeing what would happen three weeks hence—how vividly these despatches bring before us the picture of Hugo's "Napoleon the Little"!

By comparison with her stricken, nerveless—shall we say deluded and betrayed?—husband, the Wife's figure becomes almost colossal. Her hopefulness, her tenacity, her inflexible will had their effect upon some at least of those with whom she was in feverish consultation day and night. From the Emperor, even at this early stage, there was nothing to hope for. What could he have done in Paris, save precipitate the Revolution, which was already in gestation?

The man to whom the Empress turned for advice was the chief of the Bonapartist Parliamentary party—Jérôme David. "In 1867," says M. Bapst, "during the debates on the Press laws and the right of public meeting, acting by the Empress's request, he had endeavoured to procure the withdrawal of the projected laws, which had originated with the Emperor himself. David's appeal for assistance in his task prompted a member of the Senate to reply, with not unkindly humour, that it seemed to him to be a question of a little Ministerial intrigue springing into existence from under the folds of a petticoat!"

After a meeting of Ministers, a deputation from the Chamber had an audience of the Empress, and asked her to sanction the immediate dismissal of Ollivier and his Ministers. To this mild request she answered that it was a question for the Chamber, not for her, to decide. "It would be regrettable to cause a Ministerial crisis at a moment of such gravity."

One of the deputation, M. Durangel, remained after his colleagues had withdrawn. The Empress took him aside, and, bursting into tears, said: "What do you think of the Emperor's proposed return to Paris?" Then, without giving him time to answer, she exclaimed, "It is impossible! A Napoleon cannot return to Paris unless he is victorious." The Empress kept him in conversation until half-past one in the morning! She was now taking large doses of chloral every night, but the drug did not bring her any but the most fitful sleep.

By August 8 Captain Duperré had arrived from Cherbourg. The Empress told him he must go to Metz (as he did) and prevent the Emperor, and even the Prince, from returning to Paris. "I would rather see my son killed by the enemy than become another Louis XVII.!" she exclaimed, and seemed to gain some consolation by repeating it. It was reported that the *Times* had made the Empress say, "If the Prince returns to Paris, I will immediately take him back to the army." To force her hand, the Government published an announcement that the Prince had returned to Paris!

Some troops had been ordered to station themselves in the courtyard of the Carrousel. The Empress suggested to Marshal Baraguay d'Hilliers (commanding the forces in Paris) that they should be supplied with rations from the Tuileries kitchens. "No," said the old warrior; "people would say that it was the repast of the gardes du corps" — the allusion (says M. Bapst) being to the banquet in the Orangerie in 1789, when the appearance of Marie Antoinette had aroused the troops to enthusiasm, and caused them to reject the tricoloured cocardes. Previously the Empress had told the Marshal to prevent the mob from invading the Palais Bourbon, should an attempt be made to "rush" it. "Rioters! brawlers!" he exclaimed; "I would sweep them all out, and if it was necessary to fire upon them I would do so!" Her Majesty cut him short with the question, "But not without orders, would you?" This was too much for the fiery Marshal, and he retorted that he "did not wish to retain his command." He remained intractable. Princesse Mathilde, who had been asked by the Empress to see if she could make him change his mind, told him he was a coward to desert his post, and there was nothing for it but to replace him by conferring the Paris command upon General Soumain. By August 9 Ministers had lost their authority, and at the opening of the Chambers they were overthrown.

On the morning of August 9, at the Tuileries, General Palikao was announced. The Empress was at a Council, and upon Palikao entering the room, she rose, shook hands with the old soldier, who had done good service in China, and appeared to be overjoyed at the arrival of "a Messiah, whose coming had been anxiously awaited." The Empress poured forth her soul; it was difficult for anyone else to edge in a word, so excited was the Regent—anxious, perhaps, to let the warrior see how well acquainted she was with what was happening in Lorraine. So steeped was she in military lore that, hearing her expound theories and ideas, even experts might have been betrayed into accepting her speculations as facts. Would Palikao take command of the Paris forces? Or would he prefer to replace Marshal Lebœuf as Major-General of the army of the Rhine at Metz? He could have either post. Seeing how the land lay, Palikao asked abruptly, "Will you make me a Marshal?" The Empress hinted at something of the kind; but Palikao "opted" for the army of the Rhine, and everybody was satisfied. The Regent, bubbling over with delight, could not keep the good news from "Louis" for a moment.

The Empress to the Emperor.

Paris,
August 9, 1.13 p.m.

General Palikao accepts, and leaves immediately for Metz. The Marshal [Lebœuf] must resign before he [Palikao] arrives. This step, I believe, will quiet the Chamber. Everything going well here. Order will not be disturbed. The Council and I do not agree with the view brought by M. Maurice Richard from Metz [that the Emperor should return to Paris and form a new army]. I embrace you tenderly, and also Louis. My affection [for you both] increases with events.

A cold douche soon arrived at the Tuileries. The proposed sending of Palikao to Metz surprised the Emperor.

The Emperor to the Empress.

Metz,
August 9.

I do not at all understand [the meaning of] sending Palikao to Metz. It cannot change the situation in any way. I thought it was the resignation of the Minister of War which was wanted. The other [that of Major-General] is impossible. As regards the army, nothing must be done without consulting me. Changarnier has come here to place himself at my disposal.

Napoléon.

All the clever combinations of the poor Regent were thus upset.

The Empress to the Emperor.

Paris,
August 9.

The situation would become graver than you can imagine if Palikao were not Minister of War. Marshal Lebœuf is held responsible for giving orders and counter-orders which are known in Paris. They tell me that the Chamber desires he should be replaced. I am in a Ministerial crisis. Do not disturb yourself. To satisfy public opinion it is urgent that at the opening of the Chamber Marshal Lebœuf's supersession should be announced.

Eugénie.

The Empress to Marshal Lebœuf.

Paris,
August 9, 2 p.m.

In the name of your former devotion, give in your resignation as Major-General. I beg you to do so. I know how much it will cost you, but in the actual circumstances we are all obliged to make sacrifices. Believe that it is as hard for me to take this step as for you.

EUGÉNIE.

The Regent does not let much, or many, stand in her way when beset by difficulties. She causes a communiqué to be sent to the *Journal Officiel* (in which it appeared next day) to the effect that Marshal Lebœuf and General Lebrun had resigned! This was untrue. But "À la guerre comme à la guerre." This reflection may have quieted her moral sense, at some times not as strong as at others.

While all this frantic telegraphing to and from Metz was going on, events in Paris were taking an ugly shape. While the Empress was scribbling, or dictating, her despatches, the mob took possession of the Place de la Concorde and the approaches to the Palais Bourbon (the seat of the Chamber). But, bitterly disappointed with his treatment as he had reason to be, Baraguay d'Hilliers was still military commandant at Paris. He put his foot down with a "thus far shall you go, but no farther." The mob was cowed, and did not rush into the Chamber, but contented itself with yelling in chorus (the troops joining): "À la frontière! À la frontière!" These fervent patriots did not, however, make any move towards "the frontier"; they were not "out" for that. They heard with satisfaction that the Deputies belonging to the Left had demanded that an Executive Commission should be substituted for the Ollivier Government.

> When one sees the stupidity, the powerlessness, and the disgusting attitude of Parliaments at times of crisis, one cannot refrain from admiring the old republicans of Rome, who established the Dictatorship to save the Republic when it was in danger.—
> BAPST.

The Empress now set about the formation of a new Ministry, with Jérôme David at its head and Palikao as War Minister. Schneider objected, and tried to persuade the Regent to include in the Ministry some Deputies of the Left. Her Majesty ordered Palikao to form a Government, and preside over it as well as over the War Office. Jérôme David was again ruled out of any post, Schneider (of the Creusot factories) hinting that David was too much "the Empress's man." All night Palikao was hunting about for a Minister of the Interior—anyone but David.

The Empress to the Emperor.

PARIS,
August 9, 6 p.m.

> What I feared has happened—a change of Ministry. Palikao is at its head; this is agreeable to all. The announcement of Marshal Bazaine's new position has produced the best effect. Your prestige is intact. The same cannot, unfortunately, be said of your Major-General [Marshal Lebœuf]. Everybody is making the greatest sacrifices. Our sole preoccupation is that you have not sufficient troops. EUGÉNIE.

Serious news from the Chargé d'Affaires (M. de la Boulaye) at Brussels; General Chazal, Belgian Commander-in-Chief,[92] had removed his headquarters to Namur, and had stated that the French army of Metz would probably be attacked by the massed German armies. The Regent rightly insisted upon the Metz forces being reinforced.

The Empress to the Emperor.

PARIS,
August 9, 6 p.m.

I think it is absolutely necessary you should be reinforced. According to my information, the junction of the two Prussian armies will put 300,000 men on your shoulders. Call to your aid the troops at Châlons and all others that you can get. If you approve, send immediate orders.

EUGÉNIE.

Not a solitary blade of grass does the Regent allow to grow under her feet. Having sent that telegram, she immediately occupies herself with the Paris Mobiles, the objects of much disquietude.

The Empress to the Emperor.

August 9, 8 p.m.

The proposed law [drawn up by General Dejean] authorizes the incorporation of the Gardes Mobiles with the army. I entreat you to order the Mobiles to go immediately to the camp at Châlons for formation in regiments.

I think the day after to-morrow I shall be able to send you 15,000 men from Paris. Will you have them? Palikao tells me there are too many troops at Lyons. Should some of them be sent to you?

EUGÉNIE.

All this time the Empress was reporting to the Emperor what was taking place at the Corps Législatif. Through her he learns that Marshal Baraguay d'Hilliers does not wish to retain his command [of the Paris forces]; she would like him replaced by Marshal Canrobert. She insisted upon Lebœuf resigning the position of Major-General, but the Emperor would not let the Marshal go.

On August 9 Charles Duperré reached Metz at 8 p.m., and had an immediate interview with the Emperor, with this result:

The Emperor to the Empress.

METZ,
August 9, 10.5 p.m.

I have seen Duperré, who will take my answer to you [in ref-

[92] After Sedan General Chazal conducted Napoleon III. from Belgium to Verviers (Prussia).

erence to the return of the Emperor and the Prince to Paris]. We seem to be returning to the fine times of the Revolution, when they wanted the army led by the representatives of the Convention. General Dumont can have the Lyons post in place of Montauban [Palikao]. I would bring to Metz, if I had the time and the means, the Châlons corps d'armée. I could do nothing better at the moment.

I wish to keep Canrobert at the head of his corps. As to Marshal Lebœuf, he has already resigned, but I cannot accept it until I can get someone capable of replacing him. D'Autemarre must replace Baraguay d'Hilliers, and someone must be found to command the National Guard of the Seine. We embrace thee tenderly.

NAPOLÉON.

Commander Duperré to the Empress.

METZ,
August 9, 10 p.m.

This morning the Emperor gave General (*sic*) Bazaine the direction of operations and the command of the army, nominating him Major-General. All orders are to be transmitted and carried out by him. Consequently the Emperor must be constantly with him. The post of Major-General thus becomes superfluous. It must be suppressed, and taken from Marshal Lebœuf. This is what you must say in answer to the Emperor's despatch.

DUPERRÉ.[93]

Much annoyed by the Emperor's refusal to adopt her views, Her Majesty sent a strongly-worded despatch to Metz the same night.

The Empress to the Emperor.

August 9, 11 p.m.

You do not know the situation. Only Bazaine inspires confidence. The presence of Marshal Lebœuf upsets things as much at Metz as here. The difficulties are immense. M. Schneider puts a knife to my throat for an almost impossible Ministry. I have to face this situation without troops, with disorder almost in the streets. D'Autemarre inspires the National Guard with confidence. If I displace him, they will not follow a new General. Canrobert is, then, indispensable to me. Take Trochu from his post, and you will satisfy public opinion and give me a devoted man, which at present I lack completely. In forty-eight hours I shall be betrayed by the fear of some and the inertia of others.

EUGÉNIE.

---

[93] This officer is now an Admiral. He visited the Empress Eugénie at Cap Martin in February, 1911.

The Empress, as her despatch proves, was bent upon (1) getting Trochu out of Paris; (2) having Canrobert as Commander of the Paris force; (3) making Bazaine Commander-in-Chief; and (4) preventing the Emperor and the Prince from returning from the front to Paris.

She instructed Duperré to speak "discreetly" to M. Franceschini Pietri in order that he might telegraph directly to her, without the Emperor's knowledge, all that would be likely to interest her.

By August 10 Palikao had practically completed his new Ministry, making the Prince de La Tour d'Auvergne (Ambassador at Vienna) Foreign Minister without his knowledge! The Empress wanted a special post created for Baron Haussmann, but to this Ministers objected, and Her Majesty had to abandon her idea, excellent as it was. Haussmann as administrator of everything relating to war supplies and to the provisioning of Paris would have been worth his weight in gold.

At 3 am. on the 9th the Empress, unable to sleep, telegraphed to the Emperor that Canrobert *must* come to Paris and replace Trochu; and her consort gave way!

The Empress had always admired Trochu, and it was only when, after the defeats at Reichshoffen and Forbach, he blamed everybody, and boasted that he alone had foreseen all the disasters, that her eyes were opened.

The Prince Imperial to his Mother.

Metz,
August 10.

I have seen M. Duperré, who gave me great good news from Paris. Papa is well.

Louis.

The Empress to the Emperor.

Paris,
August 10.

I send you contents of a telegram which I have received [this referred to some alarming and inaccurate news from Brussels]. Shall we send masses of Gardes Nationales Mobiles in the direction of the army? We will provide them with food and arms.

The Ministry will, I hope, be formed at 3 p.m. to-day. I shall then be able to send marine infantry—an excellent force—to Châlons. All my preoccupation is that you have not enough men. Will you authorize me to send you men whenever I can do so, and can assure them a supply of food? You have not answered several telegrams which I sent yesterday. I am quite well. I embrace you tenderly. Do not worry about us. All will come right.

Eugénie.

The Emperor to the Empress.

METZ,
August 10.

I refuse the battalions of Mobiles. I am getting the corps from Châlons. The Minister of War must occupy himself especially with arming the country people who ask for weapons. Form centres with the fourth battalions at Paris, Châlons, and Langres. MacMahon is going to re-form his corps at Châlons.

NAPOLÉON.

The Empress complained to her consort of telegrams from Lebœuf and the Emperor being so contradictory that they produced "the most deplorable effect" when they became known to the public (as she asserted was the case). The Emperor explained all this in a telegram on the 10th, concluding: "It rained in torrents last night. No fighting. We embrace thee tenderly."

Acting upon the advice given to her by Duperré in his telegram of the 9th, the Empress telegraphed to the Emperor begging him to suppress the functions of Major-General.

The Emperor to the Empress.

METZ,
August 10, evening.

It would be more impossible for me to do without a Major-General than without a Minister of War. There is no connection between those functions and those of Marshal Bazaine. For example, if I suppress the Major-General without advantageously replacing him, the army would go short of food, the cavalry would be without forage, and all the details of the service would suffer. One can know nothing about war to think that on the eve of a battle I can suppress the most important spoke in the wheel. I regret to hear that the Chamber has declared that it is sitting permanently. That is a manifest violation of the Constitution.

NAPOLÉON.

The Emperor to Marshal Canrobert.

METZ,
August 10, 2.35 *p.m.*

Continue uninterruptedly and without loss of time the movement of all your divisions at Châlons on Metz.

Canrobert was handed the above while he was waiting at the Tuileries, at 11 p.m., to see the Empress. In the face of that order how could he abandon his corps on the eve of a battle? He could not, therefore, comply with the Empress's natural, yet somewhat flighty, desire that he should remain in Paris at the head of its troops.

The Empress was now in a state of exhaustion, "living on her nerves and strength of will." All agreed that her conduct was "admirable." She could not eat, and, despite the large quantities of chloral which she continued to take, she was unable to sleep. But she slaved on. Acting on the advice of M. Magne (the financial expert) an inventory of the Crown jewels was made, and the various objects were sent to the Bank of France. Pepa, the Empress's femme de chambre, was trembling with fear, so she was sent away. The Prince de Metternich, who was honoured by the Sovereign with her complete confidence, was constantly with her. He told her of the increasing probability of a revolution, and depicted its horrors in terms which made her consent to hand him her diamonds and her other jewels.[94] These the Austrian Ambassador took away in his carriage and sent them to England. Metternich's gloomy forebodings greatly excited the Empress. She thought once more of Marie Antoinette, and felt that she might share that Queen's fate on the scaffold.

The Council of August 10 finished at midnight, and the Empress warmly thanked Canrobert for his presence. The Marshal was grieved at her changed appearance. In a few days she appeared to have aged by ten years. Her features were drawn, the wrinkles showed, her face was puffed, fever burnt in her eyes, she was shaking with cold. As Canrobert was there, she thought he had come to tell her he would not leave the capital—would remain to protect her and to keep order in the town. Taking him apart, she said: "Marshal, I wanted to see you to give you the command of Paris. I reckon upon your devotion. You have influence with the troops, and I am certain you will hold the command successfully." He showed her the Emperor's imperative telegram, and said: "Madame, I cannot accept. My corps is at this moment on the march to Metz. There may be a battle to-morrow. If I remained here while my men are fighting, your Majesty would have but a worm-eaten bâton which would give you no support. Let me go and do my duty as a soldier."

She understood, and was silent. Later, she regretted that she had not compelled the Marshal to remain by her side, had a grudge against him for ever, and reproached this faithful servant of the Empire for leaving her at the moment of danger—leaving her by command of the Emperor.

Events proved that, as regards Canrobert, she was right, while it cannot be said that the Emperor was wrong. Canrobert's refusal gave Prince Napoleon, a week later, the opportunity of making Trochu Governor of Paris, with fatal results to the dynasty.

Canrobert to the Emperor.

Paris,
August 11, 1.10 a.m.

As the Empress and the Montauban (Palikao) Ministry think that my presence here is not obligatory, I am going to Metz, where your Majesty has assembled all my corps for the decisive battle. I

---

[94] All these valuables were delivered to the Empress soon after her arrival in this country (September 8, 1870).

am leaving at once.

MARSHAL CANROBERT.

At 8 a.m. Canrobert started for Metz. All along the railway he saw indescribable disorder. The employés had lost their heads. The line was blocked. There were trains full of Failly's stragglers. One man put his head out of the window and shouted to Canrobert: "Now it is your turn to go and get a drubbing!" The Marshal dragged the ruffian from the carriage, shook the life out of him, and made him crave for pardon. At last (August 12) the Marshal, famishing, got to the Metz station, where one of his staff discovered a loaf, which they devoured. The Emperor was at the Préfecture, and at seven o'clock he gave Canrobert an audience. A conference was proceeding with Marshal Lebœuf and General Lebrun, and Canrobert was an eager listener to the talk. The Emperor, well aware of the scarcity of biscuits and also of cartridges, was endeavouring to get supplies of both. He wanted to collect 200,000 men at Metz, but Canrobert could not understand why. The Sovereign seemed to be dreaming.

While Canrobert was with the Emperor, Commandant Lanclos (one of the Marshal's aides-de-camp) witnessed a strange scene at the Hôtel de l'Europe. The house was full of officers, all much excited, and deeming the game lost. "See what fifteen years of favouritism have done for us," said a Colonel of the Staff. "The Emperor ought not to give any more orders. He should make Bazaine Commander-in-Chief, with full powers." This was openly said by a General, one of His Majesty's aides. Another General spoke strongly in favour of Bazaine, in whom all appeared to have confidence. He was "the saviour hailed by everybody." Even the most devoted friends of the Emperor had lost their faith in him. When he was at the Tuileries, Canrobert had observed the same feeling. Those surrounding the Empress no longer troubled about the Emperor—what he did, what he said, what he thought. He had become an embarrassment.

In 1867 all the "strong places" had been well supplied with biscuits by Marshal Niel; but by June, 1870, not one was left, and the Chamber (previous to the declaration of war) had refused to vote money for further supplies. Thus Metz and the frontier places were now without resources. A hurried contract had been made with the house of Rothschild for 2,500 tons of biscuits, which were on board ship at various ports, until they could be taken to Metz. The railway at Nancy and other places was blocked, so that no food, or anything else, could get to Metz. Plans were changed hourly. Orders followed by counter-orders—this was the rule.

Marshal Canrobert left the Emperor firmly convinced that the only plan in existence at the moment was to concentrate 200,000 men at Metz; what they were to do when, if ever, they arrived there was a mystery!

After forcing his way through the streets, which were in a state of turmoil, Canrobert reached his hotel, the Europe, and ordered lunch—an omelette and a cutlet. These he could have, but only in the room common to all comers.

> In a large room, on the ground-floor, was a great table; around
> it were smaller ones. At all of them were seated, pell-mell, Gener-
> als, officers of all ranks, civilians, reporters, and women of every

description—in such costumes! All these people were talking, gesticulating, and eating. Such were the avant-coureurs of defeat.

Nothing had been seen of the enemy for many days. Canrobert was furious, but he said nothing, and ordered his officers to remain silent. He rode to Woippy, saw his troops, and returned to the Emperor. His Majesty, bombarded by telegrams from the Empress and Palikao, gave way. By half-past two o'clock that day Lebœuf had ceased to be Major-General, and Bazaine was Commander-in-Chief of the French army, vice Napoleon III., resigned!

Canrobert saw at the Metz Préfecture the ghost of an Emperor. Overwhelmed, pale as death, seated at a large table, Napoleon held in one hand a pocket-handkerchief, with which he continually wiped his mouth. Either he had had a nephritic attack or had taken an over-dose of extrait thébaïgne; for he was inert.

Canrobert left Lebœuf, Bazaine, and the Emperor together at the Préfecture. The Emperor never told anyone what Bazaine and he had discussed. General Lebrun has put it on record that the Emperor told Bazaine he wished the army to retreat, and that Bazaine made no reply. In the evening Napoleon wrote to Bazaine: "See what can be done, and if we are not attacked to-morrow we will come to a decision."

Marshal Bazaine, tried by a court-martial—presided over by H.R.H. the Duc d'Aumale—for dereliction of duty, was found guilty, deprived of his military rank, and sentenced to imprisonment for life. I doubt very much whether the guilt or innocence of Bazaine will ever be satisfactorily established. The temper of the French people at the time of his trial required a victim, and he was freely offered up by his companions-in-arms on the altar of National Vanity. Nothing throughout the war was more remarkable than the discussions, the rivalries, the petty jealousies, which characterized the relations of Napoleon's Marshals and Generals. A friend of mine who was at Metz in the early period of the war assured me that he had never seen anything more pitiable than the look of sheer despondency which he saw on the Emperor's face as he sat presiding at a council of war, and listening to the noisy and even brutal recriminations of one General after another as he rose to defend his own movements, or attack the tactics of a brother officer. Naturally, Bazaine had few friends among the Commanders of Corps. They were only too glad to be able to point to his retirement on Metz, and his subsequent surrender, as the proximate causes of the overthrow of the French army. Each one felt his military honour less seriously impeached when the court-martial ordered Bazaine's name to be struck off the roll of the Legion of Honour.

I do not presume to offer an opinion on the subject of Bazaine's crime; but, from all that I have been able to gather from French military experts, the conviction is now prevalent that Bazaine was no traitor. I know that the Empress Eugénie, who suffered as much as anybody through his falling back on Metz, had nothing worse to say of him than that he was "ramolli," that all the thoughts of the old soldier were centred in his young and pretty wife and her children, and that France was secondary. At any rate, it is pretty certain that when the German armies got between him and Paris all the energy and skill and bravery of the best

General France had would have been overtaxed by the effort to pierce the barrier of fire and steel built across the roads by the Germans. Happily, there was one exception. Bazaine's Chief of Staff, his devoted friend during the siege, and subsequently his support during the trial, his comrade in imprisonment, ultimately his saviour, deserves honourable mention. He it was who planned and carried out Bazaine's escape from the Isle St. Marguerite in a little rowing-boat, and enabled his old commander to spend the rest of his days in exile instead of in prison.[95]

[95] I am greatly indebted to MM. Plon-Nourrit, the eminent Paris publishers, for most kindly permitting me to print the Sovereigns' war despatches and the summary of events in August, 1870. They are from the valuable work, "Le Maréchal Canrobert," by the well-known writer, M. Germain Bapst, an admitted authority on the subject. Five volumes of this brilliant historical work have already appeared through MM. Plon-Nourrit et Cie., and M. Bapst is engaged upon the sixth volume, to be issued in 1912.

CHAPTER XIII

WHAT OUR EYES HAVE SEEN

"Nous sommes prêts, archi-prêts. Il ne nous manque pas un
bouton de guêtre." —MARSHAL LEBŒUF.

IN the dead of the night the springless waggon containing two doctors of a
Sanitäts-Corps and myself rumbled through the streets of hilly Clermont, at that
moment[96] the headquarters of King William, first German Emperor. I had made
my way from Saarbrücken (escaping in a soldiers' train) to Pont-à-Mousson, had
seen something of the Bavarian bombardment of Toul, and had visited Commercy
and Bar-le-Duc. These eastern districts were occupied by the German troops, and
side by side on the walls of the Hôtel de Ville at Commercy were the Emperor's
placards, headed "Souscription en faveur de l'armée," and King William's announcement, "La conscription est abolie dans toute l'étendue du territoire Français
occupé par les troupes Allemandes."

I found the Prussians in high feather. "We shall be in Paris in a fortnight from
now," said some of their officers to me at table d'hôte; and I thought of the prediction when, three weeks later, I was "before," but not yet "in," Paris with them. My
greatest anxiety had been to catch up the royal headquarters, so that I might apply
for a "legitimation," which would enable me to move about free of interference;
and, thanks to Count von Podbielski, the King's Adjutant, I obtained this precious
document at Clermont. It was here that I met the King—here that, for the first time,
I saw Moltke and other giants of the sword, and Bismarck.

The one long, steep street of Clermont was ankle-deep in white mud. Each
side of it was lined by baggage-waggons and carriages—such carriages! In every
house soldiers were billeted. At No. 21 in the main thoroughfare King William
was lodged. This was the royal "haupt-quartier"—a plain, white building, nothing like the grand residence which the King had had at Saarbrücken. There was
no flag flying. Two soldiers were doing "sentry go"—that was all. As the church
clock chimed eight our hearts were stirred by the clash of music, and a Bavarian
battalion marched through the town, their band, forty-three strong, playing the
march from "Sardanapalus," to which, four days later (September 1), I stepped
at Bazeilles, while shells were flying and bullets whistling, and the mitrailleuses
furnishing a growling, snarling accompaniment.

As the Bavarians—the ill-fated King Ludwig's lissome Bavarians—passed No.

---

[96] August, 1870.

21 the King (he was seventy-four then!) came to the open window and gravely saluted the Captain of each company with a nod of his silvery head. "Hoch!" shouted the men—"hoch! hoch!" Presently came another battalion, and then the King came downstairs and stood in the street, chatting to his Staff as if it had been a review day in the Tempelhof, and not a pouring wet morning in war-time. King William was in the uniform of a general officer—tunic and trousers of blue, pickelhaube, low boots, cloak, and the blue-and-gold star common to all his Generals. All the officers of the battalion were called to the front, and forty or fifty were presented to His Majesty, who made this little speech: "Gentlemen, I am very much pleased to see the troops of Bavaria with those of Prussia. It has also given me a great deal of pleasure to observe the bravery which you have displayed and the zeal you possess. I hope that this unity of all the German armies will long endure, and that you will gain yet more glory."

Von Moltke and two or three other officers stood close by, and in attendance on the King was Count von Alten, brother of the Duchess of Manchester. (The Duke of Manchester of those days was with the Prussians for some time in the early days of the campaign.) Spectators of the incident were General Sheridan, of the United States Army, and a couple of other Americans. As I stood in the muddy streets of Clermont that morning, my attention riveted on the King, I little thought that ere the week was over I should witness two of the most sanguinary battles of the war, and see Napoleon III. and his army surrender to the white-haired old gentleman who had greeted his Bavarians so pleasantly opposite No. 21.

The hotel at Raucourt—a small town some two or three miles from the battlefield of Sedan—was full of German officers on August 31, but no hint was dropped to the three civilians (two English and one Austrian[97]) in the house that the next day would be an eventful one. The word "Sedan" was not even mentioned. But the constant passage of troops, all moving in the same direction, warned us to be on the alert. At half-past seven on September 1 two of us joined the procession, stimulated to hasten forward by the continuous roar of the guns from afar.

Pontoon bridges had been built over the Meuse, and on these we crossed with artillery and infantry—thousands of both. Here was the battlefield, extending over miles of ground, hill and valley, with sheltering woods here and there. It was a sweltering day—blue sky and fierce sunshine. The French gunners were very active, and, as we skirted the welcome coppice, their shells flew over our heads and burst at a few yards' distance. Parched with thirst, I parted company with my friend, whom I thought rashly venturesome, and retraced my steps in the direction of a large château, in the hope of getting a glass of water. On guard at the entrance-gate was a helmeted soldier, who barred my way. I produced my "permit," signed only two or three days before by the King's Adjutant, General von Podbielski; but this had no effect upon him, and, but for a happy accident—or, rather, two accidents—I should never have seen any more of the fighting. I ran up to a mounted officer, showed him my "legitimation," and had the satisfaction of hearing him shout to the man at the gate to "let me in," as I was a privileged person, entitled to go whither I listed.

[97] H. Sutherland Edwards, Edward Legge, and Victor Silberer.

Much relieved at this recognition of my status, I was tramping on towards the coppice, in the hope of picking up my companion, when a sergeant in charge of some ammunition waggons passed. To my surprise he stopped, inquiring, in my own tongue, "Are you an Englishman, sir?" I assured him that I was, and, moreover, a newspaper correspondent.

"Well, then," said this friend in need, "if you will come with me, I will take you to our battery, which is in action on the top of the hill, and introduce you to the Captain, Von Richter, who I dare say will allow you to be attached to us upon seeing your 'legitimation.' Otherwise you may find yourself in trouble."

It was soon done, and I was made free of the battery, and permitted to share its fate.

I found that this battery was part of the Fourth Army Corps, commanded by the then Crown Prince of Saxony, who became King Albert some years later. The battery was pounding away all day, and I never left it. I had smelt powder previously—at Saarbrücken, when the little Prince Imperial received his "baptism of fire," and at the battle of Beaumont, at the end of August. Then, however, I was constantly moving about, and at Saarbrücken, when Von Pestel's 1,000 fusiliers and three squadrons of Uhlans retreated, leaving the Emperor and Frossard's force of 30,000 (!) masters of the field, I had an hour's run at top speed with the defeated troops until we were out of reach of the French fire.

It was different on September 1. I was in the best position to see the fighting, throughout the day, until it was all over, and I was cautioned against roving about. On rising ground, near Richter's battery, were the King, Moltke, Bismarck, Von Podbielski, Von Alvensleben, and others—General Sheridan amongst them. I should have preferred the position of a "galloper" to that of a mere spectator, standing up, hour after hour, as it seemed to me, to be shot at. The firing from this one battery alone deafened me at first, but I soon got used to it. The time dragged on very slowly. I cannot conscientiously say that this period of looking on was particularly exciting. Our battery was engaged in a duel with a French battery on a distant hill. To these Saxon gunners it seemed not to matter what happened elsewhere. They were only an atom of a vast mosaic. What our battery was doing was being done by other batteries all over an illimitable area.

Down in the valley we watched the lines of blue-tuniced Germans always advancing. Havoc in their ranks was made by the mitrailleuses, whose diabolical grinding rattle was terrifying; but the wearers of the spiked helmets seemed to be traversing a field of poppies, so thickly was the ground strewn by the red-trousered killed and wounded. Every now and again our battery took up a fresh position, and as we advanced the closer we got to Bazeilles, Willers-Cernay, and Waldincourt, all in flames.

We did not know the "motive" of the battle, which, as General Pajol afterwards put it, was to drive the French into the "mousetrap" of Sedan. What we did know, towards the late afternoon, was that we had assisted at a great German victory, and that the white flag (which, from our position, we could not see) had been hoisted within Sedan. What we saw, about four o'clock, was the German cavalry scouring the valley and cutting down the retreating enemy. Then our battery ceased firing, but we heard the occasional growling of other guns until sunset. Next morning early, when the bands were playing "Nun danket alle Gott," General von Schöler told me many astounding things—how the Emperor Napoleon had personally surrendered, and how the whole French army had capitulated. Von Schöler, like so many others, thought the war was over, but on the 3rd the victorious armies began the famous march to Paris. And that march is a thing to remember, for by the 19th the invaders had encircled the capital.

At 8.30 p.m. on Thursday, the never-to-be-forgotten First of September, 1870, when Napoleon, although he had formally surrendered, was not yet an actual captive, General de Wimpffen said to him: "Sire, if I have lost the battle, it is because your Generals refused to obey my orders."

Towards the end of August the Emperor had confided the supreme command to Marshal Bazaine, and left Metz for Châlons, where he found the débris of the 1st Corps (MacMahon), the 5th (Failly), the 7th (Douay), and the newly-formed 12th Corps (Trochu). Napoleon followed MacMahon's corps, which was in very indifferent case.

On August 30 the whole of the French corps were at a point between Mouzon and Carignan. Failly, who had just been badly beaten, found that he was in close proximity to the greater portion of the German forces, and felt unable to march to Metz; as a consequence, MacMahon ordered him to retreat to Sedan, and told the Emperor (then at Carignan) also to proceed to that place, now the rallying centre of the army. When, at 11 p.m., Napoleon reached Sedan, he was urged to continue his journey to Mézières, where he would have been safe, and could have gained Paris. He refused, however, to leave the army, declaring that he would share its fate.

The four French corps were so placed as to surround Sedan, the left bank of the Meuse remaining open. This was an unfortunate disposition, as it made it possible for the Germans to pass round the town by that bank of the river. A Bavarian and a Prussian corps soon occupied that position, thus preventing a French retreat in that direction.

The battle of Sedan began at 5 a.m. on September 1, the Germans first attacking from the Bazeilles side, vigorously defended by the 12th Corps. MacMahon immediately roused the Emperor, who rode towards Bazeilles, followed by his Staff. On the road he met MacMahon, already wounded and hors de combat. The Emperor rode on until he came to Vassoigne's division of marine infantry, a splendid force. The Sovereign, finding that shells and bullets were coming from all sides at once, ordered the officers accompanying him to join a battalion of foot-chasseurs, who were sheltered by a wall, until the time came for them to advance in line. The Emperor, anxious to see the disposition of his troops, rode onward, accompanied only by his aide-de-camp of the day (General Pajol), his orderly officer (Captain d'Hendecourt, who was killed), his principal écuyer (Comte Davilliers), and his doctor (Baron Corvisart). Napoleon proceeded to an exposed point, where Commandant St. Aulaire's battery was in position, remaining there for an hour under a withering cannon and rifle fire.

At 6 a.m. MacMahon, wounded, had placed the command in the hands of Ducrot, who, in order to prevent the turning movement, which had been fatal to the French in previous battles, and also to preserve the one line of retreat remaining open—viz., the Mézières road—had placed on the heights of Floing two divisions of the 7th Corps, whose artillery faced Mézières; and at the same time he ordered the commander of the 12th Corps to execute his retreat in échelons by brigades. That movement was ably performed by General Lebrun (vice Trochu), whose force never ceased fighting during the operation.

General de Wimpffen now appeared. He had visited the outposts, had observed the admirable attitude of the 12th Corps (Lebrun's) and its energetic resistance on the Bazeilles side, and predicted a successful issue of the battle. It was still only nine o'clock. For three hours Ducrot had been in supreme command. De Wimpffen now handed him a letter, signed by the War Minister, in virtue of which he claimed to succeed the wounded Marshal. Ducrot at once complied, and explained to De Wimpffen all that had been done. The new commander treated Ducrot's explanation very lightly, and expressed the opinion that the enemy's movements were nothing but cavalry manœuvres!

As the Emperor now wished to proceed to the distant heights, which were apparently the key to the position, he led his Staff down to Givonne, where they met General Goze and his division. Here an officer of chasseurs-à-pied approached the Emperor, saying: "Sire, I am a native of these parts, and know the country perfectly. If we allow the Garenne wood to be turned the army will be surrounded, and will be in a most critical position."

Napoleon at once sent one of his Staff to find De Wimpffen and give him this information, which bore out what Ducrot had previously said. De Wimpffen rode up to the Emperor, remarking: "Your Majesty need not be alarmed. In two hours I shall have thrown them into the Meuse!"

General Castelnau grasped General Pajol's hand, exclaiming: "I hope to God *we* shall not be thrown into the river!"

All were now alive to the supreme danger of the French forces. The ground on which the Emperor and his Staff were standing was torn up by shells coming from all sides. The troops had already concentrated in the ravines which surrounded Sedan; the roads leading to those places were blocked by commissariat and artillery waggons and by regiments of cavalry; all these thousands were trying to escape from the storm of shells and bullets, but the majority succumbed to the terrible fire.

The result of De Wimpffen's change of plan was now evident. At one o'clock the 1st and 5th Corps got into confusion. The Generals endeavoured to re-establish order by going to the front; but all was of no avail, and the troops retreated to Sedan in such disorder that General Lebrun had the gates of the town closed. Even this was useless, for the defeated troops scaled the ramparts with the aid of ropes and ladders let down by the men within the citadel.

The Emperor had fully realized the situation since eleven o'clock. For five hours he had been in the thick of the fighting, under a cross-fire. Shells burst around him and his Staff. General de Courson and Captain de Trécesson had fallen gravely wounded close to the Emperor. In retiring the troops had compelled His Majesty to fall back, and he was jammed against the walls of the town. When, at half-past eleven, he freed himself, more than 30,000 men were heaped together in the streets of Sedan, pell-mell. The enemy's shells fell in their midst, as they were still falling on the battlefield itself, and dealt out the same destruction. On the bridge a shell burst two yards from the Emperor, killing two horses by his side. The marvel was that he escaped with his life and uninjured.

After visiting Marshal MacMahon, the Emperor tried to remount his charger. As the confusion rendered this impossible, His Majesty went to the Sous-Préfecture, and there awaited the dénouement. The commanders of the various corps soon joined him, declaring that the troops were all in such disorder in the streets that further resistance was impossible. General Pellé, who, next day, voted against the capitulation, said to the Emperor: "Sire, I am only a soldier. I want to save your Majesty, but at this moment you cannot leave the ramparts. To attempt to do so would be useless."

The Emperor replied that he would not sacrifice the life of a single soldier to save his own, and that he had made up his mind to share the fate of the army.

Having minutely questioned the Generals as to the state of affairs, the Emperor sent General Lebrun to find General de Wimpffen, and tell him, since it was useless to continue the struggle, to ask for an armistice. A full hour having elapsed without any answer from De Wimpffen, and the murderous fire of the Germans continuing, while the French guns remained silent, the Emperor himself ordered the white flag to be hoisted on the citadel. The King immediately sent an aide-de-camp to demand the surrender of the town. The Emperor, believing that in delivering himself up to the victors he would obtain better terms for the army and for France, despatched one of his own aides-de-camp to the King with the message that the Emperor placed his sword in the Prussian Sovereign's hands. On the following day (Friday, September 2), at a Council of War, composed of thirty Generals, presided over by General de Wimpffen, it was recognized that capitulation was inevitable, only two Generals voting against it.

The Emperor (General Pajol asserts it most positively) was entirely ignorant of the strategical movements which led the army from Châlons to Mouzon, and from thence to Sedan. To charge Napoleon III. with being militarily responsible for the capitulation of Sedan is an injustice, as Marshal MacMahon was perfectly free in all his movements. The Emperor has been personally charged with wrecking the army. He could but try to save the crew of the ship, of which he was no longer the captain. This is what he endeavoured to do when, at three o'clock in the afternoon, he ordered the white flag to be hoisted. Half an hour later one or other of the Generals would have given the order, but in the meantime thousands more lives would have been sacrificed.

The politicians tried to throw the whole of the responsibility of Sedan upon the Emperor, whom they would certainly not have credited with a victory, had there been one. But Marshal MacMahon, whose noble simplicity and loyal character are known to all, wrote, in October, 1870, a letter to the Emperor, dated from Pouru-aux-Bois, in which he said: "The Emperor may be assured that I should never think, for the purpose of defending myself personally, of misrepresenting the events which I witnessed in the last campaign."

These words do the Duc de Magenta honour, and cast upon each individual the responsibility of his acts.

"Such is the true story of this deplorable day. I have given the details in sober language. Desiring only to tell the truth, I have related only what I myself saw."[98]

Were the Emperor's cheeks rouged on the day of Sedan? Zola has asserted that they were so coloured "to make him appear juvenile, and even jovial."[99] Personally I can neither confirm nor deny the allegation, for, although I was with the Saxons during the battle, and remained on the field the two following days, I failed to get a glimpse of the Emperor, who had been within an ace of being captured on August 29 and 30 by the troops I was then accompanying. His Majesty (so they assured me) was bundled into a third-class carriage of the last train used by his forces, and so escaped capture by the skin of his teeth.

It is quite possible that some of those numerous informants of Zola, from whose stories he mainly compiled his marvellous narrative, may have inadvertently led him astray in this particular matter, if not on some other points. I have conversed with a French gentleman who was close to the Emperor an hour or two before the surrender and with a Prussian officer who was one of Napoleon's escort. Both closely scrutinized the captive, but neither noticed any unusual colour in his face. Zola was not the first Frenchman to accuse Napoleon III. of cowardice (for that is what is implied by the story of the painted cheeks); he may have borrowed the idea from Kinglake, who describes the Emperor at Magenta turning green, yellow, and white under the Austrian fire.

Those who enjoyed the personal acquaintance of the Emperor are unanimous in the opinion that he was less of a poseur than most men. There was nothing of the "roi du théâtre" about him. Throughout the short campaign which finished for Napoleon III. at Sedan he was, both physically and mentally, unstrung by his malady. It was indispensable that he should begin the campaign in good health, and be able to keep the saddle for several hours at a stretch. Gamble, the Scotsman, who superintended the imperial stables for many years, and stood by the Emperor on the day of Sedan, said that His Majesty "did his best to court death," despite the entreaties of his officers; and Gamble's testimony is confirmed by many other eye-witnesses.

---

[98] The narrative of General V. Pajol, aide-de-camp of Napoleon III. To the best of my belief it has not appeared in any French, and certainly not in any English, volume.

[99] "La Débâcle."

NAPOLEON III. AT SEDAN.

From an unpublished photograph, privately taken at the instance of the Comte
de La Chapelle, of the picture painted by the distinguished French artist, Olivier
Pichat. Lent for this work by the Vicomte de La Chapelle.

The late M. Paul de Cassagnac gave Zola credit for his account of Sedan, but emphatically denied the rouging story. De Cassagnac was a good witness, for he was with the Emperor at Sedan. "It was on my shoulder," he has told us, "that Napoleon III. leaned when, seriously ill and suffering terribly, he got into the carriage in order to surrender himself as a prisoner."

The question was even discussed by M. Melchior de Voguë, who affirmed that Zola was wrong.[100] Princesse Mathilde, cousin of Napoleon III., "refused to believe that the Emperor would have acted so theatrically on such a momentous occasion." She had certainly never told anyone that her relative was rouged. M. Robert Mitchell corroborated Paul de Cassagnac. He was a volunteer in the 3rd Zouaves at Sedan, often saw the Emperor, and was certain he was not rouged. M. Mitchell argued (and military experts will agree with him) that no writer, "not even Zola," could adequately describe what happened at Sedan without having been actually in the battle. We may believe Paul de Cassagnac and Robert Mitchell, and may be certain that Zola was misinformed.

I pass on to the final phase of Sedan.

In newspapers, in magazines, in volumes of memoirs, in histories of the war, there have appeared, year after year, ever since the autumn of 1870, as many different accounts of what passed the day following the battle of Sedan, at the interviews which Napoleon III. had, first with Bismarck, and next with the King of Prussia, as would fill volumes. It is natural that it should be so, for at the meeting of the Emperor and the King no third person was present, and the Emperor's talk with Bismarck was heard by only one other man. What passed between the two Sovereigns was related to his son, the then Crown Prince, by the King, and recorded by the Prince in his "Diary," in his royal father's own words. The Prince-reporter's account of the interview is as follows:

> The King began by saying that, as the fortune of war had gone against the Emperor, and as the latter had handed his sword to the King, His Majesty had come to ask Napoleon III. his present intentions. Napoleon replied that he placed himself in the King's hands. The King rejoined that it was with a feeling of real compassion that he saw his adversary in such a position; the more so as he knew that it had not been easy for the Emperor to resolve upon war. This assertion was visibly welcome to Napoleon. He warmly assured the King that he had given way to public opinion when he decided upon war. Thereupon the King remarked that, as public opinion had had that tendency, those who had excited it were the more culpable. Then, recurring to the immediate object of the Emperor's visit, the King asked Napoleon if he wished to enter into negotiations.

> The Emperor replied in the negative, observing that, being a prisoner, he had no control over the Government. And upon the King inquiring where the Government was, Napoleon replied,

---

[100] *Revue des Deux Mondes.*

"At Paris." The King then turned the conversation upon the Emperor's future, and offered him the château of Wilhelmshöhe as a residence—an offer which he immediately accepted. He appeared particularly satisfied when the King said he would give him an escort of honour which would insure his safety to the frontier. As Napoleon, in the course of the conversation, appeared to suppose that he had had against him the army of Prince Frederick Charles, the King told him that it was not so—it was the army of the Crown Prince of Saxony and my army. The Emperor having inquired where the army of Prince Frederick Charles was, the King, emphasizing the words, replied, "With the 7th Army Corps, before Metz." The Emperor, painfully surprised, took a step backwards. On his face there was a sad expression, for now it was made clear to him that he had not been opposed by all the German army.

The King praised the bravery of the French, which Napoleon willingly recognized. The conversation lasted a good quarter of an hour, and then both retired. The tall figure of the King dominated. The Emperor saw me, and held out one hand, while with the other he tried to dry the tears which rolled down his face. He uttered words of gratitude to me, and for the generous manner in which the King had treated him. I spoke naturally in the same sense, and asked him if he had been able to get some rest during the night. He replied that chagrin and the thought of his family had banished all possibility of sleep. When I expressed my regret that the war had been so terrible and so sanguinary, he said it was, alas! too true, too terrible, especially as "they had not wanted war!" He had not received any news of the Empress and the Prince Imperial for a week, and asked if he might send her a private telegram—a request which was granted. We shook hands as we parted, Boyen and Lynar accompanying him. There was something sinister-looking about his suite in their new uniforms, in marked contrast with ours, so damaged by the war. When he had gone a telegram from the Empress arrived, and I sent it to him by Seckendorff.... Some fears are expressed lest the results of the war should not come up to the expectations of the German people.

The only witness of the meeting (September 2, 1870) between Napoleon III. and Count Bismarck at Donchéry, the day after the battle of Sedan, was Colonel Freiherr Josef von Ellrichshausen (who died in September, 1906). After the Colonel had ridden out with his men to take over a convoy of wounded French officers and prisoners, and while thus engaged, the carriage with the Emperor in it appeared. At the same moment several horsemen, amongst whom was Bismarck, rode up. Von Ellrichshausen reported to the Chancellor the presence of the Emperor, whereupon Bismarck at once sprang from his horse, and, in the Colonel's own words, "approached Napoleon almost with humility, and the words, 'Sire, qu'est-ce que vous désirez?'" As conversation in the small wayside house (the only building near at hand) was impossible owing to the presence of many dead and wounded soldiers, Von Ellrichshausen and his men brought out two chairs, upon which Napoleon and Bismarck sat while discussing the situation.[101]

The late Sir Henry Drummond Wolff, accompanied by Sir Henry James (Lord James of Hereford), happened to be at Verviers when Napoleon III. was being taken to Wilhelmshöhe. Drummond Wolff found the Emperor looking anything but ill, nor did his features betray any traces of that deep emotion which other eye-witnesses have dwelt upon so eloquently. The Emperor "leant somewhat heavily on the arm of the gentleman who assisted him to alight" from the carriage which had brought him to Verviers. His Majesty read a despatch which was handed to him, "sat down at a table in the waiting-room, and was engaged in writing for some time." He then took a turn up and down the platform, returned to the waiting-room, and read *l'Indépendence Belge* until the moment came for him to enter the special train which took him to his destination, Wilhelmshöhe. Sir Henry Drummond Wolff noted with the Emperor General Chazal, who was in command of the Belgian army of observation on the German frontier, and at whose earnest request the Emperor wrote a full explanation of the causes which, in his opinion, led to his defeat at Sedan.[102]

To the list of English journalists who suffered from the spy mania in the Franco-German War, and whose cases were recorded in the *Star*, may be added the name of Mr. Edward Legge, who was at that time the youngest of the war "specials." As the representative of the *Irish Times* he was present at the first engagement (the "baptism of fire") at Saarbrücken, and the next morning started alone (the fighting having scattered the reporting battalion) to overtake the Germans, who had retreated the previous day. He was not long in coming up with the wearers of the "Pickelhaube," and in being arrested by a cavalry picket. The imaginary "French spy" was put in a springless waggon, and taken from one place to another, and before one General after the other, until he felt somewhat weary of the involuntary promenade in full view of König Wilhelm's legions. Appearances were decidedly against him, but nobody seemed disposed to give the order to put a bullet through him, although that was the fate which he hourly anticipated. The hectoring General von Steinmetz first believed and then relegated the prisoner to General von Goeben, who liberated him on condition that he went straight off to Cologne, and did not return to "the front" again. The required promise was given—and broken, and a week afterwards the correspondent was back at Saarbrücken, where he read the news of his death in the *Old Free Press* (Vi-

---

[101] This historical episode had an echo in 1888. The Colonel, then a member of the Reichstag, was unexpectedly sent for by Bismarck, who said: "The Press has been stating that I treated Napoleon with undue roughness upon the occasion of our meeting at Donchéry. You were the only eye-witness of the scene, so do you tell them the truth."

[102] This remarkable document appears textually only in "The Empress Eugénie: 1870-1910." London: Harper & Brothers. New York: Charles Scribner's Sons. 1910.

enna) and also in the *Times* (which later contradicted it under the pleasing heading of "A Revenant"). The youthful "special" passed scatheless through the battles of Beaumont and Sedan, accompanying a Saxon battery into action on the memorable First of September, and remaining "in the thick of it" until nightfall; and the next day marched with the same battery to Paris, or, rather, to Montmorency and St. Gratien, where he remained during several weeks of the siege.—*Star*.

CHAPTER XIV

ON THE EVE OF EXILE

OFTEN as the story of the Empress's escape from the Tuileries on September 4, 1870, has been told — perhaps with more circumstantiality by the late Mr. T. W. Evans than by anyone else — the version now given for the first time differs in some important respects from the Evans narrative.

This account of the episode of September 4 (not the 1st, as erroneously printed in the original French version) appeared in *L'Écho du Parlement Belge* of January 28, 1871. The writer asserts that his informant was the well-known diplomatist, Mr. Bancroft, who at the time in question was United States Minister at Berlin, and who stated that he had "had it direct from Mr. Evans"; which, to say the least of it, is curious.

This new version of an old story runs thus:

About nine o'clock on the morning of September 4, 1870, the Empress Eugénie was in the Pavillon Marsan, at the Tuileries, anxiously waiting for the domestics to come and assist her in dressing, as Her Majesty was going to hear the grand'messe at the church of St. Germain-l'Auxerrois. The Empress became impatient, and was astonished that no one had obeyed the orders which she had given. At this moment there arrived Mme. Lebreton (sister of General Bourbaki), her devoted friend, who came to report to the Empress the gloomy state of affairs in the capital. It appeared that the people were excitedly demanding the overthrow of the Emperor; everywhere menacing groups had formed; perhaps the Tuileries would be invaded.

With tears in her eyes, Mme. Lebreton entreated the Empress to fly while there was still time to escape. Her Majesty, although much perturbed by what she had heard, tried to soothe Mme. Lebreton with the assurance that General Trochu would watch over her safety — that he had promised to protect her, that he was a man of honour, that he would keep his word, and that if there should be any real danger he would not fail to send someone who would tell her what course it was necessary, in his opinion, for her to take.

Meanwhile the Revolution became more threatening. The clamour of the crowd and the cries of "Vive la République!" were plainly heard by the two ladies. Mme. Lebreton renewed her appeals, but the Empress unheeded them. "I have confidence in Trochu," she continued to repeat; "he is a soldier, and will not abandon me."

It was not until about one o'clock that, the Place du Carrousel being by this time invaded, the Empress, now finally convinced of her danger and of Trochu's defection, listened to Mme. Lebreton. Her Majesty rang for her women—rang several times; no one came. Mme. Lebreton, much alarmed, went into all the neighbouring rooms. Not a soul! All she saw was furniture upside down—the drawers all open.

The Empress was abandoned—abandoned by everybody, even by her servants! Then the poor woman fled, accompanied only by her devoted friend. For a full hour they paced through the galleries, the cabinets, the long passages of the immense, deserted palace, their cheeks paling at every noise which they fancied they heard; not daring to pass in front of the windows for fear that those outside might see them; undecided which way to go. Finally, exhausted, they arrived under the colonnade of the Louvre, at the top of the great staircase.

When, at last, they ventured to look into each other's face, a cry of terror escaped from them. In their haste and their anguish of mind they had forgotten to put on their hats and mantles; thus they could not take a step without being noticed. The Empress was en peignoir, with a simple piece of gauze thrown over her head. At this moment, before they had got half-way down the stairs leading to the street, someone close to them exclaimed, "The Empress!" Her Majesty turned pale and cried out, "We are lost!" Mme. Lebreton, preserving her sang-froid, turned towards the person who had spoken; he was a gentleman irreproachably dressed. She cast a look of entreaty at him. He understood, and pretended not to see them.

At the foot of the staircase a fiacre was passing. To spring into it was the work of a moment. The driver, astonished, and perhaps suspecting who the two ladies were, had a good look at them. The Empress, conquering her fears, exclaimed brusquely, "Boulevard Haussmann, 30!" and the fiacre moved off. As they were driving through the streets, feeling a ray of hope, Mme. Lebreton asked her mistress if she had any money with her. "Ah, mon Dieu! Did I think of that?" replied the Empress. Mme. Lebreton rummaged her pockets, while the faces of both were bathed in a cold perspiration. "Saved!" cried Mme. Lebreton, who had found in her pockets two five-franc pieces!

The cab stopped at the place indicated. At the same moment another fiacre came up. The driver of the Empress's cab was given five francs, and when he had disappeared the two ladies engaged the other vehicle. "Avenue de l'Impératrice, 57!" said the Empress. (It was to put the first cabman off the track that the Empress had told him to go to the Boulevard Haussmann.)

At No. 57, Avenue de l'Impératrice lived Mr. Evans, the Court dentist. They rang the bell, and a valet opened the door. "Monsieur is not at home," said the man; "what do you want?" Then, surprised at the tenue of the ladies, the servant seemed to be about to shut the door in their faces, but the Empress, rousing herself, said: "We are two Americans. Mr. Evans made an appointment with us here at three o'clock."

They were shown into a room, where they waited an hour. Then Mr. Evans came in. He had returned from the Tuileries, where he had vainly searched for the Empress.

Upon Mr. Evans's return the servant told him that two ladies, very oddly attired, were waiting to see him, and the dentist at once guessed who they were. "Ah, yes," he remarked, "they have come to bother me again. We must try to get them across the Atlantic as soon as possible."

He had previously arranged how the Empress was to escape. While two of his best horses were being harnessed, the Empress and Mme. Lebreton wrapped themselves in some plaid shawls which they found in Mrs. Evans's wardrobe. Then they were driven off in Mr. Evans's carriage. They stopped first at Evreux to change horses, which had been telegraphed for in advance; next, at Trouville. Nobody imagined that it could be the Empress of the French who was travelling in this fashion. Happier than Louis XVI. at Varennes, the Empress was not recognized anywhere, not even at the hotel at Trouville, to which Mr. Evans conducted her.

When the Empress and Mme. Lebreton were comfortably installed at the hotel, Mr. Evans hurried off to the harbour, where he found two yachts moored. Sir John Burgoyne, the owner of one of the vessels, when first asked by Mr. Evans if he would take two ladies to England, refused, but relented when, under a pledge of secrecy, he learnt that it was a question of saving the Empress.

In this version of the Empress's flight from the Tuileries no mention is made of the prominent part played in the episode by the then Austrian Ambassador (the husband of the still-living Princess Pauline Metternich, who gave herself the very uncomplimentary sobriquet, the "singe à la mode"), and the Italian Minister, Chevalier Nigra, who died at Rapolla in July, 1907. When Nigra's death was announced, the English newspapers published a variety of versions of his share in the Empress's escape, but I am disposed to think that the vérité vraie is to be found in the subjoined brief narrative, from the pen of M. Maurice Dumoulin.

The gates of the Tuileries were forced open by the excited, exasperated crowd. The déchéance had been pronounced on the steps of the Corps Législatif, and the Republic proclaimed. The Empress must quit. Early on that terrible Sunday afternoon M. Franceschini Pietri half opened the door of the Empress's salon and exclaimed, "Madame, there is only just time!" Prince Richard Metternich (the Austrian Ambassador) and Chevalier Nigra were with him. "Make haste, Madame!" said Nigra, who watched from the windows the progress of the émeute; "make haste!" The Empress snatched up a waterproof, a hat with a brown veil, and some portraits.

Nigra again exclaimed: "Be quick, Madame! I can hear them; they are coming up!" The Empress took Metternich's arm. Nigra walked by her side. Like a whirlwind the Empress and the Ambassadors, followed by Mme. Lebreton, M. Conti, and Dr. Conneau, flew across the salles of the Louvre Museum, making for St.-Germain-l'Auxerrois, where Prince Metternich's carriage had been ordered to wait; but the vehicle was not there, and the Prince went in search of it. Nigra remained alone with the Empress and Mme. Lebreton. Meanwhile the crowd increased. As the little group stood in the street, a boy, who was watching them, recognized the principal figure, and cried out, "Tiens! Voilà l'Impératrice!" Nigra's presence of mind saved the situation. "What, you little scamp!" exclaimed the Ambassador; "you dare to shout 'Vive la Prusse!'" Just then, before the bystanders could realize who was in their midst at the most critical moment in her life, an unoccupied fiacre jolted by. Securing it, Nigra pushed the Empress and her companion into the cab, saying: "Get in, Madame. We cannot wait for Metternich's brougham."

Not only was Nigra possessed of great intellectual powers, he was the handsomest of men, and that fact contributed in no small degree to his success in diplomacy. Count Cavour had a great friend in the Comtesse de Circourt, née Anastasie de Klustine, whose salon was the resort of many political and literary celebrities. She helped to "launch" Nigra, to whom she wrote: "What strikes one so forcibly is the perfect harmony of your youth with the maturity of your look. M. D— — says your profile reminds him of a Greek statue. And he is right." Nigra took up his abode at the hotel of the Italian Embassy (formerly the home of the Piedmontese Legation), at the Rond Point of the Champs-Elysées, and was soon made much of, for his reputation had preceded him. Cavour had written to his friends in Paris: "Nigra knows all my thoughts," and that alone was sufficient to insure the young diplomatist's success.

Nigra's rôle was a very difficult one. He had to conciliate French diplomatists, to keep "well in" with the Emperor, and to avoid creating jealousy amongst the foreign Ambassadors and Ministers. Above all, he had to secure the goodwill of the Empress Eugénie, who had no love for a Government which was attacking the temporal power of the Pope. But Nigra succeeded. How he did it is still a mystery. He got on terms of intimacy with the Emperor and Empress, and even stifled the jealousy of Prince Metternich.

Nigra was not only a diplomatist and a handsome man—"beau comme Apollon"—but a poet. One afternoon (it was a soft June day in 1863) the imperial hostess and some of her guests were trying a Venetian gondola on the lake at Fontainebleau. The Empress asked the gondolier to sing something appropriate; but the man declared that Nature had not endowed him with a voice. But Nigra was there, and Nigra would sing. He warbled in those beautiful, seductive tones which had struck responsive chords in the hearts of many before he had bewitched the imperial lady, the favourite "Gondola," which he had himself written and submitted to Prosper Mérimée, who was pleased to approve it. The singer ended with these daring lines:

> Oh femme, si parfois ton lac paisible doit voir voguant sur tes côtes le muet Empéreur, dis-lui que sur les rives de l'Adriatique, pauvre, nue, exsangue Venise souffre et languit. Mais elle vit ... et elle attend encore. (Oh lady, if sometimes thy peaceful lake sees wandering by thy side the dumb Emperor, tell him that, on the shores of the Adriatic, poor, naked, bloodless Venice suffers and languishes. But she lives ... and she is still expectant.)

It has been even said that it was Nigra's poetic skill as much as anything which impelled the "dumb Emperor" to hand over Venetia to the young Kingdom of Italy. What is more certain is that Nigra made two powerful friends of the Marquis d'Azeglio and the celebrated Signor Manzoni by writing, when he was a humble clerk in the Sardinian Foreign Office, a poem dedicated to d'Azeglio's daughter on her marriage to Comte Matteo Ricci, the Marquis at the time being Prime Minister. That poem gave Nigra a step in the "F.O.," but had not Cavour made him his secretary he might have had no opportunity of showing that he could do something better than pen little lyrics, copy despatches, and warble a chanson to the Empress's eyebrow. In his most poetical moments he could hardly have imagined that a day would come when he would be aiding the subject of his love-song to escape from the fury of the mob by pushing her into a common fiacre and refusing to "wait for Metternich's carriage."

In one of his interesting volumes Comte d'Hérisson appears to have narrated the story of the Empress Eugénie's voyage from Trouville to Ryde after her flight from the Tuileries. A letter to Sir John Burgoyne on the subject brought the French author the following reply:

Cowes, Isle of Wight,
December 27, 1889.

Sir,

I have the honour to acknowledge the receipt of your letter of December 14, and I beg to express my regret that I am obliged to reply to it in my own language.

With reference to the statements published in your "Letters of an Aide-de-Camp" concerning the passage of H.M. the Empress Eugénie from France to England in 1870, I have never seen the book, but only an extract from it, concerning myself, sent to me by a friend, and which statements you now tell me were communicated to you by Dr. T. W. Evans.

It is difficult to recall details after the lapse of so many years, but my recollection is that Lady Burgoyne and myself were on board the Royal Yacht Squadron cutter, *Gazelle*, forty-two tons, in Deauville (Trouville) harbour during the first week of September, 1870.

On the morning of September 6 Dr. Evans's card was given to me; I went on deck, and one of two gentlemen introduced himself as Dr. Evans. He told me that Her Majesty the Empress was in Deauville, and he asked me to take her on board the yacht at once, as she was in danger and in distress.

I acknowledge that at the moment I thought the story so unlikely that I did not believe one word of it, and I have no doubt that I expressed myself to that effect.

I asked Dr. Evans to speak to Lady Burgoyne, and she told me that Dr. Evans was the well-known American dentist in Paris, and that his statement was probably true. There was but one other yacht in the harbour, and that was a small schooner, hired by the late Lord Charles Hamilton. No American yacht was at or near Trouville, and the statements as to Dr. Evans having had to threaten to embark Her Majesty the Empress in such a vessel never occurred.

Deauville Harbour is a tidal basin, and vessels can only enter it and leave it at the time of high water; and the only objection I am aware of having made was that, as the yacht could only leave the harbour at about seven o'clock, night and morning, it would be injudicious to attract attention by endeavouring to embark Her Majesty the Empress during daylight. Dr. Evans agreed to this suggestion, and it was arranged that Her Majesty should embark at midnight, which she did, accompanied by Mme. Lebreton, Dr. Evans, and a nephew of that gentleman, who left the yacht before we sailed.

I was captain of my own yacht, and I navigated her myself, and to the best of my recollection the only conversation I had with the Empress during the time she was on board was that early in the morning of September 7 I asked Her Majesty's permission to get the yacht under weigh. Once during the night, when there was a great noise on deck, owing to a boat washing adrift, Her Majesty sent for me to ask if anyone was hurt; and shortly after we anchored off Ryde, Isle of Wight. On the following morning I was ordered to thank the crew for their exertions during an unusually rough passage across the Channel.

I am much more amused than angry at the account of my tears, fears, and entreaties to Dr. Evans to put me on shore. The fact is that that eminent practitioner was seasick in my berth from the time we left Trouville until just before Her Majesty the Empress landed at Ryde, and if he had had a little experience of the sea he would have known that anyone who had to stand for many hours at the tiller of a small yacht in a gale of wind (and I may mention that this was the same night that Her Majesty's ship *Captain* was lost) might charitably be allowed to wipe the salt-water out of his eyes before consulting the chart without being accused of shedding tears of fear.

I wish to add that any story which may have got abroad implying what you are pleased to term a "tardy recognition" on the part of the Empress of the slight service it was my good fortune to render to Her Majesty is absolutely untrue.

The Empress, on leaving Ryde, went to Hastings for a few days. From that place she sent Lady Burgoyne an autograph letter of thanks. This was followed by a magnificent jewel, which will ever be a cherished heirloom in my family. I may further mention that His Majesty the Emperor sent for me to Chislehurst a short time after his arrival in England and thanked me in the kindest manner. From that day to this Lady Burgoyne and myself have received from the Empress the most unvarying kindness and hospitality.

I am, Sir, your obedient servant,
J. MONTAGUE BURGOYNE.

Sir John Burgoyne subsequently made the appended extracts from the logbook of his yacht. With this addition the narrative may, for the first time, be considered complete:

> The Empress told Lady Burgoyne how shamefully she had been deserted by all about her at the Tuileries, and that her very servants had pilfered things in her apartments.
>
> 2.45 a.m.—Ran close in shore off Ryde and let go anchor. At 3 a.m., thanks to smartness of steward and cook, had a capital supper on the table, and Her Majesty came and joined us at supper in the main cabin.
>
> The emotions of the previous four-and-twenty hours produced a natural reaction, and the Empress was very cheerful at table. Her health was drunk in champagne, and she returned thanks in a few hopeful words. But now that she was no longer in danger of capture or death, and that a hundred new possibilities in life presented themselves to her mind, she was more reserved in talking about politics. Here might have been a curious study for a psychologist.
>
> The lady who had come on board, abandoned and almost heart-broken, complaining in the bitterness of her heart of those by whom she had been forsaken, was transformed once more by hope—and very rapidly—into an Empress who looked with some philosophical indifference upon the baseness of men.

The writer to whom Sir John Burgoyne gave these extracts from the *Gazelle's* logbook adds, amongst many other piquant details of the terrible voyage from Deauville to Ryde, that the Empress personally thanked the crew who had risked death in order to save her life, and presented them with five pounds.

A story which is told of Louis XVIII., in somewhat analogous circumstances, may furnish a pendant to the above. The King, being compelled to evacuate Courland, engaged the Captain of a Danish merchant ship to convey him and his suite to Prussia. The Captain had a cargo for the Baltic, but, anticipating a handsome reward, he consented to change his course. For this service the King gave the skipper a gold watch and a written promise that, if he regained his throne, he would liberally recompense the Dane. As the Captain did not land his merchandise in time, it could not be disposed of, and the consignees made him pay them heavy damages, with the result that the poor man was ruined. After the King's restoration the promissory note was presented to His Majesty by the Danish Minister at

Paris. Louis XVIII. did not shirk his liability, but handed to the diplomatist what he considered a suitable reward for the Danish Captain who had rendered this service—fifty napoleons and the Cross of the Lily!

If it was an American citizen who, at no little risk, escorted the Empress from Paris to Deauville, it is well to remember that it was a British officer who really saved and brought her to our shores. Sir John Burgoyne, Bart., entered the army in 1850, and retired (Lieutenant-Colonel) from the Grenadier Guards in 1861. Eton should be very proud of its gallant son. Sir John resides at Sutton Park, Sandy, Bedfordshire, and is widely known in clubland as a member of the Carlton, the Travellers', and the Royal Yacht Squadron (Cowes).

There is yet another version of the Empress's escape from Paris—that which Her Majesty related at Chislehurst to Lord Ronald Sutherland-Gower, who very kindly allows it to appear here:

> How well she described the hurried flight through the Palace and the galleries of the Louvre, followed by only two or three attendants; the respect with which the guardians of the galleries received her, and their emotion at seeing her almost a deserted fugitive in the Palace of which she had been so lately the idol; her great danger of being recognized while alone with Mme. Lebret-on in the Rue de Rivoli, where for hours they had to remain, the street being blocked with a mob of mobiles and the rabble forcing their way to the Hôtel de Ville to proclaim the Republic; and another terrible long period of suspense when, at some station near Paris, her only safety from detection while waiting hours for a train was a newspaper that saved her from recognition and probably death.
>
> She said such a death as that had terrors for her which, could she have remained and faced the dangers in the Palace, she would not have felt; and, indeed, it made one shudder to think what would have happened had that mob guessed who one of the two ladies in black was in the cab in the roaring street that bright September day. I believe the Empress has regretted ever since having left the Tuileries, and she had almost to be forced to leave the Palace. She had the courage and the will to stand alone against the mob, but then her fate might have been that of Hypatia.

In the course of the story the Empress became somewhat excited and brushed off the table an alabaster bust of Marie Antoinette, which she had given Lord Ronald. He picked it up, minus its head!

No one has hitherto told us the precise time at which the Empress quitted the Tuileries on Sunday, September 4, 1870.

She actually left the Palace at 1.30 in the afternoon by the Louvre entrance.

Towards four o'clock all the servants left, the National Guard having previously taken possession of the Palace.

These facts are recorded in his register[103] by M. J. Maillard, chef du service de l'argenterie, who records that the troops did not give him time to "put things in their places." He did not fail to observe that the National Guard had "written everywhere" the simple words, "Death to the thieves." It was the parting shot of the gallant "Nationals," whose commander was that modern Bayard, General Trochu.

PALAIS DES TUILERIES,
Septembre 4, 1870.

Départ de S.M. l'Impératrice à une heure et demie par le Palais du Louvre.

Départ de tout le personnel du service vers quatre heures de l'après-midi, après l'occupation du Palais des Tuileries par la garde nationale. Ils ont écrit partout, *Mort aux voleurs.* Je ne pas pu faire remettre le matériel en place—l'on ne m'en a pas donné le temps.

J. MAILLARD.

[Extract from the register kept by M. Maillard, who had charge of the silver.]

Baron Imbert de Saint-Amand holds that the Empress would have had less prestige if the Empire had not been overthrown. "The world is most interested, not in the châtelaine of the Tuileries, not the Juno reigning over an Olympus of Emperors and Kings at the Exhibition of 1867, but in the mother who weeps and prays in Zululand on the spot where her son had fallen after fighting like a young lion. What posterity will prefer to contemplate on the brow of the Empress Eugénie is not a crown of Empire, but a crown of thorns."

"The Empress's conduct after Sedan," said an ex-Minister of the Empire, "was heroic. It is impossible to conceive a nobler courage than she showed on September 4, 1870. When she speaks of the Empire or the Emperor it is always with regret that the aims of Imperial institutions had been misrepresented and that the Emperor was misunderstood. On one occasion she observed that 'English journalists would not understand the democratic basis of the Empire. The Empire wanted to give a direct voice in the government to all Frenchmen, whereas other régimes would give a monopoly of power to the bourgeoisie, and make the people pay the taxes and remain voiceless. If turbulent Frenchmen had only the calm in political matters of the English public!'"

Immediately after the overthrow of the Empire an amazing plot was concocted to defraud the Empress. It was alleged that Her Majesty had abstracted French Crown jewels valued at 6,650,000 francs (£266,000), and had sent them by one Manuel Perez to her mother at Madrid.

M. Franceschini Pietri says:

Swindlers and exploiteurs began in 1870-71 to benefit by our troubles and grief, and some of them went so far as to produce

[103] From the late Duc de Conegliano's volume (1897), "La Maison de l'Empereur," preface by Frédéric Masson. Paris: Calmann Lévy.

forged autograph letters of the Empress Eugénie. I have held those letters in my hand, and I assure you that the imitation was marvellous. The object was invariably the same—to attract silly people or thieves by telling them of the existence of secret treasure, and asking them to advance money towards the expense of discovering it, and dividing it among those who had found money for making the search. As you will see, it was an old and well-known trick, but it was sometimes so well carried out that many persons fell into the trap.

I remember the case of a peasant of Metz, who, attracted by the prospect of gain, sent 3,000 francs to a person from whom he had heard on the subject, and waited a long time in anticipation of news concerning the fortune which was promised to him. Tired of the delay, he had the effrontery to come to Chislehurst and demand to be reimbursed the 3,000 francs which he had invested! You can imagine that he was sent away without the least consolation. But that is only one out of a hundred cases. All who believed in the existence of a secret treasure were not dishonest people; many of them, after receiving mysterious letters on the subject, informed the Empress Eugénie of what had occurred.

To give you an idea of the extent of this swindling affair, and of the amount of information which we received at Chislehurst, I may tell you that we had printed forms to answer the communications, and put an advertisement in the *Times* warning the public to be on their guard against these attempts to obtain their money.

It may be pointed out that many of these letters inviting the credulous to "bite" were dated from the gaol at Madrid, and that Spain supplied the strongest contingent of these "Imperial treasure" swindlers. They spread themselves over all Europe—Italy, France, England, Portugal, and other countries. The story received so much credence in Portugal that the King sent one of his Ministers to Chislehurst to confer with the Empress Eugénie on the subject! As you see, it became a Cabinet affair.

Time passed, and these attempts at swindling decreased; but we occasionally get wind of timid efforts in the same direction, and doubtless the photograph which you have shown me comes from the same quarter as the previous letters.[104]

---

[104] Statement by M. Pietri to "Le Matin" in 1910.

CHAPTER XV

"THESE THINGS ARE LITTLE;
BUT, THEN, THEY'RE ALL"

BETWEEN December 23, 1870, and January 25, 1871, a minute record was made, by order of the new Government, of all the objects found in the imperial apartments at the Tuileries, and admittedly belonging to Napoleon III., the Empress Eugénie, and the Prince Imperial. The list was most carefully drawn up by the Delegates of the Commission of Liquidation of the former Civil List and Private Domain of their Majesties, and when it was completed everything was transferred to and put under seals in a room on the fifth floor of the Pavilion of Flora.[105]

Not one of this heap of cherished articles was of any particular intrinsic or artistic value, yet it was this fact which gave, and gives, them their charm. It is not the State décor, seen and known by all, that we can reconstitute with the aid of these multifarious knick-knacks, but they form the milieu intime, comprising a thousand familiar objects, a thousand personal souvenirs, in the midst of which the occupants of the Tuileries lived their daily life. It is more than interesting or curious to handle these old-fashioned bibelots; it is often touching, even painful.

In the Emperor's apartments were an eagle (from a flag) in gilded bronze, embraced by Napoleon I. when he took farewell of Fontainebleau; a hand of the Empress Eugénie in white marble; a portfolio of music (containing the "Marche des Impériaux," from the tragedy of "Jules César"), by Hary de Bülow; a meerschaum pipe, representing Napoleon III. and the Prince Imperial; a silver fountain, the gift of Queen Pomaré to the Emperor; a dagger, with damascened blade, given to him by his mother-in-law, the Comtesse de Montijo; a walking-stick, made of a bulrush stalk; a crutch, in rock-crystal, ornamented with fine stones, the Empress Catherine of Russia's present to Frederick II.; a tin box, containing water from the Jordan; a candle used at the Prince Imperial's first Communion; a black leather case, containing the Emperor's costume of Knight of the Garter; a man's head, in crayons, signed "Joséphine"; a plan in relief of the château of Ham (the prison of Napoleon III. for six years); a photograph of the Prince Imperial in his cradle; boxes, cases of medals, addresses, diplomas, vases, cups, tea and coffee services; a thousand articles which have gone out of fashion, in all styles; albums of photographs and engravings, portraits of Sovereigns, hundreds of paper-weights, inkstands, and wafer-boxes; a collection of French and foreign military models in

---

[105] This pavilion was not destroyed by the Communards in 1871. It contains the kitchens of the Tuileries (*vide* p. 108).

coloured plaster—amongst them two Prussian soldiers, one Bavarian, two Würtemburgers, and a White Cuirassier; figures of a merchant, a woman, five soldiers and peasants—Russian; and two mahogany boxes containing the plaques and decorations of Napoleon III., with the stern official notification, opposite the French ones, "Two plaques and decorations missing—taken away by the Emperor."

Among the numerous "Souvenirs intimes de Napoléon I. et de sa famille" are a Prayer-Book ("paroissien") which belonged to Mme. Mère,[106] and a black snuff-box with her portrait, enclosing some locks of hair of her daughter, Princesse Pauline; a gold folding lorgnette, which belonged to the Duc de Reichstadt; a packet containing handkerchiefs from the death-bed of Queen Hortense, and a packet of handkerchiefs which belonged to Napoleon I.; a gold ring containing a tooth of Michel Montaigne, and one of Goethe's visiting-cards; the grey capote of Marengo, and the scarf worn by Napoleon I. at the battle of the Pyramids; a morocco blotting-pad, ornamented with a painting under glass representing a Spanish bandit, painted by Queen Hortense; a blue velvet sabretache, embroidered in gold, the gift of Prince Eugène; two gold epaulettes; the garniture of buttons, grenades, and plaques; the grey capote worn by the Emperor at the battle of Waterloo; a quantity of breloques, bibelots, snuff-boxes, objects in hair, miniatures, porcelain and crystal ornaments, bonbonnières, pocket-knives, etc.

In the Empress Eugénie's apartments were found Perrault's stories, a Spanish edition of "Paradise Lost," an "Imitation de Jésus-Christ," the "Mémorial de Saint-Hélène," and the "Chansons Populaires du Piémont"; photographs of the Shah of Persia, Mme. Carette (the Empress's "reader" for many years, and a reliable chronicler of Second Empire days), the Princesse de Metternich, the daughters of the Duchesse d'Albe (the Empress's nieces), the Royal Family of Spain, the Sultan Abd-el-Kader, and Princesse Bacciochi; a miniature of the Prince Imperial and his "guardian angel," in a velvet frame; an egg, on which is painted the battle of Malakoff; two dumb-bells, in granite, with silver handles; one of Orsini's bombs, seized on the memorable January 14, 1858, the date of the "attempt" at the opera; two pairs of satin shoes, which belonged to Queen Hortense and the Empress Joséphine; and the hat worn by Napoleon III. on the night of his attempted assassination by Orsini.

In the Prince Imperial's apartments were statuettes of the Virgin and the Infant Jesus, the dome of the Invalides in painted cardboard, stuffed birds, geographical games, a three-masted vessel in a glass case; a reliquary, containing relics of St. Eugénie and the brassard worn by the "little Prince" at his first Communion; a garden rake and two hoes, in steel; three summer hats, in white silk, and two black ones; a cantata dedicated to the Prince by Pellegrini; trophies of the imperial hunts at Fontainebleau and Compiègne; and the Prince's Orders and decorations.

There were chairs and fauteuils, settees (poufs) in tapestry and red satin, with silk fringe; étagères in black wood and bronze; a prie-Dieu in carved oak, covered with blue velvet; tables, with feet of bamboo, covered with tapestry and adorned with fringe; a carved fire-screen in gilded wood; and many other objects.

---

[106] Mother of Napoleon I.

Finally, there were several boxes of cigars ("regalias" and "Londres") and "Imperial" cigarettes (the Emperor was a great smoker of these), which were sent by the Delegates of the Commission of Liquidation, by order of M. Picard, to M. Jules Simon, at the Ministry of Public Instruction, and sold for the benefit of the wounded soldiers. Forty years have flown since France was weighed down by the disasters, but the past appears so recent that, in stirring its ashes, we fancy them still warm, still living; neither the tears nor the blood poured upon the souvenirs of so many misfortunes have yet made them cold.

CHAPTER XVI

THE EMPEROR AND THE COMTESSE
DE MERCY-ARGENTEAU

ALTHOUGH the name of the Comtesse de Mercy-Argenteau is a very familiar one, it seems desirable to put on record some details of her family history, if only in order to explain what might otherwise appear somewhat of a mystery—the selection by Napoleon III. of this beautiful and gifted woman as his secret political emissary, both during and, to a certain extent, after his six months' captivity at Wilhelmshöhe.

She is the daughter of that Prince de Chimay who was the head of the younger branch of the Riquet-Caramans; she is, consequently, the granddaughter of Mme. Tallien, whom the "Directory" named "Notre Dame de Bon-Secours." Mme. Tallien was the idol of Barras; she was the divinity of the Revolutionary epoch, the worshipped of France. Many people speak of the Chimay family as if it were Flemish. It is Franco-Austrian-Belgian, and had its origin in Gille Paul Riquet, a worthy bourgeois of Béziers—the man who founded the Languedoc Canal, and was ennobled by letters patent, granted by Louis XIV., in 1666. The house of De Mercy has been thrice ennobled, receiving from three different heads of State the coronet which it has worn proudly and with dignity. The actual head of the house in 1871 was Charles François Joseph, whose two sons married the Comtesse de Caraman (Marie Louise de Riquet) and Mlle. Alix de Choiseul-Praslin; his two daughters became the Comtesse d'Oultremont and the Duchesse d'Harcourt.

The Comtesse de Mercy-Argenteau was, then, born Comtesse de Caraman-Chimay. It has been said of her that, "like Cleopatra, she would have thrown pearls into the goblet or her heart out of window, according to the caprice of the moment." When she made her appearance in Paris the Second Empire was at its zenith; the world's gaze was riveted upon it. All was gaiety and sunshine. It was a magnificent Court, that of the Tuileries in the reign of Napoleon III. and his consort. Only the Cassandras of the period went about predicting, and rightly, that it would not last.

The Comtesse de Mercy-Argenteau was a contemporary of some very celebrated women whose names, at least, are still remembered. There were notably the Princesse de Sagan, the Duchesse de Mouchy, the Comtesse Edmond de Pourtalès, and the Marquise de Galliffet, wife of that dashing cavalryman of whom so many amusing stories are told.[107] Our Comtesse shone at the head of the famous

---

[107] Of these four ladies, two survive in 1911—the Duchesse de Mouchy and the

"Décameron," and was counted the most beautiful of the lovely group. They wittily said of her that her grandmother was a goddess, her mother a queen, and she herself a "moderne." For the first there was Olympus, for the second a throne, for the third the little English cart, which, said one of her sprightly friends, "takes to the Allée des Acacias every morning our mondaines semi-garçons."

As already hinted, the young Comtesse de Mercy-Argenteau made a sensation in Paris society—in the Faubourg as well as at the Tuileries, at Compiègne, and at St. Cloud. The Empress Eugénie admitted her into close friendship. The Emperor paid her his most respectful homage. If a particularly delicate mission had to be undertaken, who so fit to carry it out as this charming woman? We need not wonder, then, that Napoleon III., in the hour of his despair, appealed to her devotion, and charged her to go, as his ambassadress, "séduire le vainqueur et tenter de sauver la France." Many women envied the Comtesse her mission to Berlin, foredoomed to failure as it was.

The Comtesse was renowned for her jewellery. In diamonds she outshone the Empress; her pearls were the finest in the world; she possessed the family jewels both of the Chimays and the De Mercys. After the war she devoted herself to study. She shines as a musician, in languages she is proficient, she paints miniatures à merveille, and she has always been a sportswoman.

Napoleon III. had been in captivity at Wilhelmshöhe about five months when he began an active correspondence with the Comtesse de Mercy-Argenteau, who, on at least one memorable occasion, acted as the intermediary between the dethroned monarch and the late Emperor William. The letters addressed to the Comtesse by the Emperor Napoleon are distinguished by their poignant interest and frank outspokenness; they are, indeed, a revelation of the unhappy man's innermost thoughts, his aspirations, his fears, and, finally, his apparent abandonment of hope, although we know that, later, his ideas underwent a great change.

Not the least curious feature of the correspondence given to the world in 1906 through the medium of an important German review, the *Verlagen and Klasing Monatshefte*, is the fact that we hear for the first time of the Comtesse de Mercy-Argenteau as figuring prominently in the Bonapartist propaganda of the autumn of 1870, throughout 1871, and up to September, 1872, the Emperor's final letter, surcharged with gloom, bearing date, Chislehurst, September 9.[108] There is no doubt about their authenticity, for, with one or two exceptions, the epistles are contained in their original envelopes, properly stamped, and bear the postmarks "Cassel" (Wilhelmshöhe) and "Terwagne" (near which Belgian town the château of the Mercy-Argenteaus is situated).

The first letter of the series was written to the Comtesse from the Tuileries, and is a graceful reference to the Count's naturalization.

When Napoleon III. was at the Tuileries.

<u>*November*</u> 7, 1869.

Comtesse E. de Pourtalès.
  [108] The letters are reproduced by arrangement with Herrn Paul Lindenberg.

MADAME,

It is with pleasure that I announce to you that yesterday I signed the Decree which gives to your husband the rights of naturalization. I congratulate myself upon having one Frenchman and one Frenchwoman more.

Believe, madame, in my affectionate and devoted sentiments.

NAPOLÉON.

Written at Wilhelmshöhe.

WILHELMSHÖHE,
February 4, 1871.

MADAME LA COMTESSE,

The attachment to me of which you give evidence touches me deeply, and causes me to answer the questions which you have put to me with all the frankness inspired by your high-minded sentiments.

The state of France is deplorable, and I do not see how it can be improved unless the Emperor of Germany displays that chivalrous mind which everybody knows him to possess. To-day we are completely vanquished; the interests of Germany, however, are mingled with ours. To re-establish order, to suppress the revolutionary spirit, to re-create the prosperity which alone can enable us to pay the cost of the war and assure peace—these are the results which must be desired in both countries.

Unfortunately, the convocation of the National Assembly makes all that very difficult, for that Assembly, if it makes peace, will be incapable of establishing a Government which can execute the conditions, and if it does not do so the country will be a prey to new convulsions.

If I were in the place of the Emperor and King, and the Assembly had accepted peace, I would demand that the people should be consulted for establishing a Government sufficiently strong to fulfil the engagements entered into. If, on the contrary, the Assembly refused to make peace, I would enter Paris at the head of my army; I would scatter the demagogues who have usurped power; I would decline to treat with any but the legitimate Government; I would propose to that Government a less onerous peace than that offered to the Assembly, and an alliance based upon an equitable appreciation of the interests of both countries.

It remains to consider what would be the conditions of such a peace and such an alliance. They are not easy to divine; but if the two were in accord, doubtless a favourable solution would be arrived at, for there are compensations when one is, like the King of Prussia, the arbiter of Europe.

All these ideas have, I believe, been put before Comte de Bismarck, and his high-mindedness has led him to grasp them; but events often upset plans, and force even great statesmen to bend under the yoke of stern necessity. No glory is lacking the Emperor and King but that of making a great peace. I mean a peace which, instead of leaving in its wake ruin, despair, and anarchy, would display the greatness of his character and the depth of his political views.

You see, madame, that I have permitted myself to tell you all my thoughts. I hope you will forgive me for this long letter, but you know how much pleasure it affords me to talk to you.

Pray say everything good on my part to your husband, and believe in the sentiments of high esteem and sincere and affectionate friendship which I have for you.

NAPOLÉON.

Napoleon III. sends a Letter to the Emperor William I. by the Comtesse.

WILHELMSHÖHE,
February 6, 1871.

MADAME,

The charming letter which you have written to me emboldens me to tell you that I think you may perhaps be able to do me a great service; but I hardly dare express here all that I think. It is a question, like the dove, of carrying a message of peace.

NAPOLÉON.

After the receipt of this letter the Comtesse de Mercy-Argenteau journeyed to Wilhelmshöhe, where the illustrious captive gave her verbal instructions and a letter addressed to the Emperor William. She crossed the German lines under an assumed name, accompanied only by her maid, saw Count Bismarck, through him obtained an audience of the Kaiser, and handed to the Kaiser Napoleon's autograph letter. These proceedings were barren of result. Napoleon III. then sent the Comtesse the following letter:

"My Gratitude is Very Sincere."

WILHELMSHÖHE,
February 23, 1871.

MY DEAR COMTESSE,

I learn with great pleasure of your arrival, and I am happy to think that your little daughter is quite well again. Need I tell you of the sweet remembrances and regrets that your visit has left? I really do not know how to recognize such loyal and disinterested devotion as yours; but you know at least that my gratitude is very sincere. I await impatiently news from the quarter to which you have been. I often fear lest people should accept that which is put before them without thinking of the future. The eagerness with which the neutrals have recognized the sovereignty of M. Thiers is a proof of the little dignity which animates the foreign Courts.

Accept, madame, the new assurance of my sincere and affectionate friendship.

NAPOLÉON.

"Writing to Bismarck Useless."

WILHELMSHÖHE,
February 25, 1871.

MY DEAR COMTESSE,

I send you the line that you wanted. It is a pale reflex of my sentiments towards you. It is very good of you to think of writing to M. de B—— [Bismarck], but I believe it would be useless. In the first place, I have asked M. de F—— to do so, and he has left; then, again, it is too late now to enable me to profit by it. Things have taken a bad turn for me. We must put up with the d'Orléans, who have numerous partisans amongst the middle classes; and then I cannot be pardoned for having been served so badly and so unfortunately.

Accept, dear Comtesse, etc.

NAPOLÉON.

"I admit we were the Aggressors."

WILHELMSHÖHE,
March 2, 1871.

MY DEAR COMTESSE,

How can one fail to be discouraged in presence of the conditions of peace imposed upon France? I admit that we were the aggressors; I admit that we were defeated, and that, therefore, we were compelled to pay the cost of the war or abandon part of our territory; but to condemn us to make both sacrifices is very hard. Where is the Government which will be able to stand with a material and moral burden like that upon its shoulders? With such conditions it is not a peace which the Emperor of Germany has concluded—it is to kill us; instead of re-establishing peace, it will sow hatred and distrust in the future. Is this a good plan, even for Germany? I do not think so. The state of civilization in which Europe finds itself demands that the nations bind themselves together by a crowd of common interests which would make the ruin of one react upon all the others.

The work of France stopped for several years, thirty-eight millions of people delivered up to anarchy, and having in their hearts only a desire for vengeance—this is to keep a wound open in one of the principal members of the social body. If the Emperor of Germany and M. de Bismarck had thoroughly reflected upon the state of Europe; if, instead of allowing themselves to be dazzled by the extraordinary success which they have obtained, they had desired to put an end to revolutions and to war, they had declared that as long as France had no stable, and consequently liberal, Government, they would only sanction a suspension of hostilities in the nature of a truce, and would take steps to put themselves in a more favourable military position in case the struggle should recommence, but as soon as there was a Government based upon law and accepted by the whole nation they would feel more certain of peace in the future than they could be by holding dissatisfied departments, detached from a nation profoundly ... that would have been de la grande politique; the hatred against Germany would have disappeared as though by magic, peace would have been assured for many years, there would have been renewed confidence, there would have been a revival of commercial affairs, and the Emperor of Germany would have obtained a glory far greater than he will acquire by the possession of Metz and Strasburg.

I am writing to you as if you were my Minister for Foreign Affairs; but I find it a consolation, in the midst of the preoccupations which beset me, to open my heart to you.

Accept, etc.

Napoléon.

Bismarck's Brusque Telegram to the Emperor's Intermediary.

Two short letters of no particular importance follow, and then comes this very brusque telegram from Bismarck to the Comtesse, dated Berlin, March 27, 1871:

To the Comtesse de Mercy-Argenteau, Château of Ochain,
near Terwagne, Belgium.

Your allusions to the conditions of peace surprise me, and prevent me from replying to your letter. It is absolutely impossible.

V. Bismarck.

Letters written at Chislehurst.

"The Future is Very Dark."

That telegram probably led to the Emperor writing to the Comtesse as follows, a few days after his arrival in England from Wilhelmshöhe:

CHISLEHURST,
April 1, 1871.

MY DEAR COMTESSE,

I thank you for all that you have written and done. No one could have acted with more intelligence and heart. Unfortunately, we are dealing with pitiless people. We must wait for the second answer, but I do not think it will be better than the first. I believe it would be completely useless to take any kind of step respecting Marshal M. [MacMahon] or others. The time has not yet come for taking any initiative whatsoever as regards internal affairs. I thank you, nevertheless, for the intention. The future is very dark, and one must leave Providence to guide the will of men. I am very grateful for your unfailing devotion, and I again assure you of my affectionate friendship.

NAPOLÉON.

"I have not Forgotten You."

There is a silence of nearly three months. The Emperor was very ill, and unable to write to the Comtesse between April and June. In the subjoined letter he explains why he had not written:

CAMDEN PLACE,
June 14, 1871.

MY DEAR COMTESSE,

What a long time it is since I wrote to you! Perhaps you think I have forgotten you, but it is not so. I have been suffering so long that it was impossible for me to write. To-day I am, happily, well again. I will not speak of what has happened since we met. Many of the plans have come to naught; but I do not regret it. Each thing must come at its own time, and the favourable movement which has been spontaneously produced in France ought to make us hopeful for the future, even if it is hopeless to charge oneself with the destinies of so frivolous a people as the French.

Accept, my dear Comtesse, the assurance of my affectionate friendship.

NAPOLÉON.

The Trap laid for the Comtesse.

CHISLEHURST,
December 9, 1871.

MY DEAR COMTESSE,

Your amiable letter makes me look at the coming year in brighter colours. I have happily convinced myself that your long silence was the result of chance, and was not caused by forgetfulness. I am indignant at what you tell me about the trap which was laid for you at Brussels. It is sad to see the police have recourse to such devices. I am much touched by the offers of service made by you, but for the moment one can only await events, and endeavour by propaganda to obtain a plébiscite and better election results.

Accept, etc.

NAPOLÉON.

The Emperor's Final Letters: "Clouds cover the Horizon."

On May 5, 1872, the Emperor wrote thanking the Comtesse for sending news. His Majesty added:

I will not speak to you about politics, for it is sad to see what is happening; but there are instances of devotion which make one forget the ingratitude of some and the wickedness of others.

Under date June 2, 1872, the Emperor wrote to his fair correspondent condoling with her upon the death of a relative. The last letter is dated September 9, 1872, just four months prior to the Emperor's death. He again expresses his sympathy at her bereavement, and concludes:

The future appears to me very uncertain. Clouds cover the horizon, and one can hardly perceive the blue sky.

From the Emperor's Secretary (M. Pietri) to the Comtesse.

CAMDEN PLACE,
CHISLEHURST,
June 16, 1871.

MADAME LA COMTESSE,

I have just received the reply to the telegram which I had the honour to address to you at Liége, and I hasten to forward the letter that the Emperor has directed me to send to you, as to which I congratulate myself upon not having put an incorrect address.

The Emperor is to-day entirely recovered. He has resumed his occupations and his usual life. He has been cruelly pained by all the evils which overwhelm our unfortunate country, and of which we cannot yet see the end.

We have before our eyes only the material ruins of Paris. They have turned our looks away from the ruins of all France, and from the appalling situation which must result from the surrender of Alsace and Lorraine and the occupation of Metz by the Prussians.

At Versailles they accuse us of conspiracy. They are wrong, and they must know well that it is the contrary. We have only one way of usefully conspiring—that is, to wait; for time will conspire for us, and will help Truth to come out of the well in which they have kept her enclosed, while those standing upon the lid preach error and lies. They will get tired, and then she [Truth] will appear. Already she begins to see daylight. It is upon her that we must count, in not adding to the evils of the country intrigues which could only aggravate them. We must content ourselves with following what is done at Versailles.

Accept, Madame la Comtesse, etc.

F. PIETRI.

CHAPTER XVII
THE EMPEROR'S CORRESPONDENCE

Besides the epistles addressed by Napoleon III. to the late Comtesse de Mercy-Argenteau, many interesting letters from the imperial pen are scattered about in the vivid pages of Comte d'Hérisson, M. Pierre de Lano, and other French authors. Those now for the first time translated for this work from Comte d'Hérisson's "Le Prince Impérial" and M. Pierre de Lano's "L'Impératrice" will be fresh to English readers, who will obtain from their perusal a better insight into the character of Napoleon III. than they previously possessed.

Napoleon III. and the Press.

For the first few days after his arrival, early in September, at Wilhelmshöhe, where he remained until the following March, the fallen Emperor seemed to be resigned to his fate. In reply to one of his friends, who had written to him asking to be informed of his plans, the Emperor wrote:

Wilhelmshöhe,
September 28, 1870.

I thank you for your letter, which has given me great pleasure. The sentiments which you express do not surprise me, for I have always reckoned on your friendship. In the actual state of affairs I believe there is nothing to be done unless it be to correct, through the Press, erroneous statements, and to act as much as possible upon public opinion. Conti,[109] whom perhaps you have seen at Brussels (his address is 2, Place du Trône), is very useful to me in this respect. May God grant that the siege of Paris be soon finished, for I dread all kinds of excesses in the country!

Napoléon.

Against the advice of many staunch friends of the Emperor, in November, 1870, it was determined to make an attempt to replace Napoleon III. on the throne, and that the movement should be directed by the Emperor and Empress. The Imperialists regarded the co-operation of General Changarnier as indispensable, and the Emperor (and, later, the Empress) worked to this end. General Fleury, furnished with private instructions by the Emperor himself, went to Brussels and had an interview with Changarnier, who, after much wavering, finally declined to take part in the restoration plot. The Emperor put himself directly en rapport with

[109] The Emperor's former Secretary, and later a Deputy.

Changarnier by writing to General Fleury the subjoined letter, which shows the ignorance in which Napoleon III. was kept respecting the events of the day:

Napoleon III., General Changarnier, and "L'Indépendance Belge."

WILHELMSHÖHE,
November 16, 1870.

... At Brussels you will see more people and become acquainted with many things of which we here are ignorant. I should therefore much like you from time to time to send me your impressions of what you hear talked about, and what you hope or fear for the future. They tell me you often see our enemies. If it is to appease them, all the better; but I fear their evil influence. Already Bourbaki and Maréchal Canrobert have, I fear, been circumvented by them. If you see General Changarnier, get him to write a word to the papers in favour of Bazaine. I have already advised him to do so, but he replied that the editor of "l'Indépendance Belge" did not insert his letter. Upon Changarnier asking the reason of its non-appearance, he was told that they could not publish it except by accompanying it with some remarks very detrimental to Bazaine; whereupon Changarnier withdrew his letter. I am sorry for this, because Changarnier's words would have made a great noise, whilst the attacks of the journalist would have passed unnoticed. Try to get Changarnier to change his mind.

NAPOLÉON.

"Arrange an Interview with Changarnier."

A few weeks later the Emperor wrote to Fleury on the same subject, but more pressingly, as follows:

W. [WILHELMSHÖHE],
December 11, 1870.

This letter will be handed to you by M. Levert, formerly Préfet of Marseilles, a very devoted and very distinguished man. He should talk to you about the steps to take respecting General Changarnier to maintain him in my cause. I beg you to arrange that he may have an interview with the General.

NAPOLÉON.

"Keep Changarnier well disposed."

General Changarnier weakened daily in view of the solicitations of which he was the object at Brussels, and yet another letter to Fleury from the Emperor at Wilhelmshöhe showed how necessary for the success of their plans did the Bonapartist party regard the General's intervention and adhesion:

[WILHELMSHÖHE],
December 23, 1870.

I thank you for the good relations that you maintain with General Changarnier. It is necessary to keep him well disposed by telling him that, when the moment comes, I shall have recourse to his advice. According to what they tell me in letters, Claremont [British Military Attaché] said Paris cannot hold out more than three weeks. But what will happen then? The attitude of certain French officers in Germany is very bad; but they are "worked" by emissaries of several colours.

NAPOLÉON.

"Everybody desires Peace."

All endeavours to secure the active assistance of General Changarnier failed. On January 4, 1871, the Emperor wrote from Wilhelmshöhe:

Unfortunately, you are not better informed at Brussels than we are here respecting future events. One does not know what to believe owing to the diversity of the opinions on the subject of the probable resistance of Paris. Everybody desires peace, but nobody knows how it can be brought about.

NAPOLÉON.

The Emperor to Sir John Burgoyne, "The English Moltke."

Immediately after the fall of Metz, General Sir John M. Burgoyne, Bart., who had taken part in the Crimean campaign, and had brought the Empress to Ryde, wrote to Napoleon III. in sympathetic terms, and expressed his opinion of the causes which had led to the French reverses. The Emperor replied as under:

WILHELMSHÖHE,
October 29, 1870.

MY DEAR SIR JOHN BURGOYNE,

I have received your letter, which has given me the greatest pleasure, because it is a touching proof of your sympathy for me, and also because your name recalls to me the happy and glorious time when our two armies fought together for the same cause. You, who are the English Moltke, will have understood that our disasters arose from the circumstance that the Prussians were ready before us, and that, so to speak, they surprised us *en flagrant délit* of formation.

The offensive became impossible for me. I resolved to take the defensive, but, prevented by political considerations, the march in retreat was stopped, and then became impossible. Returned to Châlons, I wished to lead to Paris the last army which remained to us; but again political complications forced us to make that most imprudent and least strategical march which finished with the disaster at Sedan. Such, in a few words, was the disastrous campaign of 1870. I have given you these explanations because I value your esteem.

NAPOLÉON.

THE EMPEROR'S LETTERS TO HIS FOSTER-SISTER, MME. CORNU.

"Let us hope for Happier Days."

The five following letters appeared for the first time in "La Revue" (Paris) in October and December, 1908, and were contributed by M. Seymour de Ricci, who is in possession of 297 letters, hitherto unpublished, addressed by the Emperor to Mme. Cornu, who visited Chislehurst in 1871. The whole of this interesting correspondence will be published by M. de Ricci.

WILHELMSHÖHE,
December 14, 1870.

MY DEAR MADAME CORNU,

You cannot doubt the pain which I have felt upon learning of the death of your husband. You know the great friendship which I had for him for so many years. I fully share all your emotions, and wish to know how you are getting on in the midst of the war which is surrounding you. I will not refer to my troubles; it is those of France which overwhelm me most.

The Empress and the Prince are well—this is a great consolation to me.

Let us hope for happier days, and believe always, my dear Hortense, in my sincere friendship.

NAPOLÉON.

"I am engaged upon a Work which will explain Many Things."

CHISLEHURST,
January 14, 1872.

MY DEAR MADAME CORNU,

It is always with pleasure that I hear from you, for the friendship which binds us is of such long standing that absence and misfortunes cannot weaken it.

I was very happy also to see you once more, and I hope you will return to us this summer. I see by your letter that you have not been to Italy, as you had proposed to do. Have you not been able to sell your property? We often have visitors from France, who are the echo of what is happening in our unhappy country.

I am engaged upon a work which will explain many things. It will not be amusing, but it will contain the truth.

Receive, my dear Madame Cornu, the assurance of my sincere friendship.

The Empress wrote you two letters from Spain. Did you get them? She sends a thousand amiable things to you, as does the Prince.

Napoléon.

"The Empress has been suffering."

Chislehurst,
May 5, 1872.

My dear Madame Cornu,

I take advantage of a post to tell you that the Empress has been suffering very much, but that she has now recovered, and that the Prince and I are quite well.

I received your letter of the 30th [of April], but have only time to thank you for it in the Empress's name, and to renew the assurance of my sincere friendship.

Napoléon.

"I am Responsible to the Country."

Marshal Baraguay d'Hilliers presided over a Council of Inquiry appointed to investigate the circumstances in which fortresses capitulated and battalions surrendered to the invaders. It was decided that the whole blame for the disasters at Sedan rested with Napoleon III., "a culprit beyond reach of the national vengeance," as he was residing at Chislehurst. The Exile defended himself in this letter, which he addressed to the Generals who had served under him at Sedan:

Camden Place,
Chislehurst,
May 12, 1872.

General,

I am responsible to the country, and I can accept no other judgment but that of the nation regularly consulted. Nor is it for me to pass an opinion on the report of the Commission on the capitulation of Sedan. I shall only remind the principal witnesses of the capitulation of the critical position in which we found ourselves. The army commanded by the Duc de Magenta nobly did its duty, and fought heroically against an enemy of twice its numbers. When driven back to the walls of the town, and into the town itself, 14,000 dead and wounded covered the field of battle, and I saw that to contest the position any longer was an act of desperation. The honour of the army having been saved by the bravery which had been displayed, I then exercised my Sovereign right, and gave orders to unfurl a flag of truce. I claim the entire responsibility of that act. The immolation of 60,000 men could not have saved France, and the sublime devotion of her chiefs and soldiers would have been uselessly sacrificed. I obeyed a cruel, but inexorable, fate. My heart was broken, but my conscience was easy.

NAPOLÉON.

The Emperor's Brochure.

August 29, 1872.

MY DEAR M.ADAME CORNU,

I need not tell you how much pleasure your wishes give me. I have been accustomed for so many years to receive proofs of your friendship; and you know how they touch me.

We shall return to Chislehurst towards October, and you will not doubt the pleasure we shall have in seeing you again.

I send you a photograph of the Prince. As to the brochure,[110] they (*sic*) are all at Camden Place.

Receive, my dear Madame Cornu, the renewed assurance of my sincere friendship.

NAPOLÉON.

The Emperor's Final Letter to Mme. Cornu.

CHISLEHURST,
November 17, 1872.

MY DEAR MADAME CORNU,

I send you a line for Charles Thelin;[111] to thank you for your letter; and to tell you that I shall be pleased to see M. Charbet, if he comes to England.

I hope you are better, and that we shall see you here when it is not so cold.

My poor boy is at Woolwich, and finds the apprenticeship somewhat hard.

Receive the renewed assurance of my sincere friendship.

NAPOLÉON.

This was probably one of the last letters written by the Emperor, who passed away within two months. When writing to his foster-sister he had evidently no presentiment that his end was so rapidly approaching.

---

[110] "Les Forces Militaires de la France en 1870."

[111] Charles Thelin had been the Emperor's valet at Ham, and was employed in a confidential capacity during the reign.

CHAPTER XVIII

CITIZEN—PRESIDENT—EMPEROR

THE date is December 20, 1848, and. M. Marrast, President of the National Assembly, invites Citizen Charles Louis Napoleon Bonaparte to take the oath required by the Constitution on his election as President of the French Republic.

The Citizen, in evening dress, with the riband of the Légion d'Honneur en sautoir, ascends the tribune, raises his right hand, and, with the slightest tremor in his voice, says, "I swear."

What is his record?

1836.—Deported to America for attempting to procure a military rising in his favour at Strasburg.

1840.—Sentenced to perpetual confinement in the fortress of Ham for a similar attempt at Boulogne.

1846.—"Broke prison" and reached London.

In August, 1849, the Prince-President was at Tours, where he opened a new railway. Miss Howard was of the party, and was found lodgings at the residence of the Receiver-General, the Préfecture. That functionary was at "the waters" with his wife, and when he heard that the English lady—the Prince's "favourite" for so many years—was actually staying under his Prefectorial roof-tree he "made trouble." Louis Napoleon wrote on the subject to Odillon Barrot:

> Your brother has shown me a letter from a M. André, to which I should disdain to reply did it not contain some false statements which it is right to refute.
>
> A lady in whom I take the highest interest, accompanied by one of her friends (a lady) and by two persons of my household, wished to see the carrousel at Saumur, and from there they came to Tours. But, fearing they might not find lodgings, they asked me to take steps to obtain them some.
>
> When I arrived at Tours I told a counsellor of the Préfecture he would oblige me by looking for an appartement for Comte Bacciochi and two ladies of my acquaintance. Chance, and their evil star, led them, it appears, to the house of M. André, where—I know not why—it was thought that one of them bore the name of Bacciochi. She has never used that name, and if such a mistake

has been committed it is by strangers, and unknown to me or to the lady in question.

I should like to know why M. André, without having taken the trouble to ascertain the truth of the matter, wishes to make me responsible for the use made of his house and for the false name attributed to one of the persons. Does a proprietor make a good use of hospitality whose first care is to scrutinize the past life of anybody whom he receives? How many women, a hundred times less pure, a hundred times less devoted, a hundred times less excusable than the lady who lodged at M. André's would have been received by him with all possible honours because they would have borne the name of their husbands to conceal their culpable liaisons!

I detest this pedantic strictness, which badly conceals the âme sèche, indulgent for himself, inexorable for others. True religion is not intolerant. It does not seek to raise storms in a glass of water, to make a scandal for nothing, and to change into a crime a simple accident or an excusable mistake.

M. André, who I am told is a Puritan, has not sufficiently meditated upon the passage of the Scriptures where Christ, addressing those as little charitable as M. André, says on the subject of a woman they wished to stone, "Let him, etc." Let him practise this teaching. As to myself, I accuse nobody, and I admit I am culpable for seeking in illegitimate ties an affection of which my heart is in need. However, as until now my position has prevented me from marrying, as in the midst of the cares of government I have not, alas! in my country, from which I have been so long absent, either intimate friends, or youthful liaisons, or relations to give me the sweetness of the family, I may be pardoned, I think, for entertaining an affection which does no harm to anybody, and to which I do not seek to afficher myself.

To return to M. André, if he believes, as he declares, his house to have been soiled by the presence of an unmarried woman, I beg you will let him know that, on my side, I greatly regret that a lady of a devotion so pure and of a character so elevated should have stumbled by chance into a house where, under the mask of religion, there remains but the ostentation of a formal virtue without Christian charity.

Make whatever use you like of this letter.[112]

In November, 1851, the imminence of the coup d'état was talked about all over Paris as being necessary and anticipated. In the salons it was a topic of "chaff";

[112] "Mémoires inédits sur Napoléon III.," par le Baron d'Ambès. Recueillis et Annotés par Charles Simond et M. C. Poinsot. Paris: Société des Publications Littéraires Illustrées.

at the Elysée (the Prince-President's abode) it was studied in detail; the Church hoped for it; the people expected it; the army reckoned upon it. The plan (says the pseudonymous Baron d'Ambès) was sketched at the end of October by Saint-Arnaud and Maupas, whom Louis Napoleon informed, about this time, of Changarnier's conspiracy against the Elysée. To wait longer would be fatal. The lists of those who were to be proscribed were prepared in September. The programme for December 1 was drawn up to the most minute details. From 3 to 4 a.m. the police commissaries were to be received by the Préfet. At 5.30 the Palace of the Assembly would be occupied. At 6 arrest of Generals, representatives of Parliament, heads of societies, and dangerous democrats. At 6.30 proclamations were to be affixed to the walls, troops to be posted near the houses of those persons who were to be arrested, and positions for fighting were to be taken up by the military. By 7 o'clock it was to be "all over." At 8 the Minister of the Interior was to send instructions to the Préfets.

The "men of the coup d'état" were divided into three classes:

First, Saint-Arnaud, Morny, and Maupas.

Second, General Magnan, Persigny, and Fleury.

Third, Baroche, Rouher, F. Barrot, De Parieu, Dumas, Véron, Romieu, Fould, Magne, Drouyn de Lhuys, De Royer, Schneider, Fortoul, Espinasse, Billault, etc.

The programme was carried out to the letter on December 1, and a year later the Prince-President had exchanged that title for the supreme one of Napoleon III., Emperor of the French. The Bonapartists' excuse for the "coup" was that it was absolutely necessary to "sweep the board" of the President's opponents in Parliament and out of it, and also in the army. There was sanguinary fighting in the streets, it is true, and the President was branded throughout the World as a perjurer and a criminal of the deepest dye, who had "waded through blood to a throne." To many historians of the period he remains the "Man of December." To later writers, not overburdened with a knowledge of the facts, he is the "Man of Sedan," a pitiful and an ignominious figure, unworthy of sympathy.

The new Constitution was promulgated on January 14, 1852. It confided the Government of the French Republic for ten years to "Prince Louis Napoleon Bonaparte, the present President of the Republic." (Prince Jérôme, ex-King of Westphalia, was President of the Senate.)

On November 4 the Prince sent a message to the Senate, saying that the nation had "loudly manifested its will to re-establish the Empire." This message was dated from the Palace of St. Cloud. The Prince had now governed France for four years. A Committee of the Senate was appointed to draw up a report, and on November 6 it submitted to the Senate several resolutions, the series being known as "Senatus Consultum." Article I declared that the "Imperial dynasty is re-established. Louis Napoleon Bonaparte is Emperor of the French under the name of Napoleon III." The imperial dignity was made hereditary from male to male, "to the perpetual exclusion of the females and their descendants." The Senate passed and signed all the articles, and on Sunday, November 21, the voting "for the Empire" began, and lasted several days.

MR. ALFRED AUSTIN (POET LAUREATE)

Mr. Alfred Austin (Poet Laureate) was Special Correspondent of the *Standard* during the Franco-German War in 1870-71. His accounts of his interviews with Bismarck were everywhere read. Mr. Austin is one of the two English survivors of the campaign. His sonnet on the Prince Imperial, written a few days after the news of the tragedy in Zululand was received, is reproduced by the Poet Laureate's special permission. The photograph of Mr. Austin, taken in 1870, was kindly lent by Mrs. Austin.

On December 2, 1852, the anniversary of the coup d'état, in the afternoon, the Emperor, who had been "proclaimed" at St. Cloud the previous evening, made his official entry into his capital. It was wet and cold, and, although all Paris had turned out to see the military pageant, the enthusiasm might have been greater than it was. The Emperor, mounted on a showy charger, looked anything but bright. He did not once take off his General's plumed tricorne, but contented himself with acknowledging the salutations of the crowd by occasionally touching his hat. By his own orders he rode alone; the escort, separated from his own by a considerable space, front and rear. This was an example of the pluck which he invariably displayed both as President and as Emperor.

During his four years' Presidency of the Republic he had been surrounded by open foes in France and by opponents who lay in ambush awaiting opportunities to strike. Foreign opinion, however, was less hostile prior to than it became after the coup d'état, which was the signal for an outburst of almost universal execration. Even Queen Victoria, who, some three years later, was entertaining, and was entertained by, the Emperor and Empress, condemned the act of December, 1851. Early in 1852 the Queen, in a letter to King Frederick William of Prussia, wrote:[113]

> The political stratagem in Paris will have taken your Majesty back to the days of your youth.... Louis Napoleon had tried to freshen up the memories of all European Governments by the reintroduction of the eagle on the standards of the French army, and by allusions to changes of the boundaries, etc. In spite of this, I firmly believe in the maintenance of peace. But I am made much more anxious by the thought that those Continental Governments which have gone too far in their blind reaction, led astray by the Paris example, are of the erroneous opinion that a State is likely to last eternally which has been raised on the ruins of civil liberty with the blood of the middle classes of France, and that they may be encouraged to widen the breach between them and their peoples, and completely destroy the belief in the political morality of Governments in general.

---

[113] "Memoirs of General von Gerlach." Published, in German only, in 1891.

CHAPTER XIX

THE PALE EMPEROR

HIS "EXPLANATION": WRITTEN BY HIMSELF.

THE whole House was on its feet, threatening, shaking its fists at a man with a waxen face who protested against this last humiliation inflicted on his master. Like the Jews demanding of Pilate that he should deliver Jesus to them, we cried to posterity at the top of our voices: "Crucifige, crucifige eum!"

I do not know which of the two attitudes has left the more painful impression on my mind—that of Conti [the Emperor's former Secretary], surrounded, almost struck, but meeting these threats with the most magnificent coolness; or that of the seven hundred and fifty representatives of the French nation, raging against a man who for six months had been little more than a corpse. He had been very guilty; but we, in our turn, were very cruel.[114]

The visit of the Emperor and Empress to Queen Victoria and the Prince Consort in 1855 was heralded by the issue of a placard thus conceived:

England's disgrace. The Real Day of Humiliation.[115] Louis Napoleon, the Murderer, the Oath-Breaker, is coming to England.

Englishmen, do your duty!

The Empress had, we know, complained to Queen Victoria of the bitter attacks rained upon the Emperor by our newspapers, and was scarcely comforted by the Queen's assurance that the English Press was free and could not be censored.

Bismarck, who, when he was Prussian Minister to France, professed the warmest friendship for Napoleon III., and became a favourite of the Empress and the Court, soon turned against the Emperor, speaking of him slightingly, if not contemptuously, and deprecating Napoleon's suggestion of a Franco-Prussian alliance.

To Vambéry Napoleon III. was "this thick-set man, with his flabby features

---

[114] "Men and Things of My Time," by the Marquis de Castellane. London: Chatto and Windus. 1911.

[115] Probably a reference to a public religious service in connection with the Crimean War.

and pale, faded eyes." Vambéry[116] could not discern in the Emperor a trace of the greatness of which he had heard so much. "His pale eyes and artificial speech soon betrayed the adventurer who had been elevated to his exalted position by the inheritance of a great name and the wantonness of the nation."

Mme. Cornu, Louis Napoleon's foster-sister, who had had a sincere affection for him prior to the coup d'état, execrated him for that act, declined to see him when he called upon her, and, as he stood at the bottom of the stairs, shouted to him from above that she would have nothing to do with "a man whose hands were covered with blood." Her resentment continued for years; then, one day, she went to the Tuileries, saw the Emperor and Empress, took the little Prince in her arms, and "made it up."

I would fain hope that we may find the "true truth" in these eloquent words of the statesman who knew the real Louis Napoleon better, perhaps, than most men, excepting De Morny, De Persigny, Fleury, Conti, and, I will add, Franceschini Pietri—I mean, as will have been guessed, M. Émile Ollivier:

> Despite all that has been written on the Emperor Napoleon III., no personage is less known. He has been described as un esprit nébuleux; in reality, no one had a clearer mind. He has been called an egotistical calculator: no one was more disinterested or more preoccupied with the national grandeur. But he placed that grandeur very high. He believed that France was the soldier of God; that his mission was not to gratify miserable cupidities, but to work for the freedom and happiness of peoples. He did nothing on behalf of dynastic interests, but he neglected no opportunity of advancing the principle of nationalities, which is that of justice, peace, and civilization. And that will be his immortal glory in the future. He would not have sent the French fleet to prevent the brave Cretans from uniting themselves with Greece, if they desired to do so. He would not have made France the synonym for egotism and platitudes. All his dreams were those of one of the most beautiful minds which ever ruled over men since the days of the Antonines.[117]

The value of that glowing tribute, that certificate of character, depends upon the impartiality and capacity of the person who penned it. I myself consider M. Émile Ollivier—Napoleon's last Prime Minister, upon whom and his colleagues was imposed the dire duty of declaring war—an impartial witness. He may not—I fear he will not—be accepted as such by all. Is he not the Minister who said he entered upon the war "with a light heart"? He is the selfsame man; only it is too often forgotten that he qualified that expression at the moment he uttered it by explaining that he was "light-hearted" because of "his conviction that Prussia was in the wrong and was deliberately attacking France."[118]

---

[116] "The Story of my Struggles," by Arminius Vambéry.

[117] In Roman history the period of the reigns of Antoninus Pius and Marcus Aurelius was generally characterized by domestic tranquillity.

[118] "The Development of Nations," by J. H. Rose. London: Constable. 1905.

It must be remembered that while M. Ollivier was devoted to Napoleon III. he was regarded with not over-friendly eyes by the Empress Eugénie. He necessarily had frequent formal and informal audiences of the Emperor, and that some of these interviews took place unknown to the imperial lady we know from the Emperor's letter asking the statesman to enter the Tuileries on a certain occasion by "the little door" in the garden, in order that the Empress might not know he was in the Palace!

M. Ollivier, as the historian of "L'Empire Libéral," intends to be absolutely unbiassed and impartial. He has taken upon himself the Herculean task of defending that Liberal Empire, the Liberal Emperor, and the Liberal Premier of 1870 (himself), and he has had to make the best case possible for all three. His work is a monument of research, memory, and industry. His fifteen great volumes are for the world's criticism; some may see in them only a brilliant plaidoirie, admirably conceived and ingeniously executed—the whole a phenomenal literary performance, yet, of course, written with parti pris, and as such challenging critical comment. But may we not accept without carping, and with faith in his sincerity, his estimate of the Man Napoleon III., the Pale Emperor, in whose words, "The crown has thorns, and often some of them sink deeply into the head,"[119] we seem to see the epitaph he would have wished?

The responsibility for the war of 1870 has been laid, firstly, to the charge of the Empress Eugénie, and, secondly, to that of the Emperor. In a previous volume I printed the complete text of what, since its publication in that work, has become known as "the Empress's Case"—Her Imperial Majesty's Reply to her Accusers. One of my numerous very appreciative American critics took occasion to remark that, in order to prove the Empress's blamelessness, something more was required than the mere word of M. Gaston Calmette.[120] To remove all misapprehension, I now put it on record that the document in question contained the Empress Eugénie's ipsissima verba; otherwise it neither could nor would have been published.

I pass on to a consideration of the measure of the Emperor Napoleon's responsibility for the war with Germany.

Those who have taken the trouble, and who have the competency, to investigate the numerous causes which were the genesis of the war have satisfied themselves that, to employ a colloquialism, Napoleon III. was "dead against" entering into a conflict with Prussia. These investigators now know, although they may not all have known it twenty, or ten, or even five years ago, that the Emperor was forced into the field, partly by the diplomacy of the then Count Bismarck (other diplomatists aiding), partly (and to a greater extent) by the practically unanimous voice of his own subjects.

Let there be no longer any doubt about this: the French themselves, not primarily, but ultimately, were responsible for the war. It was not Paris this time, but the entire nation, and, with very few exceptions, the Press, which made it impossible for the Emperor and his Government to refrain from throwing down the gauntlet. That the Empress should have sided with the "war party" is not surprising, for the

[119] Napoleon III., January 3, 1870.
[120] Editor of "Le Figaro."

"war party" was the country, and she would have been voted anti-patriotic (and we know what that means) had she not fallen into line with those millions who professed their anxiety to get "to Berlin," although they knew no more how they were to get there than they knew how to reach the planet Mars.

We forget the vacillations of the Emperor, we forget his moral lapses, we forget the coup d'état, we can even forget the hideous Mexican blunder, when we remember his noble hesitancy to plunge the country into a war which he knew could have but one ending—disaster. He knew it from Stoffel and he knew it from Niel. As Baron de Mackau has most truly said, Napoleon III. *"submitted* to the war." There is the whole matter crystallized into four words. The Emperor sanctioned the war because he had no alternative. He had to submit to pressure from within and pressure from without. If ever a Sovereign was driven into making war it was that most unfortunate of men the Emperor Napoleon III.

Baron de Mackau was one of the Emperor's most intimate friends, and after the battle of Solferino he was entrusted with the duty of presenting Niel with his Marshal's epaulettes. The Baron says:

> The Emperor did not wish for war. It is only just to him to say that he submitted to it. It would be equitable to seek for the reasons of the defeat of France in the refusal of Parliament to contribute, during the years preceding the war, to the work of national defence proposed by Marshal Niel. In 1867, after the Italian war, Niel, as Minister of War, demanded the modification of the military law and the creation of reservists. He was not allowed to finish his speech. The Magnins, the Favres, the Simons, and all those who formed the Opposition at that date, prevented the vote. They said to the Marshal: "You want to make France a vast entrenched camp." I heard the Marshal reply, with a gravity well calculated to move those who were present: "May you, gentlemen, not make it a huge cemetery."

On the day following the declaration of war, when the Delegates of the Corps Législatif took leave of Napoleon III., His Majesty said to them: "Ah, gentlemen, we are undertaking a heavy task!" As he left the Emperor's study at St. Cloud, Baron de Mackau said to his colleagues: "We are done for!"

The Baron continues:

> The eagerness with which, a few days previously, people had heard of the possibility of avoiding war; then the order given suddenly by Marshal Lebœuf, the Emperor's friend and confidant, to stop all preparations; the Marshal's resignation when, at the last night council, war was decided upon—these things have been always, to me, proofs that the Emperor only submitted to the war. The truth is that public opinion in France, grievously over-excited, urged on the war; and that the Left, represented by those whose names are noted above, and always taking heed of outside rumours, followed the current of public opinion, as did, lat-

er, Marshal Bazaine. The Right, as a whole, advanced hesitatingly and defiantly, animated by the desire to weaken the Emperor's Government abroad, and only made up its mind when our colleague, Talhouët, a member of the delegation to whom the secret documents had been communicated, declared at the Chamber that, as a matter of honour, war was inevitable.

While the Emperor was in his "prison" at Wilhelmshöhe (September, 1870, to March, 1871) he spent the greater part of his time at his desk.[121] In this former palace of his uncle, Jérôme, King of Westphalia, Napoleon III. wrote, from memory, aided by extracts from State papers which someone copied for him, an elaborate statement of his policy during his eighteen years' reign, so far as it regarded Germany. This very frank apologia (De Persigny having refused to figure as its "author") was fathered by his old friend, the Marquis de Gricourt, who had been his companion in London when he was awaiting the call which came to him in 1848. That the statement was written by the Emperor himself is guaranteed, in his Memoirs, by General Count von Monts, to whose custody at Wilhelmshöhe the august captive was confided by King William.[122]

General von Monts writes:

"The Press had obtained excessive liberty; the Republican party, the Empress, and the clergy had too much power for the welfare of the Dynasty; and the Emperor damaged himself by obeying the suggestions of several French Ambassadors abroad. That Napoleon himself was also culpable for the war against us [Germany] is a fact which cannot be disputed, inasmuch as we know his letter of July 12, 1870, addressed to Gramont, in which he formulated his exigencies in respect of Prussia, and begged Gramont to explain them to Benedetti. Napoleon never, in my presence, alluded to this letter, but he recognized his culpability by writing, in his brochure, 'Les Relations de France et Germany sous Napoléon III.':

    'Toutefois, nous le disons franchement, le devoir de l'Empereur était d'être plus sage que la nation, et d'empêcher la guerre, même au prix de sa couronne.'

"The cover of the brochure gave the name of the Marquis de Gricourt as the author; *but I know for certain that the Emperor was the author of it, for he wrote it during his captivity at Wilhelmshöhe, and gave me a copy of it.*"

This highly-interesting document is so little known—I will venture to say it is <u>unknown—that</u> I will quote some of its principal paragraphs in full, fortified by

[121] His Majesty's own detailed statement of the causes which, in his opinion, led to the defeat of his army at Sedan appears textually in the volume, "The Empress Eugénie: 1870—1910" (and, I think, in no other work). London: Harper and Brothers; New York: Charles Scribner's Sons. 1910.

[122] "La Captivité de Napoléon III. en Allemagne," par le Général Comte C. de Monts, Gouverneur de Cassel. "Souvenirs traduits de l'Allemand," par Paul Bruck Gilbert et Paul Lévy. Préface de Jules Claretie, de l'Académie Française. Paris, Pierre Lafitte et Cie. 1910.

This positive statement of General von Monts is confirmed by M. Émile Ollivier ("Le Figaro," October 22, 1910). The Marquis de Gricourt was a Chamberlain of Napoleon III. and also a Senator.

the conviction that I shall be thereby clearing the Emperor's memory (as I have already cleared that of the Empress) from many reproaches and sneers which have been accepted as gospel by all who have not waded through M. Ollivier's fifteen volumes, which are not likely to be translated into English, although possibly they may be issued in German; but even that is doubtful, for the author of "L'Empire Libéral" is a very outspoken historian.

The Emperor wisely says: "We must not judge of things as they are, but as they *might have been*. Certainly, since Königsgrätz the power of Prussia has increased amazingly; hence her crushing France with considerable forces, outnumbering her own by hundreds of thousands.... Before 1866 there was no possibility of forming an alliance in the centre of Europe. Austria was irrevocably joined to Germany, and Italy did not then exist as a Power. But might it not likewise be argued that in 1870, also, France remained alone? Central Europe then permitted her to form alliances. The Austro-Hungarian Empire might have been won over, and Italy, reconstituted, led to join in the war. Had these events taken place, the policy of the Second Empire doubtless would have triumphed; for facts could have proved that, in spite of the augmentation of Prussia, there existed in Europe a serious counterpoise to her gigantic power.... From January 2, 1870, France[123] became entire mistress of her own destinies. And what use did she then make of the liberties so largely accorded to her? The country desired peace; the Chambers and Government desired peace; and yet the climax to the situation was War."

With these preliminary words Napoleon III. proceeds:

> When M. Émile Ollivier accepted the task of forming a Ministry, his programme—as submitted to the Emperor—frankly acknowledged the principle of nationalities,[124] recognizing the right of Germany to reconstitute herself in a manner thought best suitable to her. He likewise expressed the most pacific intentions.[125] Soon after the installation of the Ministers on January 2, 1870, Comte Daru, Minister for Foreign Affairs, proposed to Prussia, through the intervention of England, a general disarmament. To support this demand, it was suggested, in the Chambers, to reduce the annual contingent by 10,000 men. This last measure was adopted; but as to the proposition of Comte Daru only a formal and evasive answer was returned. Nevertheless, it may be said that the year 1870 began under favourable auspices. Nothing seemed to threaten the repose then enjoyed by Europe. The only thought in France was to develop, under a Liberal Government, the moral and material resources of the country.[126]

[123] Through the Liberal Empire.

[124] One of the cardinal points of the Emperor's policy, foreshadowed by him when he was in London in 1839-40.

[125] M. Ollivier's critics condemn him for disregarding Marshal Niel's earnest appeals to increase the military forces of the Empire, and so put the country in a proper state of defence. The annual contingent was, in fact, as the Emperor notes, *reduced* by 10,000 men!

[126] His Majesty ignores the fact that for at least two years there had been throughout the country a growing feeling of discontent, aroused, to a large extent, by M. Henri Roche-

But it has often been said, "He who sows the whirlwind shall reap the tempest." For four years the Opposition—including all sections—had caused the Tribune and the Press to resound with most bitter lamentations on the increase of Prussian power.... These constant assertions, these perpetual attacks, had penetrated to the remotest parts of the country. The army, even, had not remained insensible to the reproaches of weakness hurled at the Government; it felt humbled by the successes of Prussia, as if those very successes had been obtained against itself.

Again, when the news reached France of the likelihood of a Prussian Prince becoming King of Spain, it had the effect of a spark falling on inflammable matter; all hatred, jealousies, and envyings were at once aroused. This incident, which at another time would only have provoked an exchange of diplomatic Notes, now fired the whole nation.

The Ministry, it must be owned, committed the serious fault of carrying to the tribune a sort of challenge, which rendered any diplomatic arrangement difficult. Nevertheless, on the Prince of Hohenzollern withdrawing his son's name as candidate for the Spanish throne, it was hoped that peace might still have been maintained; but public opinion had been too violently agitated: it spurned all conciliatory measures. The journals of nearly every shade of opinion cried out for war. The provinces partook of the exultations of the capital. Whatever may be said of the confidential messages sent by the Préfets, and of which only garbled accounts had been given, the majority of these high functionaries announced, in the aggregate, that in the Departments the public mind was animated beyond precedent; conditions of peace, however honourable, would in no way satisfy them. Of this we need no further proof than the following despatches, found by the Prussians in the Palace of St. Cloud, and published in the "North German Gazette":[127]

"PERPIGNAN, *July 15, 1870.*—The Préfet to the Minister of the Interior, Paris. In consequence of the last news we have had great excitement here. The idea of war with Prussia is warmly received by the bulk of the population. Even the Radicals say that in a week's time hostilities will commence, and that by August 15 our soldiers will celebrate the Emperor's fête at Berlin. No one, for one moment, doubts the results of the war. Everywhere, in town

fort's denunciations (in the "Lanterne") of the Emperor, the Empress, and the Court.

[127] These extracts were doubtless translated by the Emperor himself, for not one of those who were with him at Wilhelmshöhe could speak a word or read a line of German! Napoleon III. had an almost better acquaintance with German than with French, and he spoke French as many Germans speak it, the result of his early education in Germany and Switzerland.

and village, there is the same confidence shown."

"MARSEILLES, *July 16, 1870.*—The Préfet to the Minister of the Interior, Paris. There has just been a great manifestation here, a torchlight procession parading the streets of our town, followed by 10,000 to 15,000 people, singing 'La Reine Hortense' and the 'Marseillaise.' The cries of 'Vive l'Empereur!' 'A bas la Prusse!' 'À Berlin!' resounding on all sides. The crowd is full of enthusiasm, and no disorder."

These sentiments found expression, nearly as energetic, in language uttered by the representatives of the country. The wish of the Corps Législatif was no longer doubtful. It appears that there had been a moment when the Ministers inclined towards peace. An order of the day by MM. Clément-Duvernois and Jérôme David—the latter Vice-President of the Chamber[128]— nearly overturned the Cabinet. This occurred on July 13. Two days later the Chamber was called upon definitively to pronounce on the conclusions drawn up in conformity to the Commission of which M. de Kératry was a member, and which had been unanimously approved of. *The vote was for War!* The majority numbered 247 against 10. Seven members only were absent. The Radical Opposition was divided in opinion. To use the words of M. Thiers: "This was, in truth, the expression of an overwhelming approval of the country; the Legislative Body siding with the people."

When the Emperor, in his proclamation to the French army, foretold the difficulties of the enterprise, so certain appeared success to all that the sober "Journal des Débats" expressed an opinion that His Majesty "showed too much diffidence in his address to his troops."

*   *   *   *   *

Every soldier in the streets was made the subject of popular ovation. In the theatres public feeling manifested itself by the noisiest demonstrations. Who can forget that representation at the Opera when the whole audience rose to a man and thundered out the "Marseillaise"?

In Paris such was the enthusiasm felt that the Emperor could not leave his Palace without being cheered by an immense mob, crying out, "Vive la guerre!" At the moment of his departure for the army His Majesty purposely refrained from driving through the capital owing to reports that the populace would indulge in wild demonstrations, intending to unharness the horses from his carriage and drag it themselves in triumph to the railway station. This same people, one month later, destroyed the emblems of the

---

[128] A Bonapartist intransigeant who greatly influenced the Empress.

Empire and broke the statues of their Ruler![129]

If we have recalled facts known to all, it is not to exonerate the Emperor from the responsibilities he assumed, but to prove what was then the state of public opinion in France.

On Sunday, July 19, 1870, Napoleon III. held, at the Tuileries, a Council of War, which lasted several hours. The Emperor and his Ministers agreed, without exception, after mature deliberation, that a declaration should be made rendering peace still possible. But the same evening the Ministers repaired to St. Cloud and amended their resolution of the morning, M. Ollivier informing His Majesty that if the document agreed upon at their last meeting had been published the disappointment would have been such that "the Ministers would have been received with hisses and their carriages pelted with mud."

Certainly, although the Chief of the State was a Constitutional Sovereign, he might have prevented the war, but at the cost of his own popularity. They would again have reproached him—as they already had—for being humble to the strong and arrogant to the weak. His conduct would have been for ever denounced by a malevolent Opposition as basely culpable towards a designing adversary.

At the same time, we own that the duty of the Emperor was to have shown himself wiser than the nation, and avoided war even at the cost of his crown.

His excuse is that he accepted the contest, but without ardour, as a man who engages in a duel because his honour and duty demand it, not considering that his opponent may be stronger than himself. Doubtless, he may have been carried away at the moment by national élan; by unlimited confidence in the power of his army; and that dreams of military glory, perhaps even of territorial aggrandizement, then stifled in his breast the calm reasoning of the statesman.

Without, however, ignoring the responsibility of His Majesty in recent events, we cannot admit, as recently stated by M. Jules Favre, that the Emperor made war of his own accord and in the interests of his Dynasty.

Who could believe that, after receiving a new consecration by universal suffrage, when 7,000,000 voices freshly ratified former Plébiscites, and showed the most incredulous how deep-rooted the Empire was, Napoleon III. should have thought it necessary, two months later, to have recourse to such a terrible expedient as war to sustain his power and strengthen his Dynasty? Why, even successful warfare would in no way have added to the security

[129] Strictly speaking, it was exactly five weeks later.

of the Empire. Alas! it could only lead to the disturbing of every-thing. The Emperor led the élite of his army, leaving behind him his wife, with no armed force, no tried and daring military chief, to guard her, in an immense capital always in agitation, imbued with Republican ideas, worked upon by SOCIALISM, a prey to 700 journals, and invested with the rights of public political meeting. On the least reverse of arms, disorders, riotings, perhaps even a revolution, had to be dreaded.

It is quite evident, then, that war, taken all in all, was palpably against the interests of his Dynasty, and it cannot be just to Napoleon III. to say that he either desired or imposed it on the country.

Furthermore, a Vice-President of the Government of Defence, had he not always upheld the institution of Ministerial Responsibility as a wise and efficient system? Why, then, be false to his principles now? Why impute to the Emperor alone the errors that have been committed in the management of State affairs? Surely his Ministers were equally blameable. The honest truth is that the country desired the contest, and that His Majesty, unfortunately, did not resist the overwhelming enthusiasm of the nation.

In conclusion, let us remark with what care Napoleon III. endeavoured, from the commencement, to show how consistent his conduct had been with national sentiment.

In his Proclamation to the French people[130] he says:

"Frenchmen! There are moments most solemn in the life of nations—when the national honour, violently excited, with irresistible force commands all interests and directs the destinies of the country. One of these decisive hours has just struck for France.

"Against the new pretensions of Prussia our objections made themselves heard. They have been evaded, and followed by contemptuous proceedings. At this our country has felt a profound irritation; and immediately a warcry resounded from one end of France to the other. Nothing is now left us but to confide our destinies to the fate of arms."

When, on July 23, the Legislative Body took leave of the Emperor, he answered the President's address in these words:

"We have done all we could to avoid war. We can now say that it is the whole nation which, by its irresistible élan, dictated our resolutions."

Thus, then, in accepting the responsibility which devolved upon him, the Emperor—before, as since, his overthrow—desired

____
[130] July, 1870.

to establish before the world the following simple fact: that he did not launch the country into a perilous enterprise on account of contemptible motives, but felt himself encouraged, if not compelled to it, by the determined manifestations of public opinion.

The reader who has followed the above recital of the principal events of the reign of Napoleon III. must be convinced that he who became a prisoner at Wilhelmshöhe employed eighteen years of undisputed power in making France the most flourishing country in Europe, in allaying international hatred, and in protecting the independence of foreign States. When his personal efforts appeared to him unequal to realize all he meditated for the universal welfare, he voluntarily gave up Authority and called on the representatives of the people to take the most active part in the direction of affairs, thus establishing in France the widest and most complete system of liberty.

And now, because fortune has abandoned him, this great man is only considered by some in the light of a tyrant, who, to establish a Dynasty, ruthlessly precipitated his country into all the horrors of a merciless war.

We have recorded facts. Posterity will be the judge.

When the Empress read the telegram announcing that the Hohenzollern candidature was withdrawn, she said, in the presence of General Bourbaki, "It is infamous! The Empire will fall to rags!" ("L'Empire va tomber en quenouille!")[131]

An extraordinary story, told by M. Welschinger, makes one wonder whether some of those surrounding the Empress in July, 1870, were in their right minds. It was proposed that the King of Prussia should be asked to write a letter to Napoleon III. to satisfy the énergumènes (fanatics, "of whom the Empress was one"), and the Duc de Gramont actually drafted and sent to the King a note of what His Majesty was to say! King William had been very pleased when he thought that all danger of war had vanished by the withdrawal of the Hohenzollern Prince from the Spanish candidature, "and in so uselessly and gratuitously wounding him the French Cabinet alienated the only person who could check Bismarck."

King William was disgusted. "Was there ever such insolence?" he wrote to Queen Augusta. "They want me to appear before the world as a repentant sinner."

When Benedetti asked the King to give "guarantees" that there should be no renewal of the Hohenzollern candidature, His Majesty said: "You ask me to make a promise for all time, and that, for every reason, I cannot do."

Bismarck did the rest.

"There was neither insulter nor insulted at Ems. There was only the Chancellor's manœuvre." The French Cabinet played into the hands of Bismarck, whose one desire was that France should be responsible for the declaration of war. "It

---

[131] "Les Causes et les Responsabilités de la Guerre de 1870." Par H. Welschinger. Paris: Plon. 1910.

was Bismarck who wanted war, and we rendered him the service of declaring it." M. Ollivier was pleased at the Hohenzollern's withdrawal, and there the affair ought to have ended; "but," says M. Welschinger, "a section of Deputies and of the Court—the Empress in particular—urged war.[132] While the business world was all in favour of peace, an artificial atmosphere environed the Cabinet—an atmosphere composed of M.P.s and hot-headed journalists—and accused Ministers of weakness. The numerical inferiority of the army was not the fault of the Emperor and his Ministers, but of the elected representatives of the nation. The Emperor's health grew worse and worse, until he could no longer resist the war party.... We had an army numerically inferior, could not reckon on allies, and were in no way prepared for war. On July 6, after the Duc de Gramont's speech, I heard on all sides, 'It is war, it is war!' The Cabinets of Austria and of England both blamed the declaration of war."

On the day of the departure from St. Cloud of the Emperor and the Prince Imperial for "the front" (July 28) gloom prevailed at the château. "One would believe there was a coffin in the house," said a lackey. But the aides-de-camp who were accompanying the Emperor were in boisterous spirits. They were inclined to say, as Pandore said to his brigadier, "Majesté [Brigadier], vous avez raison."[133] The Emperor wore the uniform of a General of Division de petite tenue; the Prince Imperial that of a Sous-Lieutenant of Voltigeurs of the Guard. As the boy strolled about, taking farewell of everybody—his pretty cousins, the Empress's nieces, daughters of the Duc and Duchesse d'Albe, were there—he tapped the scabbard of his sword and gave himself airs, to the delight of the admiring group. Tears were in his mother's eyes when, as the train moved out of the special station, she exclaimed, "Do your duty, Louis!" "We shall all do it," answered the Emperor; and to the Prime Minister he shouted, "Ollivier! Je compte sur vous!" It was their last meeting.

As the imperial party left the château on their way to the station there was a shout of "À Berlin!" "Don't say that," exclaimed the Emperor reproachfully; "the war will be a very long one, in any case." And one remembers that, a few days before, when the streets of Paris were paraded daily and nightly by crowds yelling "To Berlin!" the Emperor had written to the Duc de Gramont, "Enthusiasm is a fine thing, but sometimes very ridiculous." If the Empress had illusions, her consort had none.

We must take it, however, that he had allowed himself to be, I will not say actually deluded, but, to a certain extent, led away by General Frossard, the Prince Imperial's inflexible "governor"—a man of many "plans." Plan No. 1 was to "take" Saarbrücken, and five days after the Emperor left St. Cloud Saarbrücken was duly "taken," Napoleon III. assisting (was he not Commander-in-Chief?), and the Prince Imperial being "baptized" by shells and bullets.

Frossard (we are told by M. Émile Ollivier[134]) was to cross the Saar on Au-

---

[132] To similar assertions the Empress Eugénie, in her Reply to her Accusers, gives an emphatic denial.

[133] Part of the chorus of one of Nadaud's popular songs.

[134] *Revue des Deux Mondes* (January 1, 1911). "La Guerre de 1870: Notre Première

gust 2 at daybreak, and take possession of Saarbrücken, supported by portions of the 2nd and 3rd corps d'armées, while the 4th corps watched the débouchées of Saarlouis. Bazaine was to command three corps destined to co-operate in the scheme. As the event proved, Bazaine was against the occupation of Saarbrücken, and "thus revealed the fatal inertia which lost himself, the army, and France."

Even thus early the "hauts chefs," to fill up time, had sent for their wives. "The camp was full of them." Prince Napoleon wrote in his notes, "Trop de femmes d'officiers."[135]

M. Émile Ollivier's exposure of the "désillusion diplomatique" is, it goes without saying, very illuminating. Prince Napoleon attributed the check of the alliance "to our wish to save the Temporal Power. It has become a historical commonplace to say that if we had given Rome to the Italians we should have had with us Italy and Austria, and we should not have sacrificed the country by protecting a decrepit Sovereignty." M. Ollivier continues:

> It was the "Spanish fanatic," the Empress, who determined our resolutions. "I prefer," she is reported to have said, "to see the Prussians in Paris rather than the Italians in Rome." De Gramont is reported to have said: "I could do nothing. I was tied by the Empress."
>
> The Empress never used the abominable words attributed to her, and De Gramont never made the unjust accusation against her that was put in his mouth. She approved the Cabinet's refusal of Beust's suggestion to give Rome to Italy, but she did not originate that refusal. The initiative was taken apart from her by De Gramont and me. If she had been the Ultramontane fanatic she was said to be, she would not have supported the protestations of Mackau[136] and his friends that it was necessary to maintain our occupation of Rome. It was, on the contrary, upon her eloquent demonstration that the Council of Ministers, taking no heed of the representations of so many of the Catholic nobility, approved the evacuation of the Pontifical territory.
>
> In the matter of alliances, as in other matters, the Council did not adopt the opinion of the Empress, except when it was in accord with its own Opinion. The Council never submitted to an influence which the Empress never had over any of its members, and which she never attempted to exercise. It was the Cabinet, not the Empress, which must be held responsible for the course followed in this negotiation.

All this will come as a pleasurable surprise to the Empress's friends, and as a disagreeable shock to her critics — or would vilipenders be the better word? Moreover, the venerable Minister's clear-cut, incisive, unanswerable statements amply

---

Défaite."
[135] *Ibid.*
[136] The Baron de Mackau (previously referred to in this chapter).

confirm the Empress's assertions in her "Case," which, in the light of M. Ollivier's pronouncements, is immeasurably increased in importance. What is printed above concerning the precise relations which existed between the members of the last Imperial Government (for Palikao's "scratch" Ministry is of little, if any, account) and the Empress is, I allow myself to say, particularly satisfactory to one who has been considered, in a few quarters, to have unduly "bolstered up" the consort of Napoleon III. The American critic who desired something more than the assertion of a journalist to make the Empress's "Case" thoroughly acceptable now has his not unnatural desire gratified—he has the word of honour of the historian of "L'Empire Libéral" that the imperial lady's vehement assertions (which, until 1910, had been buried in the columns of a newspaper) are true in substance and in fact, and may no longer be questioned.

But M. Ollivier has more to say on this point:

> The Empress and the Duc de Gramont were convinced that, the war over, it would have been easy for us [the Ollivier Cabinet] to have established the Papal Sovereignty had it been overthrown by revolutionaries. The Emperor and the Duc did not realize the situation in which we should then have found ourselves.... The withdrawal of our troops, in the circumstances in which it took place, was equivalent to the abandonment of what remained of the Temporal Power.

> Even had Victor Emmanuel sent troops to our aid, he could not have done so before the first week in September; consequently, such help from Italy would not have saved us from Spicheren, Wörth, and Sedan.

> *The real motive of the abstention of Italy was not the refusal to give up Rome. The Italian Ministers from the first subordinated the question of participation in the war to the initiative which Austria might have taken. Italy could do nothing without Austria.*

> The causes which led Austria to refuse to come to our aid and to bring Italy with her are infinite. *But the one cause which dominated all others was the known intention of Russia*[137] *to put her army at the service of Prussia if Austria sent her troops to the assistance of France.*

> *This is confirmed by King William, who, on the morrow of his victory, wrote to the Emperor Alexander II.:* "NEVER WILL PRUSSIA FORGET THAT SHE OWES IT TO YOU THAT THE WAR DID NOT TAKE EXTREME PROPORTIONS. GOD BLESS YOU! YOUR GRATEFUL FRIEND FOR LIFE, WILLIAM."

To this outburst of gratitude the Tsar replied: "I am happy to have been able to show you by the evidence of my sympathies that I am a devoted friend. May the friendship which unites us assure the happiness and the glory of the two countries!—ALEXANDER."

[137] Known at the Foreign Offices, but unknown to the outside world, the Press included.

We may not question the sincerity of M. Ollivier's avowal, extorted from him by bitter memories of, as Napoleon III. says, "what might have been": "*La Russie a beaucoup à réparer à notre égard.*"

At this point it is germane to the diplomatic question—which, as we have seen, was at the root of everything—to recall the doubtless forgotten fact that on July 24, 1870—five days after France had declared war—a Conference took place in Paris on the vital question of the proposed alliance of France, Austria, and Italy. Prince Napoleon and the Duc de Gramont represented France, Prince de Metternich (husband of the celebrated Princess Pauline) and Count Vitzthum represented Austria, and Count Nigra (a great admirer of the Empress) and Count Vimercati Italy.

The Duc de Gramont produced the draft of a proposed Treaty, which was agreed to. The Conference was about to break up when Prince de Metternich and Count Nigra simultaneously introduced a condition making it a sine quâ non that France should give up Rome to Italy. Prince Napoleon refused to accept the condition, and the Duc de Gramont announced that the Conference was at an end. Napoleon III. at once informed Prince de Metternich and Count Nigra that only in the last extremity would he agree to a diplomatic conference on the question of abandoning Rome to the Italian Government.

On August 1—the day before the first engagement at Saarbrücken, when the Prince Imperial received his "baptism of fire"—the Emperor Napoleon, at his urgent request, was presented by Austria and Italy with a new project of alliance, containing these important clauses:

1. The diplomatic campaign projected against Prussia will be commenced only after September 15 [a fortnight, as it happened, after the French defeat at Sedan], and only if France shall have already victoriously invaded South Germany.

2. Austria-Hungary undertakes to effectively support Italy, in order that that country may obtain conditions favourable to her interests in the Roman question.

In opposition to Prince Napoleon, the Emperor demanded the withdrawal from the Treaty of the paragraph relating to Rome and the fixing of a date for changing the phrase "armed neutrality" into "armed co-operation." To this proposal Austria and Italy gave a point-blank refusal. Thus France was left to carry on the struggle single-handed.

Nevertheless, the military party at Vienna pushed on preparations for war. The Tsar was highly incensed, and the Austrian Ambassador at St. Petersburg telegraphed that His Imperial Majesty had spoken to him "very bitterly" concerning the Austrian preparations. This had its effect at Vienna, and the war party subsided. The result of the failure of Austria and Italy to join France was that the Emperor Napoleon, who had confidently reckoned upon the armed support of those countries, took the field, with fatal consequences.[138]

---

[138] From the hitherto unpublished correspondence of Count Beust, Chancellor of Austria-Hungary, July, 1870.—"Deutsche Rundschau," 1910.

CHAPTER XX

THE EMPEROR'S COLLABORATOR

I HAVE told, in "The Empress Eugénie: 1870-1910,"[139] how, on January 9, 1873, upon hearing of the unexpected death of Napoleon III., I hastened from the Temple to Chislehurst on behalf of the "Morning Post," whose editor (he was not yet proprietor), the late Lord Glenesk (then Mr. Borthwick), had for many years enjoyed the intimate friendship and confidence of the Emperor. I told how, on my arrival at Camden Place, I sent in my card to Sir Henry Thompson, who blandly declined to open his lips except to assure me that the Emperor was dead, and that he, the eminent surgeon, would himself relate the facts "some day"—a day that never arrived. M. Pietri was too overcome with grief to say anything. But there was at hand—I have always found it so—the friend in need. He was the Grand Chamberlain, the Duc de Bassano. All that could be hastily told he told me, between his sobs. "Come to-morrow, ask for me, and you shall see our dear Emperor." I went, and the veteran led me into the chamber of death. Two Sisters knelt by the bedside. I was alone with them—and the Dead.

There was at Camden Place, when I sought out Sir Henry Thompson, one who could have greatly enlightened me; at the moment I did not know him, even by name. Later I enjoyed the friendship of the Comte de La Chapelle, and I have retained it to this day. Moreover, I am honoured by the friendship of his eldest son, the Vicomte, who has rendered me infinite service in this essay to portray the Comedy and the Tragedy of the Second Empire.

The Comte de La Chapelle of the sixties and seventies—to-day, alas! but the shadow of his former self—was the confidant, the trusted and devoted friend and collaborator, of the Emperor, and equally the ami fidèle of "Napoléon IV." He was a born fighter—with the pen, which, in his hand, was of more account than the sword. Much of what I thirsted to know on the Ninth of January, 1873—the fatal day at "Camden"—the Comte de La Chapelle could have told me at the moment. I console myself with the reflection that had he told me all he knew, and had I written it, the "Morning Post" would assuredly never have printed it—it was too tragic. I published in 1910 what this chivalrous friend of Napoleon III. knew a few hours after those last words had been murmured—"Etiez-vous à Sedan, Conneau?" And it gratified me not a little to find that many of the eminent critics who reviewed "The Empress Eugénie" in such generous terms selected that particular passage for comment or for quotation.

-----

[139] London: Harper and Brothers. New York: Charles Scribner's Sons. 1910.

I must explain the status of the Comte de La Chapelle, who is the Empress Eugénie's junior by four and M. Ollivier's by five years. He descends from an essentially French Royalist family of Périgord, in the department of the Dordogne. His father was an officer of the bodyguard of Louis XVIII., and it was only a few years before his death that he forgave his son for seceding from the Royalist party and devoting himself heart and soul to the Imperialist cause. Perhaps it was the surviving Count's Gascon blood which made him so energetic in the defence of Bonapartist interests at a time when they had fewest supporters.

After twenty years of travel in America and Australia the Count returned to Europe in 1869, and throughout the campaign of 1870 did the "Standard" splendid service as one of its war "specials," a post for which he was eminently fitted. His admirable volume, "La Guerre de 1870," was the first war-book given to the public. In 1872 there appeared, with the Count's name on the title-page, "Les Forces Militaires de la France en 1870." The authorship of this striking work was immediately attributed to Napoleon III., it being argued that none but the Emperor could possibly have obtained so much official information concerning the condition of the army at the beginning of the war. It was generally believed that this "Comte de La Chapelle" was a pseudonym adopted by the Emperor. This was an error, the fact being that the Count had become the collaborateur attitré of the august Exile at Chislehurst, who wished his friend to assume the nominal authorship of the volume. In 1873 the indefatigable and versatile Count—the most genial and generous of men—issued "Les Œuvres Posthumes de Napoléon III."; and among his other works were "Paysans, on vous trompe,"[140] "Les Représentants du l'Appel au Peuple," and "Déclarations des Napoléon," this last containing a characteristic message from the Prince Imperial, whose claims to the throne were fervently and cogently set forth by the Count.

When "Les Forces Militaires de la France en 1870" appeared the Bonapartist journals, as well as papers of another colour, declined to review it! The Comte de La Chapelle was the man to get it "noticed." At the Emperor's request he took several copies of the brochure to Paris, for personal distribution among the editors and reviewers of the leading papers. In one copy the Emperor wrote his own name, and commended the work to the attention of the well-known publicist, M. Saint-Genest (a nom de plume), of the "Figaro," which at the time was hostile to Napoleon III. Saint-Genest was himself inimical to the fallen Sovereign, but he was an eminently just man, and a day or two after he had received the brochure from the Count he wrote an elaborate, and scrupulously fair, review of it in the then unfriendly "Figaro." Other papers followed Saint-Genest's courageous lead, and in the end the Emperor's convincing pamphlet was widely reviewed. We may be certain that the Emperor did not think the less of the Comte de La Chapelle for this triumph.

In those days the Emperor was generally derided by the French Press, which, as M. Émile Ollivier has recently shown in the fifteenth volume of his masterly work, "L'Empire Libéral," and also in the "Revue des Deux Mondes," drove him into the declaration of war. The Comte de La Chapelle and Paul de Cassagnac

[140] "Peasants, you are being deceived."

were almost the only supporters of the Emperor. Inertia prevailed amongst a large section of the Bonapartists, and probably they felt somewhat ashamed of their slackness when they read De La Chapelle's fiery and pungent exhortations, which afforded the Emperor the greatest consolation. But there was reason in what the admiring Prince Imperial said to the Count after His Majesty's death: "Not everybody here likes you."

It is with sincere gratification that I now introduce as narrator the venerable Count's eldest son.

Reminiscences of Bazaine, Napoleon III., and the Prince Imperial.[141]

Marshal Bazaine,[142] immediately after his escape from the Island of St. Marguerite, came direct to London, saw my father, and sought an interview with the Empress Eugénie at Chislehurst. It was reported at the time that the Marshal did not, as he was originally said to have done, escape from the fortress by means of a rope, but owed his liberty to a friendly (and bribed) gaoler. Bazaine himself, however, told my father that he freed himself with the aid of a rope, and he showed his much-lacerated hands as evidence of the truth of his assertion. My father was once discussing with Napoleon III. the question of the Marshal's generally assumed treachery, when the Emperor said: "Pas traître, pas traître; mais, mais!"—accompanying the two last words with a significant shake of the head and a very serious look.

My father often had confidential talks with the Emperor, sometimes for hours together, and at such times Napoleon would get the Count to relate his adventures and experiences in the various countries which he had visited. These little stories greatly interested and diverted the Emperor, and aroused his old enthusiasm.

Some time before the death of Napoleon III. determined efforts were made to bring about a restoration of the Empire, and my father and a few — very few — others were let into the secret.[143] I remember, as a small boy, my father concealing in the lining of the hat which he wore when travelling important documents entrusted to him by the Emperor for transmission abroad, especially to Paris. At the same time my father was "shadowed" everywhere by the detectives of the French Republic, and subjected to the greatest annoyance. The propaganda for the restoration of the Empire continued even after the Emperor's death.

When, after his release from captivity at Wilhelmshöhe, the Emperor arrived in this country, in March, 1871, he was very short of money, and through my father's untiring efforts large sums were raised for His Majesty and for the Resto-

[141] Communicated by the Vicomte de La Chapelle (1911). The Comte de La Chapelle's dramatic description of the painful scene at Camden Place, Chislehurst, on the day of the Emperor's death is given in the volume, "The Empress Eugénie: 1870-1910." London: Harper and Brothers. New York: Charles Scribner's Sons. 1910.

[142] He had been convicted of treason in December, 1870, but the death-sentence was commuted to twenty years' imprisonment. He escaped on August 9, 1874.

[143] The Vicomte thus confirms the assertions on this point published in "The Empress Eugénie: 1870-1910." London: Harper and Brothers. New York: Charles Scribner's Sons. 1910.

ration propaganda. I mention this because it was falsely reported that the Emperor had left France taking a great deal of money with him. As a matter of fact, when the Emperor reached Chislehurst his finances were at a very low ebb. In my father's own words, "Il était très gêné" (he was very short of cash).

THE COMTE A. DE LA CHAPELLE.

Collaborator and Friend of the Emperor Napoleon III.

A private photograph, lent for this work by the Vicomte de La Chapelle.

The Prince Imperial, as many are probably aware, was an excellent swordsman. He attended regularly at Bertrand's fencing academy, in Warwick Street, Regent Street, where the courteous maître d'armes, a fencer of the old school, used to put the Prince through his lessons with much dignity and infinite ceremony. M. Bertrand passed away long since; but there may still be seen in the academy over which he so worthily presided a bust of the Prince, his foils, his épées de combat, and other of his weapons, which, on one occasion, the veteran professor, with pathetic solemnity, allowed me to handle when I was a favoured pupil many years ago.

The Prince was also a first-rate rider, and my father has often told me with what agility the imperial youth would vault into the saddle. It was really this cleverness in mounting which cost him his life when he and his party were surprised by the Zulus on June 1, 1879. Lieutenant Carey (who, whatever may be said to the contrary, *was* in command of the ill-fated reconnoitring-party) gave the order to mount, and the Prince, in attempting to vault into the saddle, put a great strain either on the flap or the girth, with the result that it gave way, and the Prince fell to the ground. By this time the Zulus were close upon him, but were checked in their advance by two of the troopers (who had not "bolted"), until they were both killed by assegais. Then our dear, brave little Prince drew his sword, and, with a skilled fencer's natural instinct, endeavoured to ward off the spears, which were now thrown at only a few yards' distance. With his sword he contrived to deflect some of the assegais, but they came so rapidly and numerously that ultimately he was struck in one of his eyes and pierced in various places. I need say no more.

The exuberant spirits of the Prince Imperial may be illustrated by this little story: One day, at Camden Place, he invited my father to a bout at singlestick. The result of a very unequal match was that in a few minutes the Prince so belaboured my father that he was black and blue all over his body, and scarcely able to move for three or four days! My father often laughed over this incident, but my mother was very angry with the Prince.

CHAPTER XXI

FINANCING THE EMPEROR AND "THE CAUSE"

COMTE DE LA CHAPELLE'S LETTERS TO NAPOLEON III.[144]

The "Subscription" Assured.

To His Majesty the Emperor.

Undated.

SIRE,

I do not know how to express to your Majesty how grieved I am because of the mishap which has occurred, and of which I am the involuntary cause.

Mr. — —, instead of going to Cowes on Friday, as had been arranged, was obliged to spend the day in the City, and he sent word to me in the evening to inquire whether he might present himself before your Majesty on the following day, and whether I could accompany him. As for me, believing that he was going away, and thinking that I had two or three days' time, I went to Belgium, and only returned yesterday evening.

As Mr. — — did not find me, he thought that he ought to wait for me, and it was only this morning that I was able to get this explanation. He is annoyed to think that your Majesty waited for him. He again repeated to me what he had intended to say himself to your Majesty on the subject of the subscription. He only requires a few more days to complete his business connected with the railways. "And then," he said, "I shall carry out my promises to a large extent, and you can, in presenting my humble respects and excuses to the Emperor, give the assurance to His Majesty that I and my friends ..." [The concluding words are undecipherable.]

(Signed) A. DE LA CHAPELLE.

Anxious Moments, but "Good Results" hoped for.

To His Majesty the Emperor.

August 6, 1872.

[144] Communicated by the Vicomte de La Chapelle (1911).

Sire,

I have been very busy taking various measures, but I regret to say that for some weeks past I have encountered obstacles which seem likely to delay the realization of promises.

In a number of instances the impression produced by the [war] loan has cooled the ardour which had been first shown, and has deferred the engagements; in other cases I have to combat the animosity or the actions of people who, after having had relations with the Empire, have had the indelicacy to borrow on their own account and to speculate on their relations with the Emperor.

Thus I am obliged to reassure myself of the co-operation of those who were most inclined to subscribe large amounts. I must confess to your Majesty that these matters cause me anxious moments, and the disappointments which I meet with would discourage me if I did not summon all my energy and call to mind that it is absolutely necessary for me to attain the object proposed.

Finally, Mr. — — is expected in London on Saturday next, and as soon as I have been able to see him I shall telegraph to inquire on what day your Majesty could receive him.

I am still in hope that all promises in this direction will be fulfilled, and that, with his co-operation and that of his friends, we shall obtain good results.

(Signed) A. DE LA CHAPELLE.

£10,000 Available for the Emperor, in Instalments of £2,000.

To His Majesty the Emperor.

Undated.

Sire,

I have this morning imparted to Mr. — — the idea which your Majesty had the kindness to express in a telegram, and I explained, moreover, how urgent it seemed to me to procure funds for the French Press.

Mr. — — replied that he would certainly bring to a happy conclusion the combination entered into by himself and some friends, in order to realize a substantial subscription, but that he still required a little time.

"Nevertheless," he added, "I can already place at the Emperor's service a sum of 250,000 francs [£10,000], as an instalment of the subscription which I and my friends are collecting, but I should desire that this amount be [? payable] by instalments of 50,000 francs [£2,000] each, at intervals of a few days."

Mr. — — will leave for Paris on Saturday next, to remain there eight days, and if your Majesty would kindly at once send his orders, the address of his offices is....

As for me, I shall await your Majesty's decision as to whether I should go to Cowes or remain in London.

Your Majesty will, perhaps, think that [our] success is still far from being equal to what was looked for; but, notwithstanding all [the] steps taken, and all my zeal, more time is required than I had expected; this worries me very much.

(Signed) A. DE LA CHAPELLE.

M. Rouher receives £2,000 for the Emperor.

To His Majesty the Emperor.

September 8, 1872.

SIRE,

M. Rouher has received the 50,000 francs [£2,000] announced, and since the Emperor will be back at Camden Place on October 1, I shall have the honour to explain the situation to your Majesty.

Mr. — — has received his picture of the Battle of Sedan, and he asks me to inquire of your Majesty whether he would be allowed to have it taken to Camden Place for inspection by the Imperial Family.

Having been obliged to give up the publication of the "International," I have made arrangements to begin next week the publication of a little daily paper, in English and French, with the title "Paris and London News."

The principal object which I aim at is to resuscitate the "Telegraphic Despatch," begun last year, but appealing to the English and French public, as well as to the Press.

I shall remain anonymous in order not to be annoyed in France, and in order to lend more force to my pathetic telegrams.

In order to keep the secret I have acquired a little printing-office ... for pamphlets and books.

... All my plans, but altogether the desire to be of use, which I trust your Majesty will pardon me.

(Signed) A. DE LA CHAPELLE.

The Count in Contact with "Influential Persons of all Countries."

To His Majesty the Emperor.

September 15, 1872.

SIRE,

Having returned to London, I hasten to place myself at your Majesty's disposal.

In compliance with the request made, I called on M. Rouher on Thursday morning, the 12th inst., to ask him at what time he would receive Mr. — —. I was told that he had not arrived, and that the date of his arrival was not known.

At Mr. — —'s request, I returned the next day, the 13th, but was no more successful than the previous day, so that Mr. — — left Paris without being able to comply with the letter which your Majesty had the kindness to write him, and in which your Majesty expressed the wish that he should spend the 12th with M. Rouher. He wished to know to-day what he ought to do.

M. de — —, an intimate friend of a relation of mine, has sent me a booklet, which I enclose for your Majesty. He is the author of it, and he would be glad, when publishing another edition shortly, to insert any rectification which might be pointed out.

During my stay in Paris my business in connection with railways brought me into contact with influential persons of all countries, and I was convinced that solid progress had been made in favour of our cause, and that people were looking forward to the future. A crisis is believed to be inevitable in connection with the interest on the loans,[145] and this is thought to be the rock which will wreck M. Thiers's boat.

The propaganda against the Empire is prosecuted at Paris, and as for us, we do not seem to have any organization.

(Signed) A. DE LA CHAPELLE.

"Fully Subscribed."

To His Majesty the Emperor.

September 17, 1872.

SIRE,

Mr. — — gives orders by this evening's post to pay to-morrow a sum of 50,000 francs [£2,000] at M. Rouher's, and in a few days' time he will pay 200,000 francs [£8,000]; the remainder of the subscription will be paid as soon as his business with the "Era" is terminated.

I am busy with various matters which I hope will have good results, and as soon as I have succeeded I will hasten to inform the Emperor. May your Majesty deign to accept the homage of my profound respect and my perfect devotion!

(Signed) A. DE LA CHAPELLE.

---

[145] The loans for paying the war indemnity of five milliards (£200,000,000).

P.S.—The funds of Mr. — —'s subscription will be paid in Paris through the intermediary of Mr. — —, his agent.

Payment Delayed.

To His Majesty the Emperor.

Undated.

Sire,

M. — —, agent to M. — — at Paris, has several times called on M. Rouher without being able to see him. It seems that he is in the country.

The paying of the funds is consequently delayed, which is not our fault. I will ask them to see about it again.

The picture of the Battle of Sedan, with the report of the Prince of Prussia, has been bought by M. — —, and as the Government has caused the photographic negatives to be broken, I have suggested that the picture should be reproduced in London on a large scale, and that copies should be distributed in France.

If the Emperor does not disapprove of the project, it will be carried out as soon as the picture reaches London.

In a few days' time several persons who have promised to subscribe will have returned to town, and I shall call on them and remind them of their promises.

I have several times been tempted to go to Cowes to have the honour to present my respects to the Emperor, but have feared to be troublesome.

(Signed) A. DE LA CHAPELLE.

A "Subscription," not a "Loan."

To His Majesty the Emperor.

Undated.

Sire,

Mr. — — having sent for me and asked me whether, because of a letter received from the Emperor, he ought to change what had been arranged between us with regard to payments, I replied that I did not know, but that it seemed to me that in the letter the purchase of newspapers had been mentioned, and that he would be able to settle the question at the rendezvous at M. Rouher's to which he is invited for September 12.

He then added: "I shall arrange to pay a larger amount at one time for the needs of the cause and the purchase of newspapers."

I take the liberty of again repeating to your Majesty that it is here only a question of *subscription*, and not a *loan*; and if I dwell on this point it is because I desire to make it plain that I have never departed from the letter of the mission confided to me.

I intend leaving London for five or six days, but if your Majesty had any command or instructions for me, I should be happy to get a telegram, and to delay my departure, which was to be to-morrow, Saturday, evening.

My journey is connected with the reappearance of my paper; for I was obliged to give up the plans of the "International," partly because promises have not been kept, and partly in order to separate myself from a circle which might have injured our cause.

(Signed) A. DE LA CHAPELLE.

Telegram to "Comte de Pierrefonds."[146]

*From Count de La Chapelle to Comte de Pierrefonds,
Marine Hotel, Cowes (Isle of Wight).*

Have seen Mr. — —, and have arranged matters with him. Shall write particulars by next post.

Received telegram. Could not meet yet Mr. — —. Shall endeavour to see him to-night, and shall telegraph his answer.

"Before long I will give you the Highest Mark of Confidence."—*Napoleon III.*

To His Highness the Prince Imperial of France.

March, 1873.

MONSEIGNEUR,

Being entirely deprived of the happiness of seeing your Highness, I take the liberty of addressing these few words to you.

His Majesty the Emperor was kind enough to count on my devotion, and until a few days ago[147] I was honoured by His friendship and His valued confidence.

I loved the Emperor with all my soul. He commanded my life, and He knew it.

One month before the terrible catastrophe which has so grievously befallen us, the Emperor pronounced these words: "Before long, dear M. de La Chapelle, I will give you the highest mark of confidence which I can give you." I bowed. I felt myself the happiest of men; I felt that I could do anything if the Emperor commanded. These kind words I shall always guard in my memory, and I have long since vowed that I would be to the son what I had desired to be to the father.

[146] The Emperor.
[147] The Emperor died on January 9.

Thus you see, Monseigneur, that, happen what may, whether or not I shall be allowed to see you often, you will always find me ready to abandon everything, and place my devotion and my humble services at your disposal, only too happy if your Majesty will deign to accept them.

(Signed) A. DE LA CHAPELLE.

Comte de Clary to the Comte de La Chapelle.

CAMDEN PLACE, CHISLEHURST,
December 30, 1871.

DEAR FRIEND,

I have duly received your letter, and I at once handed the enclosure to the Empress. Her Majesty read it with interest, and thanks you. Moreover, she charges me to tell you that if during your stay in Paris, you should hear anything of interest, she would be pleased to hear of it. Au revoir, dear friend. Please present my respects to Mme. de La Chapelle, and accept my sincerest wishes on the occasion of the New Year. It is terribly cold here.

Very affectionately yours,
(Signed) COMTE DE CLARY.

From the Same to the Same.

CAMDEN PLACE, CHISLEHURST,
January 1, 1872.

Just a line, dear friend, to let you know that the Empress and the Prince Imperial will be most happy to see you to-morrow, Sunday, in the afternoon. Till to-morrow. And I shall be very happy to shake hands with you.

Yours faithfully,
COMTE DE CLARY.

Conversation with the Prince Imperial.

March 9, 1873.

The Prince said to me:

"I know what great confidence the Emperor placed in you, and I know how fond he was of you. I know how devoted you were to him. Not everybody here likes you; but, as for me, do not forget that I feel for you the same attachment that my father did, and I hope that you will often come to see me and speak to me of my poor father."

Then we went on to discuss the situation. The Prince confided to me certain secrets regarding the organization of the party; then he asked me what the intentions of his father might have been on this or that point.

I answered.

"Well, then," he said, "I shall act in the same way when the opportunity occurs, and, as regards what is now going on, I intend to make a complete change in a year's time, and to take the initiative myself, which is my due."

After having given an account to the Prince of the plans of my friends, finances, and the elections, he repeated that he depended on me ... and I was to come and see him often.

(Signed) A. DE LA CHAPELLE.

Letter from Émile Zola to the Comte de La Chapelle.

MÉDAN,
July 15, 1892.

DEAR SIR,

I thank you heartily for your kindness in sending me the reply which you were good enough to send to the question of the "Figaro."

It is calculated to make me feel very proud, and I assure you that I am greatly touched because of the solid support which it gives to the historical portion of my work.[148] I shall always be extremely grateful to you.

Believe me, Sir,
Very truly and cordially yours,
(Signed) ÉMILE ZOLA.

THE EMPEROR'S LETTER TO M. ROUHER.[149]

CHISLEHURST,
le 12 J., 1871.

MON CHER MONSIEUR ROUHER,

Je vous écris pour vous faire faire la connaissance de M[r.] de La Chapelle, littérateur distingué, qui a publié un récit très bien fait de la campagne de 1870, et qui m'a donné des preuves de dévouement dont je suis fort touché.

Recevez la nouvelle assurance de ma sincère amitié,

NAPOLÉON.

---

[148] The Comte de La Chapelle had supported Zola in the Press respecting one of the historical passages in "La Débâcle."

[149] See the facsimile on the previous page.

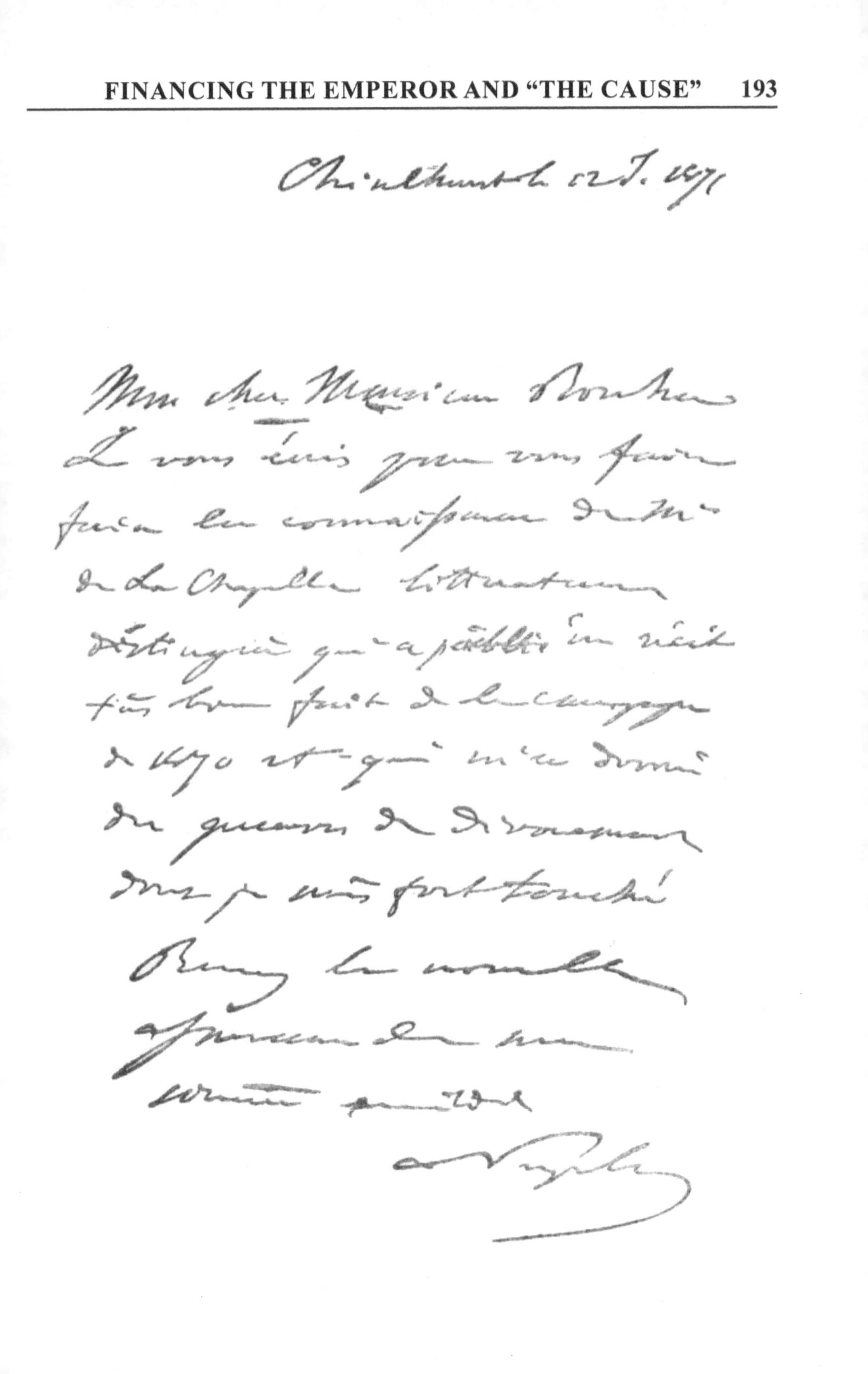

TRANSLATION.

CHISLEHURST,
June 12, 1871.

MY DEAR MR. ROUHER,

I am writing in order that you may make the acquaintance of M. de La Chapelle, a distinguished littérateur, who has published a very admirable account of the campaign of 1870, and who has given me proofs of devotion which have greatly touched me.

Receive this new assurance of my sincere friendship,

NAPOLÉON.

CHAPTER XXII

THE MAN WHO GAVE THE WARNING
—M. PIETRI'S LETTRES RÉVÉLATRICES

The Man was Colonel Baron Stoffel.

And Colonel Stoffel was the French Military Attaché at Berlin from 1866 until 1870.

This clear-headed artillery officer, ever on the alert, saw what would inevitably happen sooner or later, and he bombarded his Government with warning reports, which were either pigeon-holed by Ministers, after a perfunctory glance at their contents, or perused and treated as waste-paper. Those who assume (which I do not, and never shall) that Napoleon III. was, as a Ruler, as black as his detractors have painted, and continue to paint, him, will now learn for the first time that, while in the highest military circles Stoffel's repeated warnings of Prussia's preparations for war were scoffed at, and he himself regarded by many at the Tuileries as a bird of ill omen, the Emperor attached the utmost importance to his Military Attaché's reports,[150] insisted, through M. Pietri, upon being kept fully informed of what was being done by Prussia, and did his best to prepare his forces for the struggle which he, like Stoffel, foresaw in the near future. We know all this now, and how we know it I will presently show. As, however, Stoffel[151] is the hero of this chapter, his personality must not be neglected.

His career was a remarkable one. From 1862 until 1865 he was prosaically employed in superintending the excavations at Alise, which had been begun in 1861 by that enthusiastic archæologist, Napoleon III. In 1860 Stoffel, then an artillery Captain in garrison at Auxonne, saw for the first time Mont Auxois. He went over the ground, Cæsar's "Commentaries" in hand, and noticed how closely the locality tallied with the description given of it by the conqueror of Gaul. Shortly afterwards Stoffel published in the "Moniteur" (August 6 and 7, 1860) "Une Étude sur l'Emplacement d'Alesia," which attracted the attention of the Emperor, who was then working upon his "Histoire de Jules César," a work of which he himself said, one day, he wrote very little, owing to his somewhat slight knowledge of Latin.

Stoffel was rewarded by being made Chef d'Escadrons and Officier d'Ordonnance to the Emperor. In 1862 the Commission de la Topographie des Gaules published Stoffel's "Étude" through the medium of the imperial printing-office. Stof-

---

[150] Colonel Stoffel's Reports were published in 1871 under the title, "Rapports Militaires Ecrits de Berlin: 1866-1870." Paris: Garnier.

[151] The Colonel died in 1907, aged eighty-eight.

fel showed that Cæsar's statements were absolutely accurate, and that the whole army of Vercingetorix might well have been located on Mont Auxois and not have lacked a water-supply. In 1866 Stoffel became Military Attaché at Berlin.

At the Tuileries, one morning, the Emperor, accosting Stoffel, said: "General Bourbaki assures me that you take an exaggerated view of the qualities of the Prussian General Staff, and that you do not sufficiently recognize the abilities of our own Staff." Stoffel, a very outspoken man, replied: "Sire, the General is deceived. In order to form a correct opinion of the Prussian and the French Staffs, one must have seen both of them.... Supposing there were two pictures of Rubens, one measuring six feet and the other eight feet— —" Here he was stopped by the Empress, who, seeing that he was warming to his subject, began talking to him, so that Stoffel had to break off what he was saying to the Emperor in order to listen to the Empress! And nothing more was said about the respective merits of the Prussian and French General Staffs.

General Bourbaki was as optimistic as Stoffel, fortified by his knowledge of facts and his prescience, was the reverse. Two years before the war the General, as Chef de Mission, followed the Prussian army manœuvres along the Rhine. He could not help noticing the rapid fire of the Prussian infantry, but his only official comment was this very inept one: "The needle-gun (fusil à aiguille) is certainly a formidable weapon, but in other matters we have nothing to learn from the Prussians!" Bourbaki was a brave soldier, but a corporal of the Scots Guards could have taught him much that would have been very useful to him.

One day, after the war, when the wounds of France were still open, as Stoffel was lunching at a Paris restaurant, Bourbaki entered, saw Stoffel, and, with tears in his eyes, said: "Ah, Colonel, I deceived the Emperor, but unintentionally. *Had we listened to you we should have escaped our misfortunes.* As a loyal soldier, I ask you to forgive me!" This showed a noble heart, certainly; but all the mischief had been done.

Not long after the death of the Emperor, Marshal Lebœuf, who, I remember, had been present at the imperial obsequies, again made his way to Chislehurst, mainly, it would seem, to perform an act of duty, for Colonel Stoffel (who chanced to be visiting England at the time) saw the Marshal[152] kneeling at the Emperor's tomb, contritely murmuring, "Pardon, Sire!"

While the war was still raging, the "Times" printed some extracts from Stoffel's reports, and in its editorial columns expressed the opinion—which all military experts must have endorsed—that it was a puzzle how anyone who had read those documents could ever have dreamt of plunging France into a conflict with Prussia.

Had Colonel Stoffel's warnings been acted upon by the Ministers of Napoleon III., France, in all likelihood, would have been saved from her disasters, and the Prince Imperial have been the reigning Emperor to-day. After all his great services,

---

[152] M. Émile Ollivier, writing in the "Revue des Deux Mondes" (December 1, 1910), proves that Lebœuf was absolutely accurate when, in July, 1870, he said emphatically, "Nous sommes prêts, archi-prêts" (We are ready—more than ready).

how was Stoffel treated? *Thiers dismissed him from the army on some frivolous pretext!*

M. Pietri's Letters to Stoffel.[153]

I.

BIARRITZ, *September 27, 1866.*

MY DEAR STOFFEL,

The Emperor has read the report which you sent to the Ministry of War. He waited for it two or three days, and was obliged to send for it. You did well to tell me about it. His Majesty, before receiving it, dictated to me the following questions, in all of which the Emperor is particularly interested:

1. How are the officers of the [German] Landwehr selected and named?

2. Where do they come from?

3. How many of them are there in each battalion of infantry and in each squadron?

4. Where are the horses for the squadrons of the Landwehr obtained?

5. Is the uniform of the Landwehr the same as that of the army? Or in what respects do the uniforms differ?

6. How much does the knapsack of the infantry weigh?

7. How many hospital-men per battalion follow into the battle-field?

8. How are the parks of artillery organized?

9. How are the requisite horses obtained?

The Emperor dictated to me all these questions for you somewhat hurriedly, and I think he will have others connected with them which you will be able to put and decide yourself, principally concerning the organization of the Landwehr. You have doubtless heard that His Majesty is greatly occupied with the question of increasing our military forces by the formation in France of a Landwehr system. All the information which you can send on these points will be welcomed [by the Emperor].

*   *   *   *   *

---

[153] M. Pietri's deeply-interesting and historically-important letters appeared in the influential and deservedly popular magazine, the "Revue de Paris," on June 15 and July 1, 1911. I am greatly indebted to the Editor of the "Revue de Paris" for very kindly allowing me to print some extracts from these valuable documents, which are "revelations" in the best sense of the word.

II.

Compiègne,
November 21, 1866.

My dear Friend,

I thank you for the interesting details which you have sent me. I perused them with much pleasure, and read them to the Emperor, for whom they arrived very à propos. The Commission for the Reorganization of the Army has begun its labours, and His Majesty has found in your letter ideas and appreciations upon certain members of this Commission which could not easily have been given to him viva voce; whilst, coming from afar, in a private letter, these opinions contained nothing disagreeable; moreover, it was not possible to question their sincerity. Several meetings [of the Commission] have already been held, at which there was more or less verbiage—many ridiculous ideas, and especially an immense quantity of blagues on the part of a misunderstood General T— —,[154] and of our Cousin.[155] The Emperor made them all come to Compiègne and work hard. At last they left yesterday, and will meet again a week hence. In the interval they will study the Emperor's plan [which was ultimately adopted].

*   *   *   *   *

That, in general, is the scheme which is about to be studied in detail. I wished to send it to you, but only thirty copies were printed, and the Emperor is very niggardly over them. Before closing my letter I will ask him if he will send you a copy, and if he consents you will find it enclosed.

And now I have to communicate two matters to you by the Emperor's order.

1. To send you the enclosed packet containing papers relating to the war budgets of Prussia and of France. The Emperor has been struck by the relatively small amount of the Prussian war budget as compared with that of France, and also by the figures for the maintenance of two armies almost equal in number. His Majesty wishes you to compare the figures now sent to you with the amounts which in Prussia are allocated to the same object as with us, in order to see what economic ameliorations may be made in our administrative system. Your report upon this subject will be of the greatest use to His Majesty, who has appointed a subcommission, formed of members of the Commission, and charged with the study of the administrative and economic details, discipline, etc., etc.

---

[154] General Trochu, the valiant soldier who deserted the Empress in her great extremity (September, 1870).

[155] Prince Napoleon, father of the Bonapartist Pretender of to-day.

2. Could you procure the new rifle which has been submitted to the King of Prussia?[156] The Emperor wishes you to do all that is possible to get one. Let me know if you have need of *means* for that purpose. I am not directed to mention this to you; but should you require any [funds], I will set about getting you some.

We have been at Compiègne a week. We had one essentially military evening, which was attended by twenty-four members of the Commission, yet was very gay and pleasant. If you want to know the names of some of the ladies, les voici: the sweet and beautiful Mme. de Chasseloup-Laubat[157]; Mme. Lejeune; the little Palikaos,[158] the eldest of whom is *charming*; the little Bruats,[159] etc., etc.; and Mlle. de Lagrenée, to whose memory I recalled you, thinking that it would be agreeable to you.... I have become a sportsman enragé, and I am going to ask to be admitted into the vénerie.[160]... The Emperor continues very well, better than ever.... Your offer to send some books is accepted [by the Emperor]. Select the most interesting, and send them to me—with your *bill*. Duperré[161] sends you a thousand remembrances.

III.

Paris,

January 3, 1867.

M. le Lieutenant-Colonel!
(That looks exceedingly well.)

... I am sending this letter through the Foreign Office. It will reach you slower than by the ordinary post, but more surely.[162] "Chi va piano, va sano; chi va sano, va lontano."[163] This is a proverb, and proverbs are the wisdom of nations.

You asked me in your last letter to tell you exactly the kind of rifle the Emperor wanted a specimen of. His Majesty has no choice. He wants a specimen of a rifle which might be adopted by the Prussian army; or to know the state of perfection to which the old rifle has been brought—supposing that steps have been taken to modify it. In a word, His Majesty wishes to be au courant of

[156] The needle-gun (Zundnadelgewehr), first used by the Prussians in warfare that year (1866) in the Austrian campaign.

[157] Wife of the Minister of Marine in 1851, and again from March, 1859, until January, 1867.

[158] Daughters of General Cousin-Montauban, Comte de Palikao.

[159] Daughters of Admiral Bruat (who died at sea on returning from the Crimea to France).

[160] The Imperial Hunt.

[161] A devoted ally of the Empress Eugénie. He survives in 1911.

[162] M. Pietri hints that the Prussian postal officials were "très indiscrets."

[163] "Who goes slowly, goes well. Who goes well, goes far."

the armament of the Prussian army. You need not, then, concern yourself with the various specimens which may be offered [to the military authorities], but only with the rifle which might be adopted....

*   *   *   *   *

The cost of the army will be diminished rather than increased, but you will find that the patriotism of our speakers will consider the expense still too heavy, and that they will do their best to create the belief that the French people are governed by buveurs de sang.[164] What fun the Prussians will make of us and the esprit militaire of the valiant French nation!...

... The Emperor continues in excellent health.... His Majesty directs me to put the four following questions to you:

1. What is the weight of the Prussian knapsack? What does it contain?

2. What is the weight of the Prussian cavalry saddle, and what weight does the horse carry beyond the weight of the rider?

3. How is the Prussian soldier shod? Does he wear boots, or shoes and gaiters?

4. Is the uniform of the Landwehr provided by the State, or paid for by the man who wears it?

IV.

Paris,
December 27, 1867.

My dear Stoffel,

Your two letters greatly interested me. What you tell me of the state of opinion and the ideas of the Prussians does not surprise me. I have always been among those who think that we are detested on the other side of the Rhine, and it has not been necessary for me to read the journals and pamphlets published in Germany. Although the German pamphlets are ... little read in France, we hear a long, dull buzz much resembling hostile clamours.... I believe we shall not seek vain pretexts to make war; but if we are obliged to make it, we shall not have a moment's hesitation....

I read to the Emperor the greater part of your opinions on the feelings of the Prussians towards us....

V.

Paris,
January 8, 1868.

---

[164] Literally, "drinkers of blood"; figuratively, "bloodthirsty."

My dear Stoffel,

You should have received through the Foreign Office my last letter, containing *twelve hundred* francs [£48], and informing you that another sum is being sent from the same source.[165] You will find in this envelope the bank-note [for 1,000 francs = £40] referred to, which will be, I believe, the last you will receive. The prodigality of César Romain[166] will stop there, and if we had not any other resources there would be nothing for us to do but to ask M. Plon to give us a bed in the hospital which he intends to build in memory of the conqueror of the Gauls and of his historian [Napoleon III.]....

I urged you in my last letter to send all the information which you can obtain, and not to omit using for that purpose the "crowns" you will be able to get the Embassy to advance. His Majesty would like to have to-day a complete report upon *a new system of mobilization adopted by Prussia, by which she will be able to put all her troops on a war footing in nine days.* Possibly you have already sent such a report; send another in more detail....

VI.

PARIS,
March 22, 1868.

My dear Stoffel,

... What you told me in your last letter is quite just, as far as Germany is concerned, but I do not, like you, expect to see the Emperor reconcile himself easily to events which might happen, as he has done, or been forced to do, up to now. The conditions have changed, and if we have submitted to events against which it was impossible to oppose any obstacles, to-day we are ready to face, with calmness and confidence, those [events] which may be produced, and we have only to act in regard to our interests.... We must be in a state of constant observation, and work indefatigably to make ourselves the strongest.

It is necessary, in this connection, to render justice to Marshal Niel. Since he has been at the [War] Ministry he has accomplished veritable tours de force, and from this time, by the admissions of the most difficult, of the most prudent, and even of the timorous [or "scrupulous"], we can say that we are ready for all events.

... I have read to the — — [? Emperor] several extracts from your letters.

---

[165] It may be safely assumed that these amounts came from the Emperor's purse.
[166] The Emperor.

VII.

Paris,
May 28, 1868.

My dear Stoffel,

I have read, and caused to be read—and that with the greatest interest on my part and also on the part of the persons to whom I communicated them—the letters which you have sent me for some time past, and which I have not yet answered.... You appear to be highly thought of at the Ministry of War, where your Reports are appreciated in a manner very flattering to you.... I have seen one or two of these reports when with the Emperor, who always follows with the greatest attention the questions treated in your Reports.... All the details which you give upon the [Prussian] army, and everything connected with it—armaments, fortifications, etc.—are a very useful thermometer to consult, indicating very clearly the degree of temperature in which we find ourselves.

Your private letters are of an equally appreciable interest. Your relations with the B— — family[167] place you in a magnificent position, and you have a hundred times more advantages than the most wary diplomatist to observe and seize, in the family life, a crowd of tints which should enable you to judge soundly of the hopes which they form for the future, and of the degree of confidence or of fear which they have of the success of their plans. In my opinion, they [the Prussians] have taken a step in advance by the meeting of the Custom-house Parliament [Parlement douanier]. M. de B— —[168] has tried to restore the prestige of Prussia, which had begun to weaken, by remounting his war-horse, in order to repel the foreigner who wished to mix himself up in their affairs, and by appealing to German patriotism....

*   *   *   *   *

I am happy to tell you to-day that our military situation is superb. Never have we had so many resources—never a finer army. If you receive the "Moniteur," you will have been able to read Marshal Niel's report upon our armament and the quality of our rifles. This has been published in the official journal in answer to the reports circulated in Germany, and noted by you, which tended to create the belief that we had not obtained the results which we had expected from our rifles. At Châlons they are practising assiduously with the new rifle,[169] and as the men are much pleased with it, they apply themselves thoroughly to practising with and taking care of it.

[167] The Bismarcks.
[168] Bismarck.
[169] The chassepot.

... All these military exercises, joined to the other summer dé-placements, do the Emperor much good....

*   *   *   *   *

I have given to the Emperor the various maps which you sent me. They are very acceptable to His Majesty, who desires you to continue to forward everything new which you may find, and which is worth the trouble of sending. It is understood that you keep an account of all your expenses. The small atlases which you have sent for the Prince are excellent for teaching him geography, and the Emperor has given them to General Frossard.[170] If there are any others, you can buy them.

VIII.

FONTAINEBLEAU,
August 17, 1868.

MY DEAR STOFFEL,

I send you with this letter a memorandum which was dictated to me, and which requests you to explain some things mentioned therein. I preferred to send it in the shape of a memorandum rather than to copy it and add it to my letter, as the E. [the Emperor] told me to do....

[M. Pietri notes the Emperor's satisfaction with Colonel Stoffel's last two letters, and with his last reports to the War Minister, which His Majesty said were "très bien faits." The writer proceeds:]

I must tell you, on my own account, that I should think your admiration of the Prussian army and of the country itself was ex-aggerated if I did not know that you intentionally exaggerated your views of both a little, with an object which I understand—viz., to give France a good idea of the strength and vitality of those who may one day become our enemies, as to-day they are our adversaries. I believe everybody is in accord upon this point.... It has made us feel the necessity of making great efforts in order not to be outdistanced. These efforts have been made, and are being made every day.... We are ready for every event, big as it might be. That we have committed faults, no one, I think, will deny; that we have lacked foresight is not to be doubted; but from all that we have learnt a good lesson, and it is not to be believed that in future we shall leave even the smallest things to chance. If our diplomacy has not always been skilful, we must do it the justice of saying that for some time past it has not done badly by remaining

[170] Divisional-General Frossard, aide-de-camp of the Emperor, member of the Committee of Fortifications. Governor and chief of the Military Household of the Prince Imperial from 1868.

tranquil and by giving way, while not losing sight of things, but observing them attentively. We have been out of luck up to now, and we must hope that fortune will not delay to turn, and that it will bring us some good coups, of which we shall have to take clever advantage.

*   *   *   *   *

In the first week of December, 1868, the Court was at Compiègne. M. Pietri writes to Colonel Stoffel to say that at Compiègne everything was proceeding on traditional lines: hunting, shooting, rides and walks to Pierrefonds, and in the evening "monster dinners and dances." One improvement had been made: the barrel-organ, which the Emperor sometimes "ground," was replaced by a live pianist, M. Waldteuffel.

Writing from Paris on May 27, 1869, M. Pietri reproaches Stoffel for having left Paris without hearing Rossini's Mass. "I like it less than the *Stabat*, but that did not prevent me from going to hear it three times."

On December 10, in the same year, M. Pietri wrote to tell the Colonel that Paris was going through a crisis, and that men's minds were unsettled. Matters had not improved at the date of the next letter (February 4, 1870). Victor Noir had been shot by Prince Pierre Bonaparte, and on the next day Rochefort published in the "Marseillaise" an appeal to the people. Thus what was destined to be the "Terrible Year" began most unfortunately.

I am told (writes M. Pietri) that the English Government will insist upon Prussia disarming. It is thought that nothing would come from such a step, and that it would be un coup d'épée dans l'eau.... What do you think of it? Do you think that it would be sufficient to say to the Federal Chancellor, "You must disarm," to cause him to disarm? I should be curious to know what answer he would make to anybody who made such a proposition to him, and what he would really think and express privately. I am certain that he would make many promises without intending to keep one of them. No doubt you think as I do, and if you can find time (try to find it) tell me if I deceive myself.

In April, 1870, Colonel Stoffel was in Paris, and M. Pietri wrote on the 9th: "The Emperor wishes to see you to-morrow morning at ten. Be punctual, and come and breakfast with us."

After that date there is a gap in the correspondence. In a long letter, dated March 5, 1871, M. Pietri says: "What sorrows since we parted! More than once I thought I should go mad, and that my heart would be unable to withstand so many troubles. To look on powerlessly at the cutting of the throat of one's own country; to see all that one holds dearest ruined, destroyed; and, after the disasters caused by the foreigners, to foresee others caused by the madness of our citizens—are not these things sufficient to fill with despair the heart of every Frenchman who sincerely loves his country?..."

H.H. PRINCE ROLAND BONAPARTE.

President of the Geographical Society of France.
Father of H.R.H. Princess George of Greece.

Photographed by Boissonas et Taponier, Paris, and lent for this work by the Prince.

A week later M. Pietri writes to tell Stoffel that all the news coming from France is very sad. He despairs of the future. Then comes a most remarkable passage, which I take upon myself to emphasize, for it shows, as I have always argued—years before this book was written—that Colonel Stoffel, if his warnings had been taken, might, and probably would, have saved France. M. Pietri himself admits it, and there is no more trustworthy surviving authority than the Empress Eugénie's devoted Secretary and valued friend. M. Pietri writes to Stoffel: "I have always done you justice, and to-day more than ever *I recognize that you were right, and that if you had been listened to we should not have been where we are; but all were blind—Ministers, statesmen, the Deputies who were in the majority and those who formed the Opposition. Everybody worked against the country. The Emperor alone, perhaps, saw correctly, but, blocked every moment by the remarks of some and by the ill-will of others, he was carried away* [by the current] *and unable to carry out many of the plans which he had formed. I admit that he must bear the responsibility, for in this world there must always be a scapegoat; but* [public] *opinion will calm down, and by degrees will better appreciate the responsibility of each* [individual]. *The Emperor's responsibility will then be lessened.*" These are noble words, ringing with patriotism and a desire to render justice to The Man who gave the Warning. And I rejoice that the Editor of the "Revue de Paris" has so generously afforded me an opportunity of making the English peoples acquainted with the fact that France had in Colonel Stoffel the most devoted and most prescient of servants, who made it as clear as daylight, not once, but again and again, that Bismarck meant to have war and meant to goad France into beginning it. At Grenoble most of us have gazed admiringly at the statue of Bayard, the preux Chevalier, who was "sans peur et sans reproche." When will Paris "do the right thing" by Stoffel? *When?*

CHAPTER XXIII

PRINCE NAPOLEON
THE EMPRESS IN 1910-11

[⁂ THESE POLITICAL VIEWS OF H.I.H. PRINCE NAPOLEON NOW APPEAR FOR THE FIRST TIME IN CONCRETE FORM. QUESTIONED IN LONDON, IN JUNE, 1911, AS TO HIS "PROGRAMME," THE PRINCE REPLIED: "THE NAME OF BONAPARTE IS A PROGRAMME."]

IT has been recently said that I adhere to the Republic, the actual Government. That is an exaggeration. In the actual Government there are statesmen, men of order, and, without mentioning names, I may add that there are talented chiefs. I am, above all, a man of my epoch, a lover of progress. The time has gone for coups d'état and for proscriptions in France. I could, to-morrow, work with some past Ministers, or with some who are retiring. I should have considered it an honour to have voted for the social laws enacted by the Government. I think only that the laws ought to be prepared more juridically. A Council of State should give a legal shape to the informal opinions of legislators not thoroughly versed in the laws. That could be done without injury to Parliamentary initiative.

All régimes have some good in them. Take, for instance, the family of Louis Philippe. Well, Louis Philippe did some excellent things. He prepared the way for the Empire admirably. If I am not with the Extreme Left, I am still less with the Right. I have none of the ideas, none of the illusions, cherished by the Parliamentary party of the Right. I am in the Centre, with legality. I put my country above dynastic questions; I would not disturb order. I crave for the Revolution, the mother of all of us—the Revolution, from which modern France has sprung. It has been said that yesterday I asked that the "Marseillaise" should be played. At my marriage, which was celebrated privately, no national air was played; but in the evening a local band of musicians serenaded us. I was asked if I should like to hear the "Marseillaise," with the "Brabançonne"[171] and the Italian Hymn, and I heard it with a feeling of respect. Did it not precede the Eagles across Europe? The "Marseillaise" is the only French [national] hymn the Moncalieri bandsmen know. I was pleased with it. The words of the "Marseillaise" have now only an historic sense, and it was with that air that my great-uncle led his armies across the world.

I note with the deepest interest all that happens in France—everything that is done and everything that is said. I admit with pleasure that some excellent things

---

[171] The Belgian National Anthem.

are often done there. The longer we—nous autres Français—live abroad, the more we love our France. For me the word "Republic" always preserves its Latin sense, res publica (the "public thing"), but there were, and there still are, in France men who have regarded, and continue to regard, it in that sense, and I do not hesitate to say that I approve from the bottom of my heart their actions. Excellent things have been done for the army, for the military service; but more attention ought to have been paid to the cadres, in order to have assured the re-engagement of the bons sousofficers; more especially should anti-militarism not have been encouraged.

France has especially need of order. I am often accused of not concerning myself sufficiently with politics; but there they make a mistake. I think I should concern myself with politics still less. That Ministers of the Interior and of Foreign Affairs should be political Ministers is perfectly natural; but Commerce, Public Works, and Agriculture ought to be only administrations.[172] That a pension should be given to every Frenchman upon attaining a certain age is an idea which I entirely approve; but how many millions of francs would that cost, and where would they come from? No Government which increases the taxes would be popular.

The Empire! Do you really believe that France could still exist under all the laws of the First, and even of the Second, Empire? The times have progressed. We have railways, telephones, newspapers. The conditions of the peoples have changed. A good Government, you see, is one which, above all other things, sees to the needs of the epoch in which we live.

To be unable to visit our museums in France is one of the most painful phases of my exile. So much has been done for the museums: they have been so greatly enriched. My deep love of art suffers from my inability to inspect their treasures. What emotion I should feel at seeing again Fontainebleau and the Malmaison, where there are so many souvenirs of my family! And Versailles!

It seems to me that my exile, in proportion as it is prolonged, exalts the national sentiment in me. I love France as a good Frenchman, with a particular and disinterested affection. I am with all those who contribute to its greatness and prosperity, wherever they come from, and to whatever party they belong. They know me very imperfectly, and many errors have been spread about me. I am of my time; I am a man of progress. I do not live in the past, with old-fashioned sentiments. I desire above everything the well-being of my country. Narrow political formulas embarrass me only very slightly.

In all camps I see those who work to realize the greatness of France, and I am their unknown friend. I have never abandoned my own projects. Whether it is this one or that one who secures the happiness and greatness of France matters little to me—that, for me, is a secondary question. I am with all who collaborate for that purpose. France first! I am, beside, un sage. I do not believe in adventures. In a modern country the army alone is powerless to bring about a change of régime, if it has not behind it the assent and the willingness of the country.

---

[172] It was pointed out to the Prince that "la République a bien du monde à caser; elle a fait beaucoup d'enfants qui veulent être nourris et pensionnés."

One must know how to await opportunities, and never attempt to precipitate events.

*   *   *   *   *

M. Jules Delafosse, the eminent Deputy for Calvados, and a zealous member of H.I.H. Prince Napoleon's party, has defined "Bonapartism" as being, "not a doctrine," but "an absolutism":

> It is the régime which Napoleon I. inaugurated, and which Napoleon III. adopted, that is represented to-day by their dynastic heir [the Pretender]. At present no one occupies himself with Bonapartism, and the Prince does nothing to direct attention to himself. For the indifferent and the satisfied the Bonapartist programme is only a purely speculative indication, which is of no more value in their eyes than a prospectus; it will have no value until the Republic expires, and the Republic will not die until it has lost the right to live. That may come sooner than one imagines. The accidental causes which may any day sweep away the régime include the increasing dissatisfaction caused by the horrible unpopularity of Parliament, which is the visible figure and the hidden soul of the Republic. The spectacles which it daily gives us reproduce the prophetic features which mark the "agony," generally disgusting, of dying régimes. That, perhaps, is not a reason why the Empire should necessarily succeed it; but it is a reason for thinking of it. One may think of it in all ranks of society, and even in all camps, because the Empire is not a party, but a refuge. It is not impossible that the heir of the Napoleons may attain to power by the political paths that anarchy fatally opens to the predestined man. It is by the Consulate or the Presidency that the elect of his race were conducted to the throne. There is no worse servitude than that of oligarchies, those especially which have the appetites and passions of negroes. It is to this miserable condition of affairs—in which the germs of revolution are already, thank God! apparent—that Republican Parliamentarism has led us; and that is why from all hearts there rises the same cry of desire and of hope—"Exoriare aliquis!"

The years 1896 and 1898 were marked by exceptional exultation in the Bonapartist camp. In 1896 there were serious differences amongst the rival Orleanist factions. Some of the younger and more ardent Royalists, recalling the début in political life of Napoleon III., were desirous of putting forward the Duc d'Orléans as a Parliamentary candidate. The managing committee of the party, however, decided that "a son of France should not parody a Bonaparte." The Duc d'Audiffret Pasquier communicated this decision to the Duc d'Orléans, who curtly replied that the committee should have consulted him upon the subject before expressing an opinion. Pasquier repelled this snub by resigning his membership of the committee, which, guided by Buffet, De Broglie, and d'Haussonville, was accused by the stalwarts of lack of energy in the propaganda. A cleavage seemed imminent among the Royalist sections, for many Catholics abandoned the party, and the Pope repudiated it.

Taking advantage of the misfortunes of others, the Bonapartists became more of a militant party. On August 15, 1898 (the old Napoleonic fête-day), they mustered in force at a banquet, made speeches ridiculing the Republic, and cheered to the echo a letter from the Pretender containing a promise to "appear at the proper moment," which he declared to be "at hand." In the intervening thirteen years the Royalists have done most of the "shouting," or, rather, it has been done by the "Camelots du Roy," led by the two sons of the late Paul de Cassagnac, M. Léon Daudet, and even M. Henri Rochefort!

THE MARRIAGE AT MONCALIERI.

The marriage contract of Prince Napoleon and Princesse Clémentine was signed at Brussels on November 7, 1910.

The banns of marriage were published on October 9, on which day the sub-joined official announcement was affixed to the notice-board of the Hôtel de Ville at Brussels, where it remained for ten days, in compliance with the law:

> A marriage is to take place at Moncalieri (Italy) between his Imperial Highness Prince Napoleon Victor Gerome Frederick, domiciled in Paris, 8th Arrondissement (Seine, France), living at Brussels, No. 241, Avenue Louise, eldest son of his late Imperial Highness Prince Napoleon Joseph Charles Paul and of Her Imperial and Royal Highness the Dowager Princess Marie Clotilde Napoleon, Princess of Savoy, domiciled and residing at the Royal Castle of Moncalieri, near Turin (Italy), and Her Royal Highness Princess Clementine Albertine Marie Leopoldine, Princess of Belgium, Duchess of Saxe-Coburg-Gotha, domiciled at Brussels, No. 1, Place des Palais, eldest[173] daughter of his late Majesty Leopold Louis Philippe Marie Victor, Leopold II., King of the Belgians, Duke of Saxe, Prince of Saxe-Coburg-Gotha, and of her late Majesty Marie Henriette Anne, Queen of the Belgians, Archduchess of Austria.

English people of all creeds will learn with surprise and amusement that the Government of the French Republic will not allow Prince Napoleon to be described in official documents published in France as "Imperial"; nor may his father (the late Prince "Jérôme") or his mother (Princesse Clotilde, daughter of the renowned Victor Emmanuel II.) be so designated, even in banns of marriage.

Prince Napoleon was described in the "banns" published at Brussels and at Moncalieri as having a "domicile" in the 8th Arrondissement, Paris—as, in fact, he always has had, although the law prevents him from entering his native country. The document containing an announcement of the marriage was affixed to the wall of the Mairie of the 8th Arrondissement, Paris, but the words "Imperial"

---

[173] By inadvertence the Princess was described in the "banns" as the "eldest," instead of the "youngest," daughter of the late King and Queen!

and "domiciled in Paris" were suppressed by the "Parquet" (otherwise the Public Prosecutor).

Many who read the banns of marriage were probably surprised at finding that neither in that document nor in other official papers does Prince Napoleon use the historic name of "Bonaparte." I may, therefore, explain that under the Second Empire it was decreed by a Family Statute that henceforward "Napoleon" should be the designation of those branches of the Imperial Family who might be called upon to reign. The other members of the family preserved the name of "Bonaparte," but constituted the "civil" family of the Emperor Napoleon III., and were not included in the "Imperial" Family. This distinction is noted in the "Almanach de Gotha" without explanation—an omission which should be rectified in future editions of the world's libro d'oro.[174]

In the *Times* of November 26, 1909, it was noted that "Prince Victor Napoleon Bonaparte, after a week's stay at the Savoy Hotel, left yesterday for Brussels."

Our official Court Circular of the same date described the Pretender as "His Imperial Highness Prince Napoleon Bonaparte."

Both those designations are incorrect. Upon the death of his father (1891), Victor, as eldest son, became "Prince Napoleon"; and it will be observed that in the original banns of marriage he is so styled, plus his Christian names, "Victor Gerome [correctly "Jérôme"] Frederick."

For the solemnization of these princely imperial and royal nuptials on November 14, 1910, the old château of Moncalieri shook off the dust of centuries; the chevaliers, in their suits of mail, who sleep their last long sleep under the tombstones; the more modern heroes, whose great deeds are narrated in the war-pictures adorning the immense and melancholy corridors—all these reawoke for some days. Momentarily they saw once more the venerable citadel, perched, like a great eagle's nest, on the flank of the picturesque hills leaning over the River Po, a few miles from Turin, in which, for so many lustres, Princesse Clotilde has unrolled the autumnal stages of her saintly existence, divided between penance and charity. At the jubilant strains of the "Alléluia" the old home of the Princes of Piedmont, which resembles a fortress charged to watch over the mausoleum of the Superga,[175] saw itself resuscitated.

After these rapid souvenirs we ascend the slopes of the park, arrest our steps on the terrace to admire the magnificent panorama of the immense valley of the Po; then enter this moyen-âge château, with its interminable galleries and great salles, ordinarily so solitary and indescribably sombre, but to-day rejuvenated, made comfortable, bedecked with sumptuous stuffs, with carpets and with flowers, luxuriously furnished by royal command—by the orders of the King of Italy. And it is the Administration of the Royal Domains which has sent to Moncalieri the beautiful services of plate for the wedding repast—something between a

---

[174] Napoleon I. always objected to the use of the surname "Bonaparte"; consequently, the three stones (now to be seen at the Invalides) on his tomb at St. Helena bore, and bear, no inscription.

[175] The Royal Basilica, near Turin.

State déjeuner and a State banquet. King Victor Emmanuel III. had indeed, with kindly and generous tyranny, decreed that, although celebrated with the strictest princely privacy, there should be lacking no noble and dignified elements in the solemnization of the marriage of his cousin-german—great-nephew of Napoleon I., Emperor of the French, King of Italy—and Princesse Clémentine of Belgium, daughter and granddaughter of two great monarchs, and great-granddaughter of Louis Philippe I., King of the French.

If Prince Napoleon was married at his mother's residence, and in the midst of his nearest relatives, it was far otherwise with Princesse Clémentine, who, for political reasons, had to make a long journey to obtain the fulfilment of a happiness which she had so long awaited. She had, however, even before the marriage, been received in Italy, not only as a Princess, but as a relative. The daughter of Queen Henrietta, Archduchess of Austria, the Princesse is, in fact, distantly related to the Italian royal family, and, previous to her alliance with Prince Napoleon, "dispensations" had to be obtained from Rome.

By yet another delicate attention of the King of Italy, Princesse Clémentine and her aunt, the widowed Comtesse de Flandre, mother of the King of the Belgians, who accompanied her to the altar, were not obliged, before the wedding, to face the ennui—in such circumstances—inseparable from the occupation of apartments at an hotel. The left wing of the Royal Palace at Turin was, for the special gratification of these two royal ladies, decorated as it is on great fête-days; and it was through a forest of chrysanthemums, adorning even the portraits of their ancestors, that they entered the old palace of the Kings of Sardinia. The Dowager Duchesse d'Aoste (Princesse Lætitia) presided, with her wonted taste and grace, over the installation of the apartments reserved for the two Princesses and their suite; and it was Princesse Lætitia who, earlier in the year, had chaperoned the fiancée on her first visit to her future mother-in-law at Moncalieri, the scene of the fiançailles.

H.I.H. Prince Napoleon arrived at the château of Moncalieri three days before the wedding, attended by M. Thouvenel, the senior member of the Prince's service d'honneur, and by the Marquis de Girardin (who had accompanied the Prince from Brussels). The other members of the suite were lodged at Turin. Princesse Lætitia and her son and General Prince Louis Napoleon stayed at the château of Moncalieri.

At half-past ten on the morning of the wedding the Princes, Princesses, and their suites assembled in the large salon des Suisses, in which the Mayor of Moncalieri (M. Protti) celebrated the civil marriage of the imperial and royal couple. The witnesses at this function were the Comte de Salemi (son of H.I.H. Princesse Lætitia), the Marquis Ferreri di Cambiano (Deputy for Moncalieri), Comte Balbo Bertone di Sambuy, and Comte Negri di Lamporo, the two latter being selected as residing at Moncalieri (the Italian law requiring that two of the witnesses at the civil union are residents of the place of the marriage). After the brief ceremony, the Mayor expressed his hopes that the future of the imperial couple would be of the happiest; then, on behalf of the Municipality of Moncalieri, he gave Prince Napoleon the gold pen with which the act of marriage had been signed; and to the Princesse the Mayor presented a bouquet of orchids. The procès-verbal of the civil marriage was afterwards registered at the French Consulate at Turin.

The religious marriage was solemnized in the chapel (which is decorated with frescoes) of the château. Green plants and white chrysanthemums covered the altar.

Prince Napoleon (who escorted his mother, Princesse Marie Clotilde Napoleon) was in plain evening dress, over which appeared the riband of the Order of Leopold, which had been sent to him through Prince Ernest de Ligne on the previous day by King Albert. (Some saw in the sombre garb of the bridegroom the symbol of exile.)

Princesse Clémentine, radiant in beauty and charm, looking equally majestic and amiable, came next, on the arm of her brother-in-law, Prince Philippe de Saxe-Coburg (who married, and separated from, Princesse Louise of Belgium). The bride's magnificent robe was of embroidered white satin, covered with lace; her veil and corsage, of exquisite lace, were the gift of a number of Belgian ladies — in fact, the subscribers were the "ladies of all Belgium."

Following the bride came—

H.R.H. the Duc d'Aoste and the Queen-Mother Marguerite (mother of the present King of Italy);

Prince Ernest de Ligne and H.R.H. the Comtesse de Flandre;

H.I.H. Prince Louis Napoleon and his sister, H.I.H. Princesse Lætitia, Duchesse Douairière d'Aoste;

H.R.H. the Comte de Turin and H.R.H. the Duchesse de Gênes;

H.R.H. the Duc de Gênes;

H.R.H. the Duc de Abruzzes;

Comte de Salemi (son of Princesse Lætitia and nephew of the bridegroom);

Prince d'Udine;

Duc de Pistoie;

Duc de Bergame (son of the Duc de Gênes); and

M. de Borchgrave (Belgian Chargé d'Affaires at Rome).

The witnesses at the religious ceremony were Prince Philippe de Saxe-Coburg and Prince Ernest de Ligne—representing the King of the Belgians; Prince Louis Napoleon, and the Duc d'Aoste (the former representing his brother, and the last attending as proxy for the King of Italy).

Other witnesses were—

For PRINCE NAPOLEON: M. Thouvenel, Marquis de Girardin, Baron de Serlay, Prince Aymon de Lucinge, Lieutenant-Colonel Nitot, Baron Antoine de Brimont, and Monsieur H. Beneyton (His Imperial Highness's Private Secretary).

For PRINCESSE CLÉMENTINE: Comtesse d'Ursel, Baronne d'Hoogworst, Mlle. de Bassompierre (all three Belgian ladies), General Daelman (Belgian chevalier d'honneur), and Mlle. de Bassano (a French lady).[176]

The dames d'honneur of Queen Marguerite and of Princesse Lætitia were also witnesses.

H.R.H. the Comtesse de Flandre was attended by the Vicomte de Beughem, grand-maître of Her Royal Highness's household; and by the Comtesse de Borch-grave, dame d'honneur.

Mass was said by Monsignor Masera, Bishop of Biella, who used the historical chalice presented to Princesse Clotilde on the day of her marriage by King Jérôme, who for a while reigned in Westphalia. Two of Princesse Clotilde's chaplains assisted the Bishop, who delivered a very inspiring address, recalling the great deeds of the ancestors of the bridal pair.

The music was exclusively Beethoven's and Mendelssohn's, and included the latter's celebrated "Wedding March."

There were no street or any other decorations in the little town. This accorded with the wishes of Princesse Clotilde, who took the greatest pains to avoid all possibility of political embarrassments. In this laudable task she was seconded by Prince Napoleon, who, ever since the death of the Prince Imperial and his consequent succession to the rôle of Pretender to the throne, has evinced the most commendable desire to remain outside the pale of politics.

Princesse Napoleon's wedding-presents were artistically arranged in one of the large salons. They were of the estimated value of 2,500,000 francs (£100,000). The Empress Eugénie sent Her Imperial and Royal Highness a diamond tiara; the King of Italy a diamond diadem. A group of French ladies presented the Princesse with a very handsome toilette-service (table coiffeuse is the technical name for it).[177] This artistic gift consists of a magnificent toilette, Empire style, in mahogany, on which stand the various items of a magnificent nécessaire in silver gilt, also in the purest "Empire," executed, from several famous models of the art of the First Empire, by MM. Falize, of Paris. Accompanying this "all-French" gift was a livre d'or, containing the names of all the donors. Several of the subscribers were persons in the humblest walks of life, and their names were read by the Prince and Princesse with much emotion.

When the "ladies of Belgium" asked the Princess what form she would like their wedding-gift to take, she expressed her patriotic preference for lace, because she would be stimulating a national industry. Her Royal Highness's choice highly gratified the presentation committee, at the head of which were Her Highness Princesse Ernest de Ligne and the Comtesse de Smet de Naeyer, two of the most popular leaders of Brussels society. This beautiful gift (veil and corsage) was pre-

---

[176] This lady, one of Princesse Napoleon's dames d'honneur, is a daughter of that Duc de Bassano who was the Grand Chamberlain of Napoleon III. He was at Chislehurst with the Imperial Family, and, later, was often to be seen at the Empress Eugénie's residence, Farnborough Hill. The author has occasion to remember him with gratitude.

[177] This was presented to Princesse Napoléon on April 6, 1911, by the Duchesse d'Albuféra, who was begged by the imperial couple to convey their grateful thanks to the dames Françaises for their superb gift.

sented to Princesse Clémentine at the Palais Belle-Vue, accompanied by a splendidly-bound album containing the names of all the subscribers.

The Princess's intimate friends greatly admired the Empress Eugénie's wedding-gift—a tiara of brilliants—the stones being specially selected and set in the most artistic manner. Her Imperial Majesty is a connaisseuse in precious stones of every description, especially diamonds and emeralds, of which, as well as pearls, she still possesses a large collection. The wearing of gems she has discarded for forty years, with the exception of one occasion—that of the visit to Farnborough Hill of the King and Queen of Spain—when, at the State dinner and the "At Home" the same evening, one small jewel was observable, relieving her invariable black costume. Princesse Clémentine received a number of smaller jewels, in the shape of pendants, earrings, finger-rings, and hatpins, some of which came from H.I.H. Princesse Clotilde, the Dowager Duchesse and the Duchesse d'Aoste, the Comtesse de Flandre, and the Queens of Italy, and others from her friends in Belgium.

The Empress's wedding-present to Prince Napoleon was fully appreciated by His Imperial Highness, whose collection of historical souvenirs has been increased from time to time by gifts from the august lady. The Prince's father was a cousin of the Emperor Napoleon III., so that the "relationship" of the Pretender and the Empress is of the slightest. As a result of the injunctions contained in the Prince Imperial's will, however, the imperial lady has displayed in the fortunes of Prince Napoleon as much kindly interest as if he were her second son. From his men friends the Prince received a number of presents, these including souvenirs from the Sovereigns of Austria-Hungary, Roumania, Bulgaria, and Servia, whom he visited in 1908, when he was also the guest for several days of the ex-Sultan of Turkey.

The honeymoon was passed in Italy. From Moncalieri the newly-married couple went to Rome, where they were the guests for a few days of the King and Queen of Italy at the Quirinal. The fact that they did not visit the Pope during their stay in the Eternal City gave umbrage to a section of the Belgian Catholics, one of their organs asserting that the Pretender deliberately kept out of the way of His Holiness. "The declarations made by the Prince on the day after the wedding at Moncalieri, the incident of his recent visit to the King and Queen of Italy, and his affected ignoring of the Vatican, have," it was stated, "definitely alienated from Prince and Princess Napoleon the sympathies of the Belgian Catholics, who would, as a matter of course, have been friendly to them by reason of the blind hatred evinced by the Catholics towards the French Republicans." Not since 1870, it was asserted, "has there been witnessed the spectacle of a member of a Catholic royal family visiting Rome without paying his respects to the Pope."[178]

The Belgian Liberal papers expressed their gratification at the omission of the Pretender to call upon "the prisoner of the Vatican." "Let the Prince become a real Liberal, and he will not have to complain of a lack of sympathy."

The sojourn of Prince and Princess Napoleon at Vienna was made additionally pleasant owing to the very friendly reception given to the former by the Emperor

[178] This was nonsensical. Etiquette precludes the King's guests from visiting the Pope.

Francis Joseph when the Prince was entertained by His Majesty at the Hofburg in 1908, the Pretender's "great year" of visits to foreign Sovereigns, including the ex-Sultan of Turkey. On that occasion the Emperor wore, as his only decorations, the insignia of the Legion of Honour, presented to him by Napoleon III.

The anniversary of the election of Prince Louis Napoleon (afterwards Emperor) to the Presidency of the Republic was celebrated in 1910 by a banquet at St. Mandé, at which there were present numerous prominent members of the Bonapartist party. The Marquis de Dion, who presided, expressed the hope that they would see France, "which had been struck in its beliefs and in its dreams of social fraternity," rally to the cause which his party defended. During the banquet an address expressing devotion to "the cause" was telegraphed to the Prince; and another was sent to the Princess, congratulating her upon "bringing to the defenders of the plebiscitary doctrine the support of her great charm and her tenacious energy to secure the triumph of the great name of Napoleon."

Italy—both in the official world and in the Press—was somewhat gênée by Prince Napoleon's marriage. From all that was said and printed it appeared clear that neither the Court, nor the Government, nor the more influential journals had ventured to give to the wedding of the grandson of Victor Emmanuel II. and cousin of the reigning King the importance and the éclat with which they would have surrounded the nuptial fêtes of any Prince who was not, like Victor Napoleon, the issue, through his mother, of the stock of the Savoys. M. Jean Carrère told in the *Temps*, in November, 1910, that a very influential Italian politician had said to him at the period of the nuptials at Moncalieri: "Do you not think that all the noise made in the Press will disturb your [French] compatriots, and will make them believe that Italy supports the dynastic claims of the heir of the Napoleons?"

How many others in Italy (asked M. Carrère) still believe that contemporary France is vaguely susceptible in all matters relating to the Pretenders? But times have greatly changed since the expulsion of the Orleanist and Bonapartist Princes, "and I believe that amongst all Frenchmen under the age of thirty the song of MacNab is as remote in history as are the refrains of former days upon Soubise or Marlborough. However this may be, one can only thank Italy, and especially those who govern the country, for their extreme discretion in this event. If they have exaggerated their scruples, it only proves how very correctly the Court and the people have acted in respect of the French Republic."

This intention to be agreeable to France was said to be the more meritorious on the part of the Italians because in reality the Bonapartes—or, if the word be preferred, the Napoleons—have remained very popular in Italy, more particularly the Jérôme branch. The battles of Solferino, Magenta, and Palestro, which covered the Napoleonic name with so much lustre, are legendary. It is, however, true that Mentana and the mistakes made towards the end of the Second Empire have slightly tarnished the memory of Napoleon III. The souvenirs still preserved in Italy prove that Prince Jérôme—cousin of Napoleon III. and father of Prince Victor—did not lessen the prestige attached to the name of Napoleon; he was, in fact, always very popular in Italy. Princesse Lætitia, Duchesse d'Aoste Douairière, who resides at Turin, is among the Princesses of the House of Savoy who are most loved by the people, and she is much cheered whenever she appears at theatres or fêtes. It is not betraying a secret to recall the deep personal affection always displayed by King Victor Emmanuel III. for his two cousins, the Princes Victor and Louis, whose cultivated minds and serious characters he so much appreciates.

At Moncalieri, where Princesse Clotilde's infancy was passed, and where her daughter, Princesse Lætitia, was married to her uncle, the Duc d'Aoste, the widowed consort of the Emperor Napoleon's cousin Jérôme (whom the Emperor always addressed as "Napoleon") saw her dearest wishes gratified by the union of her eldest son, Prince Napoleon, with a Princess who is exceptionally accomplished, beautiful, spirituelle, cultivated, endowed with a taste for the arts, and a fervent Catholic, with whom the Holy Father evidenced his great sympathy by sending her a magnificent gift, accompanied by a much-prized autograph letter of congratulation.

If, as in a vision, Princesse-mère, the august châtelaine of Moncalieri, evoked the brilliant, or the sad, events which furrowed her life, clouded by melancholy episodes which her ardent faith in Providence helped her to face courageously, she saw again the fêtes celebrated for her own marriage at Turin—the prelude to the union of her beloved Savoy with France; the cradle of her House offered in exchange for an independence which France—the France of the Pale Emperor—assisted the Italians to obtain; she saw again the struggle between the newly-born Italy and the Holy See; and she saw herself, the patient and devoted wife, bien Française in the moment of danger, refusing, in a charming letter, the asylum offered to her by her father, King Victor Emmanuel, when France was bleeding from the wounds inflicted upon her in the year of disaster. "At this moment," wrote Princesse Clotilde to her father, "I cannot accept your advice, because, if I fled from France, my sons would blush for me, and you know that the House of Savoy and fear have never met. You would not wish them to meet in me." Similarly noble sentiments were contained in a memorable letter written by Queen Catherine to the King of Würtemburg, when, urged by her father in 1814 to forsake King Jérôme and take refuge at Stuttgart, she loftily refused, resolved to share the fate of her proscribed husband.

If, in 1870, events proved to be stronger than the firm will of Princesse Clotilde, and if she was compelled to quit France, then in the throes of revolution as well as war, we remember how calmly and with what dignity, on September 5,[179] she drove en daumont to the Lyons railway-station, traversing the quarters where the revolutionary danger was greatest, and still saluted on all sides by a populace disarmed by this noble woman's courage. The Princess, looking back through the years—through forty years!—saw herself once more at Prangins, by her husband's side; saw her sons en pension at Vevey; then, her consort having returned to France after the chute of Thiers, she would have recalled her arrival at Moncalieri, her home ever since.

At Moncalieri, then, the Princesse Clotilde has voluntarily lived her cloistered life. Not, however, that she has ever failed to discharge her family duties. Twice

[179] The day following the Empress Eugénie's flight from the Tuileries, and the same day on which Her Imperial Majesty actually left Paris for the coast.

she journeyed to Rome—the first time in January, 1878. Her father, King Victor Emmanuel, was dying, and, despite her repugnance to enter a Rome which had become the capital, she wished, as a devoted daughter, to receive the King's last words. Learning en route, however, that her father had expired, she abandoned her intention of going to Rome, and returned to Moncalieri. Early in March, 1891, her consort, Prince (Jérôme) Napoleon, who had resided in Rome all the winter, was struck down by an attack of nephritis, complicated by pneumonia. The Princesse, accompanied by her daughter, the Duchesse d'Aoste, set out once more for Rome. Only a very few persons are acquainted with the incidents of the Prince's last illness, and I will not recall those painful episodes. One detail may, however, be recorded here, as it shows how the perseverance of Princesse Clotilde triumphed on that melancholy occasion. Twice had Cardinal Mermillod knelt by the bedside of the dying Prince, who was still fully conscious. When the Bishop of Geneva left the sick-room the second time, he seemed relieved of a great weight, and the face of Princesse Clotilde evidenced her gratitude at the "good end" made by her husband.[180] With her children she watched, praying—always praying—by the side of the dead. After the interment at the Superga (March 30) the widowed Princesse took the hands of her children, joined them in hers, and said: "Promise to remain united." They promised, and they have kept their word. Princesse Clotilde was last seen in Paris during the illness and at the death of Princesse Mathilde, the cousin of Napoleon III. On that occasion she fulfilled once again the rôle of a sœur de charité.[181]

THE HOME.

Perhaps—I do not assert it—secret party meetings have been, and are, held now and again at No. 241, Avenue Louise, in those beautiful salons, so rich in relics, or in the garden of the imperial residence, now more than ever an object of public curiosity, with its modest blue stone façade and its oak door with carved eagles, guarded only by those tall chestnut-trees which serve as a curtain to many a demeure bourgeoise of more ambitious aspect. The Prince's partisans, the associates of his hopes, evidently come and go very unobtrusively, for no one at Brussels hears or sees anything of them. The Prince's voice is raised at long intervals—whenever he thinks it desirable to formulate the Imperialist idea—in succinct and frank letters addressed, now to the Bonapartist Committees of the Seine, anon to personalities like M. Malbert. But this is done so discreetly, these letters are written in so dignified a style, without any reference to the question of personal banishment from France, that the sharpest-sighted critic is unable to trace in them the faintest infraction of the duty which an exile owes to a country which shelters him.

Prince Napoleon returns to Brussels from his rare visits to the Empress Eugénie at Farnborough Hill, and to his sister, the Duchesse d'Aoste Douairière, at Turin, without getting himself talked about; for on no account would he say or do anything which might compromise the country in which he has found an agreeable asylum for half his life. When he comes to England two lines in the "Times,"

[180] It would be idle to suppress a fact which everybody knew, and knows, that the Prince had been a Freethinker all his life.

[181] Princesse Clotilde died at Moncalieri on June 25, 1911.

"Telegraph," or "Post" sometimes announce the fact, either on his arrival or departure. His "movements" at the Carlton or the Savoy (the hotels of his predilection) are not watched and reported upon; the names of his visitors are not publicly, or even privately, mentioned. His friendly visit to King Manoel at Buckingham Palace in November, 1909, was recorded in the Court Circular (which scrupulously noted his rank of "Imperial" Highness) and mentioned in the "Times"—that was all. And perhaps it was enough; for the Prince it was certainly ample. Let him alone, and he is grateful.

It was amusingly said of him by a Brussels critic: "Prince Napoleon is a Pretender who seems to have no pretensions." Probably the author of the mot was unaware of the homage which he was paying to the Prince's correct interpretation of a rôle so difficult to sustain.

The daily life of the Prince has never ceased to be governed, in all its details, by the same prudent and admirable reserve. His existence is that of a grand seigneur, too distinguished to "make an exhibition of himself" for the entertainment of the crowd, too cultivated not to know how to vary the preoccupations of an exile by useful toil. In the morning one may often catch a flying glimpse of his tall, robust, dominating figure among the riders galloping in the beautiful Bois de la Cambre, or at the "meets" of M. Saint-Pol de Sinçay and of the Prince de Chimay. But he is seldom to be seen in the afternoon. He is then at home, studying some work on political economy or some scientific volume, or, to assist his memory concerning some historical point, turning the leaves of one or other of the 6,000 books composing his "Napoleonic" library—those 6,000 volumes of the prodigious annals of the Revolution, the Consulate, and the Empire. The Prince's library is, of its special kind, unique. Of his collection of books and relics he has said:[182] "I live my darkest hours in the midst of souvenirs of the First Emperor. Each one of these, in recalling a period of his life, teaches me a lesson. Force has driven me from the cradle and from the tomb of the great Emperor. I take refuge in his thoughts. To him alone I go to ask for inspirations."

If you have been granted an audience of the Prince—a favour not accorded to more than a very few of those who seek it, unless an application is well backed— you wait your turn in one of the rooms on the left of the entrance-hall, into which you have been shown by a footman in a light-coloured livery. Here you may find a few of the Prince's friends who have come from Paris to spend the day with him, and who will leave in these rooms some "good mouthfuls" of the air of France.

When the moment arrives for your interview with the Prince, you pass through a vestibule gleaming with white marble, and your gaze falls upon a bronze statuette of Bonaparte, at the age of twelve, reading a book. You proceed through a vast corridor, paved, like the vestibule, with white marble. Before entering the cabinet in which Prince Napoleon receives his visitors, you cast an admiring coup d'œil upon a spacious landing where portraits and statues of the imperial family form an incomparable museum, seeming to mount guard on the threshold of this last representative of the Bonapartes. They are all here—the grandfathers and the grandmothers. Here Lætitia, robust and bonne, in her ample senaro of a Ro-

[182] In a letter to Théophile Gautier.

man matron, regards reposefully her peaceable husband. Neither this Corsican—a humble deputy of the island, not long become French—nor this Florentine, by origin and temperament, seems to divine, around the head of the pale infant before them, the unperishable aureole that awaits him. There Bonaparte, at all the ages of his life, and at all the stages of his apotheosis, glances, with his cold eye, at the Kings his brothers and the Queens his sisters. Here is Joseph of Spain, whose handsome and open countenance is less that of a King than of a dilettante, épris of belles-lettres. Here is Louis of Holland, with the cunning eye, observing, not without melancholy, Hortense de Beauharnais, who seems to turn her head from him. Here is Jérôme of Westphalia, sanguine, ready-witted, adventurous, regretting that Napoleon had not allowed him to conquer the crown by his own daring. He avenged himself, however, many times—among others, on the day when, not yet having a hair upon his face, he bought, for 12,000 francs (£480), at the Emperor's expense (!), at the sign of the "Singe Violet," the famous travelling "necessary," with its ivory-handled razors and silver-plated wash-hand basins.

Then, in this marvellous gallery, come the women. Here is Pauline Borghèse, an ideal Diane chasseresse—Canova's. You remember this marvellous creature's reply to someone who had reproached her for posing for this statue in her splendid nudity, "Oh, il y avait un poêle!" (But there was a fire!). You linger a moment to gaze upon Joséphine de Beauharnais, like the lava of a sleeping volcano under the calm envelope of this warm beauty of the isles of the West—this mortal who, as someone has said, "had the audacity to love a god." And here is the Archduchesse Louise, in the midst of her parrots and her dogs, indifferent and dreamy as an Austrian woman, and also as far from Napoleon as from the Schönbrunn, which she prefers even to the Tuileries.

Napoleon III., fearing lest you should surprise him in the midst of his dreams, flies from you, his eyes almost effaced, as if lost in a mist. Here is Eugénie, reigning as much by her blonde beauty as by that imperial crown whose gold seems to be expiring in her glowing hair. Her eyes, in particular, strike you as strange—tranquil eyes, with their far-off, melancholy look; eyes like two tears; eyes which are about to weep, whose too large eyelids resemble inexhaustible wells, from which sorrow has nothing more to do but to draw the water. Last of all, there is Napoleon IV., with the eyes, the look, and all the sweet resignation of his mother: the "little Prince," in the bearskin of the Imperial Guard; the Prince, grown taller, as the Woolwich cadet; the Prince—having attained his majority—in a British soldier's cap, mournfully posed upon that languid head, already enveloped by the night of Death.

But you have arrived at the door of the Prince's cabinet, an immense room; and here is the Prince himself, giving you a hearty and hospitable shake of the hand. The Prince's broad chest, strong head, wide shoulders, and firm pressure of the hand which clasps yours indicate frankness and sympathy.

"Victor or Napoleon? Say, rather, a Savoyard!" exclaimed one of his opponents, who, however, could not more aptly have described or more pleased the Prince. Prince Victor is a Napoleon through his father, a Savoyard through his mother, whose saintly virtues do honour to the upright, proud character of her son. A little habit of the Prince amuses you: when he speaks he takes the large triple ring from the finger on his right hand and transfers it mechanically to his left hand. You note also that his deep, strong voice is well fitted to utter words of command—like that of all the Napoleons. The Republic of which he is so fond of talking is neither Liberal nor Conservative, but an "authoritative" Republic, with its hierarchical chief at its head.

His words, energetically hammered out, resound through the large salon, full of cases containing the spolia opima of nearly a century of imperial grandeurs. Here are sabres, there swords; elsewhere crosses and medals; hats, browned by powder; redingotes, no longer grey, but faded, colourless. Ah! that Napoleon— what rays of light he leaves behind him in his hats, his greatcoats, and his swords, the latter still gleaming, and all forming a noble cradle for the heir, born to pre- serve the immortal memory of the great Emperor! These bullets, mortars, swords, guns, banners, hats, greatcoats, spurs—all the conqueror's battle paraphernalia, sorted and classified—must perturb the mind of even the most stoical and unsym- pathetic; and the chances are that you will leave No. 241 without having studied the Napoleon of to-day as calmly and as thoroughly as you had intended to. In that dominating head there is a mixture of the Carignan Savoyards and the Napo- leon Bonapartes. The convex forehead, arched, low, stubborn, is that of Clotilde, his mother. The moustache, long and sèche, is that of King Humbert, his uncle; but it is in the chin, prominent and handsome as that in a Greek statue; it is in the black eyes, sphinx-like in their penetration, and as steel-bright as an eagle's (as is said of the Bonapartes), that Prince Napoleon so strongly resembles his father, as that father resembled Napoleon I. Summing up, you feel that you have seen a Prince robust alike in body and mind—mens sana in corpore sano. France, without dis- tinction of party, may be proud of this scion of a glorious race. And who knows if the Republic is not damaged by depriving itself of the services of this citizen?

Some of the privileged few who are received by this descendant of Napoleon I., in the midst of those rare prints which faithfully reproduce the episodes of that dazzling career, have dined or supped off the selfsame campaign plate on which were served the hasty repasts of the conqueror of Austerlitz or of Jena before or after the victory. "The privileged ones of whom I speak," says the most amiable and gifted of confrères, M. Gérard Harry, "are numerically few, mais de choix. By his admirable fulfilment of the rôle of a silent and studious exile, by the charm of his conversation—the talk of an érudit and an artist—and by his sportsmanlike qualities, Prince Napoleon has made, in the royal family and in the 'high soci- ety' of Belgium, friends whose circle he has restricted only from a sentiment of proud reserve, and the better to preserve himself from the bothers inseparable from 'fashionable' existence. One seldom sees him at the theatre, concealed in the semi-obscurity of a box, except when some chef-d'œuvre of French dramatic art is produced; or at the Cercle Artistique et Littéraire; or at 'Wauxhall,' when the attraction is some literary piece brought from his natal land. On such occasions he is accompanied only by one or other of the Bonapartist notabilities who come in turn from Paris, like the 'relief' of a guard of honour."

I recall an audience granted by the Prince to the "Figaro" in 1910, at which the heir of the Napoleons expressed his initiation in the art of aviation, and his pride that Frenchmen of to-day—Frenchmen of the Republic—have been the heroes and the conquerors of so many aerial contests.

The Empress.   Comte Primoli.   M. Pietri.

**H.I.M. THE EMPRESS EUGÉNIE IN THE EMPRESS JOSÉPHINE'S
BEDROOM AT LA MALMAISON IN 1910.**

The Empress Joséphine died in this room on June 1, 1814.

*Courteously lent by the Proprietors of the illustrated Paris journal, "Femina."
The Photograph by "Central-Photo," Paris.*

That so many merits should have attracted Princesse Clémentine is not more surprising than the attachment of the Prince to a King's daughter so morally royal. This youngest of the daughters of Leopold II. has the same tastes as her consort—a heart as French as his own. It was her affection for France which led her for so many years to make one of the Mediterranean plages—St. Raphael—her winter home. She is the only one of the daughters of King Leopold who did not trouble his last years; and she set a good example to others by submitting to her father's rigorous will, and by delaying an alliance which she so long desired. Her artistic education and her penchant for "glory" make her the ideal companion of an exiled Prince.

From the outset of her acquaintance with the Prince, Princesse Clémentine has been a fervent upholder of the Napoleonic legend, and has made a close study of the works of M. Frédéric Masson, M. Émile Ollivier, and other historians of the First and Second Empires. She, at all events, does not regard the imperial cause as a lost one; and her friends laughingly assert that she is really plus Bonapartiste que le Prince. In her new home she is surrounded by many historical emblems of her culte—precious souvenirs of the First and Third Emperors and of the ill-fated "Napoléon Quatre," these latter including presents from the Empress and others bequeathed to the present Head of the House of Bonaparte by the "little Prince" himself.

From her birth Princesse Clémentine was linked in relationship—very slightly, only in the seventh degree—to Prince Napoleon; for the youngest daughter of Leopold II. had for her maternal granduncle the Archduke Régnier of Austria, great-grandfather of the Prince-Pretender. But "the élans of two hearts are of more avail as a means of bringing two persons together than the drooping boughs of two genealogical trees."[183]

Prince Napoleon's exile dates from a quarter of a century ago; and some ten years have elapsed since there was an entente cordiale between His Imperial Highness and Princesse Clémentine. There was one obstacle (and, let it be emphatically said here, only one) in the way of a realization of their hopes—the fatal raison d'état! King Leopold was, or professed to be, haunted by the fear that such an alliance might possibly place Belgium in a delicate position vis-à-vis the French Republic. Has that apprehension vanished? Anyway, "Leopold the Builder" has gone to his last account, and Princesse Napoleon is not the daughter, but simply the cousin, of the reigning Sovereign.

> Machiavelli outlined the line of conduct to be followed by Princes who reign or who will surely reign. He would, perhaps, have found it difficult to formulate the troublesome rules of existence of a Pretender in exile, who is obliged to firmly maintain his historical rights to the government of a neighbouring country, and to keep them sufficiently in the background, so that they may not compromise the nation which shelters him and whose hospi-

[183] M. Gérard Harry, the celebrated Belgian publicist, author of a very pungent, detailed, and erudite criticism, in "La Grande Revue" (Paris), of the volume "The Empress Eugénie: 1870-1910." London: Harper and Brothers; New York: Charles Scribner's Sons. 1910.

tality he enjoys. How many banished Princes have known how to comply with two such contradictory conditions? The Comte de Chambord, Victor Hugo, and General Boulanger failed to grasp this essential point, and had to leave Belgian territory. It is by having known, since June, 1886, by his consummate tact, how to scrupulously respect the laws of hospitality, without in the slightest degree abdicating his dynastic claims, that Prince Napoleon has secured the respect and esteem of all Belgians, whether Conservatives or Liberals. They thank their guest because he has never been the cause of the least friction between Belgium and the French Republic; and they have admired him because, without going back upon his principles, he has never troubled the friendly relations which exist between Belgium and France.[184]

By the civil law of Belgium, Princesse Clémentine was under no obligation (her father being dead) to request permission to marry. When the Constitution was revised in 1893 a clause was inserted providing that any "Prince" who married without the consent of the King would lose all rights to the Crown. No mention was made of "Princesses." If Prince Napoleon had married the Princesse and created difficulties of an international character during her father's lifetime, the Government, by virtue of Article 1 of the Law of February 12, 1897, could have expelled him from Belgium. King Leopold's death changed the situation.

By her marriage Princesse Napoleon became connected with a reigning King (Victor Emmanuel), a former Queen (Maria Pia of Portugal), and a former Empress (Eugénie). One of her aunts (the Comtesse de Flandre) is the mother of a King (Belgium), and another aunt is an ex-Empress (of Mexico). The latter was deprived of her reason when on her fruitless mission to Napoleon III. and to Pope Pius IX. to crave their support for her consort, and was thus spared all knowledge of the execution by the insurgents at Queretaro, in June, 1867, of the Emperor Maximilian, brother of the present Emperor of Austria-Hungary. For forty-four years the Empress Charlotte has lived in complete seclusion in the residences provided for her by her brother, the late King of the Belgians—first, at the château of Tervueren, which was destroyed by fire in 1874; and then at the château of Bouchout, a few miles from the Royal Palace at Laeken. The veuve tragique (as the Empress of Austria pathetically described her) wore her imperial crown for only three years—a period of continuous anxiety, trouble, and bitter humiliations. She had a devoted friend in the late Queen of the Belgians, and she found another in Princesse Clémentine.

Princesse Napoléon's arrival at and departure from the church at which she hears Mass on Sundays is witnessed by an eager and admiring crowd of "the faithful"—and others; and she herself related this little episode to the eminent Belgian sculptor, M. Lucien Pallez, one day, when she was sitting for the bust which was completed in April, 1911. As Her Imperial Highness was leaving the church she heard a young girl of the people say to a companion: "How happy our Princesse looks!" This tribute, said the sculptor to a friend, touched her more than all

[184] M. Harry Gérard.

her wedding-presents. The impression of supreme elegance which one derives from a glance at the bust—a chef-d'œuvre of Pallez—results from the harmony of the lines and the graceful curve of the neck and shoulders. The general allure of the bust recalls the Dianes chasseresses of the Renaissance. "I had only to look at my model to get my inspiration," said the sculptor. On the imperial lady's head (coiffée in Empire style) is a diamond and pearl diadem; the delicate ears and the supple neck are unadorned. M. Pallez has previously exhibited at the Paris Salon busts of the young Queen of Spain and the Queen-Mother, Pope Pius X., and Cardinal Rampolla.

The German Emperor and Empress met H.I.H. Princesse Clémentine for the first time during their visit to Brussels in the autumn of 1910. Prince Napoléon had a long conversation with the Emperor William, whom the Bonapartist Prince had not previously met. The Kaiser had, however, made the acquaintance of the Empress Eugénie in July, 1907, when Her Imperial Majesty received him one Sunday on board her yacht *Thistle* off Bergen. It was a memorable meeting, but not a single detail of the interview has ever been published, and never will be during the Empress's lifetime.

THE IDYLL.

Some two months prior to the marriage the illustrious fiancés visited Farnborough Hill, where, in the Empress's Oratory, the nuptials would have been solemnized but for the weak health of the Prince's mother, Her Imperial and Royal Highness Princesse Clotilde.

Prince Napoléon's consort was no stranger to the august lady who entertained her in Hampshire in September, 1910; for the Princesse, her sister Stéphanie, and their father were the Empress Eugénie's guests at Cap Martin some few seasons ago. To her unfeigned gratification, the Empress witnessed the enactment, chez elle, of an idyll the consequences of which may ultimately prove to be of high import to Europe. "The legends woven by the peoples around their Sovereigns must not be destroyed," said the Empress one day. Prince Napoléon's prospects of ruling France may not be very apparent at the moment; nor, in June, 1870, was the downfall of the Second Empire deemed within the region of possibility. But one September morning that terrible "shout from Paris" went up, and the imperial crown "flew off" with a suddenness which startled and thrilled the world. In France, more surely than in any other country, it is "the unexpected" which happens oftenest; and it may be that one day there may be another plébiscite, and that another Bonaparte may be invested with the imperial purple.

It needs a Ruskin or a Matthew Arnold to depict the Nature-glories of Farnborough Hill, the scene of this idyll. The rustic gabled mansion, the terraced slopes, the bosky lanes and dells, the "forest" which skirts the imperial domain, and the smiling Arcadian landscape provide all the materials for a great painter's canvas, a poet's tuneful lay. "How many walks," says one of the venerable châtelaine's French guests, "I recall in the alleys of the park at Farnborough Hill in the evenings of glorious days; or in winter, when the great trees were powdered with frosty rime, giving to the English landscape the semblance of some phantom picture; or in the early morning, in the second park, which has been christened 'Compiègne,' planted with rhododendrons and young pine-trees. The black dogs gambol round us, now racing off like mad things, then returning at the call of their mistress. The Empress's firm voice mounts higher and higher in the pure invigorating air, as, leaning on her cane, with which she taps the sandy path, she gazes around, drinking in the freshness of the morning which she loves. Her features are more than usually animated. 'Compiègne' has revived memories of the past."[185]

In "Compiègne," those glorious autumn days, the story which is never old was once more told, to the accompaniment of the birds' music and the rustle of the falling leaves, with, for spectator, an Empress, dethroned, 'tis true, but perhaps greater in her fall than in her elevation. Amid these beautiful surroundings, gladdened by the sympathy of one who has seen the world at her feet, the lovers' days flew on lightning wing. For the Princesse, whose charm exercised a spell over all, those September days were of the nature of an imperial fête. The "auto" in which she and the Prince sped through the Hampshire and Berkshire lanes was not, certainly, preceded by piqueurs in the green-and-gold livery of the vénerie of the other Compiègne; but, to compensate for the absence of such luxe, the imperial guests revelled in that blissful solitude which is the one thing needful for the complete enjoyment of "love's young dream."

An excursion to Windsor awakened memories of happy days which the Princesse had spent at the royal château with her father as guests of the beloved "Great Queen," whose good graces King Leopold's youngest daughter enjoyed to the full. And, further, she was befriended at Sandringham by the then "Prince" and "Princess." In Victorian days, too, Prince Victor had received hospitable entertainment at Windsor. His father had presented him to the Queen at Camden Place, Chislehurst, after the obsequies of the young Prince who had willed Prince Jérôme's eldest son as his successor to the headship of the House of Bonaparte. Prince Victor could recall to his fiancée how, a score of years ago, he was taken along those same roads to Windsor, and how, at Queen Victoria's dinner-table, he had met the Tsar of to-day, who later had also his idyll on the marge of the Thames.

Accompanied by M. Franceschini Pietri, the Princesse and the Prince paid their homage to the Empress's beloved dead. They bore with them two crosses of violets, which with reverent hands they laid on the tombs of the Emperor and his son, the young victim of the assegais, who, as Monsignor Goddard said of him, had "the soul of a Sidney and the heart of a Bayard." The then newly-erected arched tomb—the "arcosolium"[186]—for the surviving member of the illustrious trio was gazed upon by the Princesse with moistened eyes; the beautiful vestments in the sacristy—some made by the Empress and by the widowed Duchesse de Mouchy, the devoted friend of nearly half a century—were unfolded, to the royal lady's inexpressible admiration; and she was shown the Sultan's humeral veil; the illuminated altar-cards, whereon is traced a passage from the Prince Imperial's

[185] "The Empress Eugénie: 1870-1910." London: Harper and Brothers; New York: Charles Scribner's Sons. This volume contains the only "intimate" account of the Empress's English home ever published.

[186] Constructed and erected in 1910, a few months before the visit of Prince Napoléon and Princesse Clémentine to the Empress at Farnborough Hill.

"Prayer" (said by Cardinal Manning to be one of the most beautiful outpourings of a pure, devout soul he had ever read); the priestly purple vestments made from the Emperor's pall, and the ecclesiastical apparel fashioned out of the Empress's wedding-robe. There were no spectators of this pious pilgrimage of the Princesse and the Prince, or they would have witnessed the pathetic figure of the royal pair kneeling side by side at the foot of the high altar, and imploring the Divine blessing upon their union. Warm thanks for his genial courtesy were bestowed upon the Lord Abbot, Dom Cabrol, who had summoned all the members of the Benedictine community to witness the arrival and departure of the visitors, and to be presented to the Princesse.

Princesse Napoléon's intimate friendship with the members of the Royal Family dates from as far back as 1895. Queen Victoria had expressed a wish to make the acquaintance of the youngest daughter, and on December 3 King Leopold and Princesse Clémentine proceeded to Windsor Castle, where they spent three days. Prince Christian and Princess (and the late Prince) Henry of Battenberg met the visitors at the railway-station, and escorted them to the Castle. Queen Victoria's guests at the royal dinner-party that evening included the Belgian Minister and the Marquis and Marchioness of Lansdowne. While at Windsor Princesse Clémentine was taken to the cavalry barracks at Spittal, where she saw a "double ride" by non-commissioned officers and men of the 2nd Life Guards. From Windsor King Leopold and the Princesse went to Sandringham on a visit, from Saturday until Monday, to the then Prince and Princess of Wales, the former accompanying them to St. Pancras on the conclusion of their visit.

Princesse Napoléon has two sisters: one, Stéphanie, married, as her first husband, the Austrian Archduke Rudolf, and, secondly, Comte Lonyay; the other, Louise, became the wife of Prince Philip of Saxe-Coburg, a son of the celebrated Princesse Clémentine (daughter of Louis Philippe, King of the French until his abdication in 1848), and consequently brother of Ferdinand, King and Tsar of the Bulgarians. Princesse Stéphanie's widowhood was brought about by the Archduke's tragic death in his hunting-box at Meyerling—a mysterious drama of which there are many versions, all of them unsatisfactory.

The story of Princesse Louise's wedded life is only a shade less poignant than that of her sister Stéphanie. It has been told, in all its harrowing details, by a young Austrian officer, Count Mattachich, in a volume which had a sale of more than 30,000 before it was seized and its further circulation in the Austrian Empire prohibited by the Government. It is a narrative of dissensions between Princesse Louise and her husband, of bills of exchange bearing the signatures of herself and her sister, the widowed Archduchess, of a charge of falsification brought against the Lieutenant, of his imprisonment, of the placing of Princesse Louise under surveillance as being of weak mind, and of a discussion on all these circumstances in the Reichsrath. The death of King Leopold led to the opening of another chapter of family quarrels relating to the manner in which he had disposed of much of his large fortune by gifts to the lady whom he had made Baroness Vaughan, and to whom, it was publicly asserted by an ecclesiastical dignitary, he had been married. Princesse Louise displayed no indications of feeble-mindedness when, in May,

1911, she contested her father's will. The little ironies of royal lives, as well as those of humbler rank, are illustrated by the fact that Prince Philip of Saxe-Coburg was among the wedding-guests bidden to Moncalieri.

H.R.H. PRINCESS GEORGE OF GREECE
(*née* PRINCESSE MARIE BONAPARTE, ONLY DAUGHTER
OR H.H. PRINCE ROLAND BONAPARTE).

Princess George and her Consort were the guests of the King and Queen at the Coronation of their Majesties. The Princess is the only member of the House of Bonaparte who ever attended the Coronation of an English Sovereign. Before leaving England, Prince and Princess George were the guests of Her Majesty Queen Alexandra at Sandringham.

Specially photographed by Boissonas et Taponier, Paris,
and lent for this work by H.H. Prince Roland Bonaparte.

The Family.

Before ending this narrative of the most important event in the history of Bonapartism since the martyrdom in Zululand of the only child of Napoleon III. and the Empress Eugénie—that tragedy which made Prince Victor, in accordance with the explicit terms of the Prince Imperial's will, Head of the House—a few lines may be fittingly devoted to the Pretender's brother and sister and their father.

At the period of the Prince Imperial's death, in 1879, the Bonapartist Pretender of to-day and his only brother, Louis, now a General in the Russian army, were being educated in Paris. Their tutor was M. Blanchet, one of the most eminent scholars in France. He lived at No. 13, Rue de la Cerisaie, and the two sons of Prince Jérôme Napoleon were his only boarders. One of my friends asked M. Blanchet if Prince Victor was clever. "Very," was the reply. "His early education was neglected, and it is wonderful how he holds his own with others who began the race long before him. [Prince Victor was then going through a year's course at the Lycée Charlemagne, under his tutor's supervision.] Before he came to me he was at a school at Vevey, and then at Vanves. He is, perhaps, best in physical sciences, history, and French. His mathematics might be better, but they were neglected in early youth. He excels in all field sports and all physical exercises. His great ambition is to be a distinguished soldier. [Later he studied at St. Cyr, the French Sandhurst.] Everything relating to military matters interests him, and he takes special pleasure in his fencing lessons, which are given him once a week. He is brought up very strictly. His father desired me to train him in the most liberal ideas, and keep him away from the many temptations which beset a youth in Paris. He hardly ever goes to theatres and races."

Both Prince (Victor) Napoleon and his brother have worn the uniform of the French army. They entered the ranks as volontaires, and served for the regulation period, one year—Victor in the artillery, and Louis in the infantry. In 1908 Prince Napoleon made his "grand tour." Accompanied by Prince Aymon de Lucinge and Colonel Nicot, he visited the Emperor of Austria-Hungary (who wore the Cross of the Legion of Honour given him by his young friend's relative, Napoleon III.), the ex-Sultan of Turkey, and the Sovereigns of Bulgaria, Roumania, and Servia. In November, 1909, he was to be seen at Buckingham Palace, in friendly converse with one who, like himself, was to become an exile—King Manoel.

Princesse Lætitia's marriage with her uncle, the Duc d'Aoste, aroused intense interest in Italy in September, 1888, owing to the high position of the bridegroom and bride and to their close relationship. The Duc's daughters were not over-pleased at the prospect of having a stepmother of only two-and-twenty, who was also their cousin. Their two brothers showed their good-feeling by desiring their father to continue to reside at the castle of Cisterna, which had come to him by his first wife. The bridegroom (a one-time King of Spain) was double the age of the Princesse, who had the ripened intelligence of much older women, and exercised great influence in the family councils, more especially over her father. No one could manage Prince Jérôme better than Princesse Lætitia. Sometimes he rebelled, but only to yield with the protest, "Where did you get that strong little head?" In consenting to the marriage, she made it a condition that she should be allowed to see her brother, Prince Victor, as often as she chose.

Princesse Lætitia was only four when, in 1870, the day after the flight of the Empress from the Tuileries, she left Paris with her mother for Prangins, on the Lake of Geneva. Five years later she accompanied her mother, Princesse Clotilde, to the château of Moncalieri, an immense square edifice, then almost uninhabitable, situated on the hills above Turin. Owls and bats had made their homes in the castle; the vast rooms contain the portraits of many undistinguished members of the House of Savoy. Here the young Princesse spent her girlhood, going daily to a school at Turin, and, later, entering the convent school of the Sacré Cœur at Lyons, where the Sisters of the Adoration supervised her education. Thirsting for more knowledge after her return to Moncalieri, she received instruction from tutors of both sexes, the present King's father (the ill-fated Humbert, who was assassinated at Monza) placing at her disposal rooms in the Royal Palace at Turin. Her principal studies were drawing, painting, music, and languages. She speaks with equal ease French, Italian, German, and English, has still a fine voice, and sings with taste and feeling. Turin society thought that a more suitable consort for the Princesse would have been her cousin, the Duca delle Puglie, then nineteen, the present head of the ducal house of Aoste, who married the Princesse Hélène d'Orléans in 1895.

Princesse Lætitia's wedding was not lacking in incidents. There was an evident coolness between the members of the House of Savoy and the Bonapartes. When the bride's father and his youngest son, Prince Louis (now a General in the Russian army), arrived at Turin nobody awaited them at the station. The Court officials had been instructed to attend, but at the last moment the order was cancelled, and Prince (Jérôme) Napoleon and his son drove to the Hôtel de l'Europe, all the other wedding-guests staying at the Royal Palace. Even Princesse Clotilde abstained from meeting her consort on his arrival, and Princesse Lætitia sided with her mother. Prince Jérôme carried his resentment so far as to refuse to meet his eldest son, the Pretender, who was consequently, to the general regret, not present at his sister's wedding. These family differences, arising out of the nomination by the Prince Imperial of Prince Victor as his successor, had their effect upon the Empress Eugénie, who did not attend the wedding, although she had given a qualified promise to be present if Prince Jérôme "made it up" with his eldest son. But even Princesse Lætitia never succeeded in bringing about a reconciliation between her father and her brother.

Prince Jérôme Napoleon (as it has been usual, although incorrectly, to style him) never recovered from the blow to his pride inflicted by the Prince Imperial. He died in Rome in 1891, refusing to be reconciled to his eldest son, and on his death-bed nominating his other son, Prince Louis, as Head of the House of Bonaparte. That position Louis declined to accept, and "recognized" his brother forthwith. Prince Jérôme's death was described by M. Duruy, son of one of the most distinguished of Napoleon III.'s Ministers, as "the end of a dream." Princesse Mathilde, Jérôme's sister, died thirteen years after her brother, and with her passed away the last niece of the "Great" Emperor.

THE LATE MARQUISE DE VILLENEUVE
(*née* **PRINCESSE JEANNE BONAPARTE, ONLY SISTER OF PRINCE RO-
LAND, AND AUNT OF H.R.H. PRINCESS GEORGE OF GREECE).**

*Photographed "for her friends" by Reutlinger, Paris, and lent for this work by H.H.
Prince Roland Bonaparte.*

One act of Prince Victor's father will always be remembered to his credit. He condemned the declaration of war in 1870 from the first. When the fatal missive went forth, he foresaw what would, and did, happen, and said to the Emperor: "Tout est fini, et nous avec." It was at Châlons, in the "blood month," August, that Prince Jérôme next saw his imperial cousin. At a council held on the 17th the Prince, in angry mood, shouted to the Emperor, racked with pain and in the deepest despair: "To take part in this war you abdicated by leaving Paris, and now, by leaving Metz, you have abdicated the command of the army. Unless you cross over to Belgium, you must do one of two things—either re-assume the command, which is impossible; or go back to Paris, which will be difficult and dangerous. But, damn it! if we *must* fall, let us fall like men!"

Prince Jérôme Napoleon disinherited his eldest son and his only daughter, and left all he possessed to his second son, Prince Louis, who has long held the rank of General in the Russian army. Prince Louis' inheritance amounted to about £100,000; and his aunt, Princesse Mathilde, Jérôme's only sister, made further provision for him under her will, leaving him also many valuable jewels and objets d'art. Scarcely anything was left by the Prince to his wife. As a Princess of the House of Savoy, the Italian Government allowed her £4,000 a year, a sum which, as she had lived a very retired and simple life since her husband's death, sufficed for her wants. Princesse Lætitia was adequately provided for by her consort, or she would have been practically sans le sou, and this despite the fact that her mother brought Prince Jérôme a very handsome dot. Jérôme dissipated many thousands in wild speculations, and lost heavily by maintaining three newspapers—the "Peuple," the "Ordre," and the "Napoléon."

The number of Bonapartist marriages since Napoleon III. ascended the throne is very limited. They include the wedding of the Emperor to "the beautiful Spaniard," Mlle. Eugénie de Montijo, "Grandee of Spain of the first class," in 1853; the late Prince Jérôme Napoleon (father of the present Pretender) and Princesse Clotilde, daughter of King Victor Emmanuel II.; the late Princesse Mathilde (sister of Prince Jérôme, and consequently aunt of Prince Victor and General Prince Louis Napoleon), who made an ill-starred marriage with the Russian Prince Anatole Demidoff, Prince of San Donato; Prince Pierre Bonaparte, who, although a first cousin of Napoleon III., made the reverse of a "great" marriage; Prince Roland Bonaparte (only son of Prince Pierre), who espoused a daughter of the late M. François Blanc, of Homburg and Monte Carlo fame; the recently deceased Princesse Jeanne Bonaparte (Prince Pierre's only daughter), who married the Marquis de Villeneuve; Princesse Lætitia (sister of the Pretender), the widowed Dowager Duchesse d'Aoste, who married as her second husband her uncle, the late Duc d'Aoste, the sometime King Amadeus of Spain; and Princesse Marie Bonaparte, the only child of Prince Roland, the consort of H.R.H. Prince George of Greece, a nephew of Queen Alexandra.

On April 2, 1910, at St. Paul's, Grove Park, Chiswick, Miss Gertrude Crowther married Mr. Napoleon Gerald Bonaparte-Wyse, youngest son of the late Mr. C. W. Bonaparte-Wyse, of the manor of St. John's, Waterford, and grandson of the late Right Hon. Sir W. T. Wyse, K.C.B., and Princesse Lætitia Bonaparte, daughter of Prince Lucien, brother of Napoleon I. There is a species of relationship—very remote, it is true—between Madame Sarah Bernhardt and one branch of the Bonaparte family. Prince Lucien, brother of Napoleon I., married as his second wife a Mlle. de Bleschamp, mother of Prince Pierre Bonaparte, Prince Roland's father. Her daughter, by her marriage with a M. Maurice Jablonowski (her second husband), had a son, who, in 1860, married an American lady, Miss Mohr. The daughter of that union, Marie Terka Virginie Clotilde, married in 1887 M. Maurice Bernhardt, son of the famous actress, one of whose most successful parts is that of the "Aiglon" (the Duc de Reichstadt).

The marriage at Moncalieri revived general interest in the period of the Second Empire. The "great year" of the régime was that of 1867, when the Emperor and Empress of the French entertained foreign Sovereigns, Heirs-Apparent, Princes and Princesses, Generals, diplomatists, and the fine fleur of European society.

> In 1911 there are still surviving several distinguished personages who were among the imperial guests in the summer and autumn of the most brilliant days of the Napoleonic reign. These include the Emperor of Austria-Hungary, whom the Empress Eugénie visited at Ischl in 1906; the King of Denmark; the King of the Hellenes; the King of Montenegro; the ex-Sultan of Turkey; Duke of Connaught; Comtesse de Flandre, Princesse Clémentine's aunt; Prince Murat; the Duchesse de Mouchy (*née* Princesse Anna Murat), the most cherished friend of the Empress; the Princesse de Metternich, who in 1910 was relating her recollections of Second Empire days to a select audience in her salon at Vienna; and the Comtesse Edmond de Pourtalès, who hastened to Chislehurst in 1870 to assist the Empress in a very practical way, and in 1911 is the valued friend of Prince Napoleon and his consort.

To this list must be added the familiar names of Mrs. Ronalds and Mme. De Arcos, both of whom have been for many years popular members of English society, and both residing in London. The last-mentioned lady and her sister, Mrs. Vaughan, are among the Empress's most attached surviving friends; and Miss Vaughan has accompanied Her Majesty on some of her recent tours. M. Franceschini Pietri remains the most invaluable and devoted of secretaries.

Illustrious *disparus* include King Edward and his brother, the Duke of Edinburgh; the King and Queen of the Belgians and the Comte de Flandre; the King of Denmark, Queen Alexandra's father; the King of Holland, father of Queen Wilhelmina; Queen Sophia of Holland; the King of Sweden, father of his present Majesty; the King of Portugal, Dom Manoel's grandfather; the Emperor William I.; the Emperors Alexander II. and Alexander III.; Ismaïl Pasha; Abdul Aziz, Sultan of Turkey from 1861 until 1876; Prince Jérôme Napoleon, father of the Bonapartist Pretender; Prince Pierre Bonaparte, father of Prince Roland and grandfather of Princess George of Greece; Princesse Mathilde, cousin of Napoleon III. and aunt of the Princes Victor and Louis; the Prince Imperial of France; the Prince of Monaco, father of the present ruler of the Principality; that Prince of the Netherlands popularly known as "Citron," Bismarck, the great Moltke, Princesse Clotilde, and

Queen Maria Pia.

THE EMPRESS EUGÉNIE: 1910-11.

Her Imperial Majesty the Empress Eugénie, who is deeply interested in the future of Prince and Princesse Napoleon, celebrated her eighty-fifth birthday on May 5, 1911. The unexpected and tragic death of King Edward, on May 6, 1910, came as a great shock to the Empress, who had known our beloved Sovereign from his boyhood—in fact, since 1855, when, some six months before he had attained his thirteenth year, he and his eldest sister (the Princess Royal, afterwards Crown Princess of Prussia, and later Empress Frederick) accompanied their august parents on their memorable return visit to the Emperor and Empress of the French. As Prince of Wales, King Edward had been present, earlier in that year, at the installation, at Windsor, of the Emperor Napoleon III. as a Knight of the Order of the Garter, and heard from his royal mother that, after the ceremony, the Emperor had expressed his gratitude for the honour conferred upon him, and, in a moment of rare expansiveness, had said to the Queen, "Now, at last, I feel I am a gentleman!"—a frank admission which much pleased, and probably amused, our beloved sovereign lady.

A week after the King's death I learnt (although no mention of the fact had been made public) that early on the morning of May 7 (His Majesty passed away at a quarter before midnight on the 6th)—the Empress Eugénie had telegraphed "heart-felt condolences" to Queen Alexandra, Princess Henry of Battenberg, and Princess Louise, Duchess of Argyll. It was also confided to me that, immediately after telegraphing, the Empress, although momentarily "stupefied" by the calamity which plunged our Empire into mourning, had written what were described to me as "very beautiful and most pathetic letters" to the three royal ladies. I was privileged to see other letters written by the Empress in May, 1910, and I do not hesitate to say that they were truly remarkable productions, revealing Her Imperial Majesty (as the Emperor once wrote of her) "in her true colours."

I have a word to add. The Empress commissioned a Paris art firm to execute a very beautiful souvenir of King Edward. This she sent to Queen Alexandra, and in the autumn it was placed near the King's tomb in St. George's Chapel, Windsor. The Empress lunched (for the last time) with King Edward and Queen Alexandra, at Buckingham Palace, on December 16, 1907, when the imperial lady was accompanied by Mrs. Vaughan (whose sister, Mme. De Arcos, represented the Empress at the funeral of Queen Victoria) and M. Pietri.

In the summer of 1910 the Empress cruised in the *Thistle* for more than two months, visiting, besides Italian ports, Corfu, Athens, the Dalmatian coast, Smyrna, and Constantinople, which she first saw in 1869, when she went to Egypt to inaugurate the Suez Canal. The Sultan of those distant days and the Sultan of these entertained her. In the August of 1910 the Empress was in the Solent, and witnessed the launch of the Orion at Portsmouth. Later in the year she lunched, for the first time, with the King and Queen at Marlborough House, M. Pietri accompanying her.

The Empress signalized her eighty-fifth birthday (May 5, 1911) by a very pleasant cruise in the Mediterranean, as the guest of Sir Thomas Lipton, Bart., on board his yacht *Erin*, and on June 24 she witnessed the review of the fleet.

In my previous volume[187] I dwelt upon the solicitude of Queen Victoria and other members of our Royal Family—notably King Edward and Queen Alexandra—for the Empress Eugénie and the fatherless Prince Imperial. I note the fact here because I am delighted to find that the details which I gave of that more than cordial—that affectionate—relationship are supplemented by M. Xavier Paoli in his volume of Souvenirs, entitled "Leurs Majestés...."[188] Some two years ago, in the "Pall Mall Gazette," I announced M. Paoli's intention to produce his reminiscences, and I emphasized the opinion that his work would contain some entertaining and piquant "indiscretions" concerning Queen Victoria and the Empress Eugénie. That my anticipations have been fully realized will be seen by what follows.

When Queen Victoria was at Nice a grave responsibility fell upon those who, like M. Paoli, the "Protector of Sovereigns,"[189] were charged with the onerous duty of guarding the royal residence without any great display of force, almost without any indication of it. The small body of infantry installed near the Queen's abode had merely to present arms when the august lady appeared, and when French official personages called upon her.

One afternoon there was a "piquante adventure," and all on account of "the" Empress. M. Paoli's amazed gaze fell upon the little infantry force drawn up in the court, and he asked the officer in command "the cause of this mobilization, which was not in the day's programme." The officer replied that he had turned out the guard at the request of the Queen's Courier, M. Dosse, who explained that Her Majesty was expecting the visit of "a crowned head." Somewhat annoyed at his ignorance of what was about to happen, M. Paoli further questioned M. Dosse, who remarked: "Then you know nothing about it?" "Ma foi, non." "Well, we are expecting the Empress Eugénie." Paoli jumped. "What!" he exclaimed, "you want soldiers of the Republic to render honours to the former Empress of the French!" "I admit," answered M. Dosse, "that I did not look at it from that point of view." "But," said M. Paoli, "I *do* look at it from that point of view;" and he requested the officer to march his men off immediately.

A few days later M. Paoli related the incident to the Empress, who said: "Oh, how pleased I am that you have told me about it! Certain papers would have made me responsible for what happened, and my very delicate position would not have been improved."

When the Empress attends a church in England other than St. Michael's, Farnborough, it is an event. On Sunday, August 14, 1910, Her Majesty, accompanied by M. Pietri and Miss Vaughan, landed at Cowes and heard Mass at the church of St. Thomas of Canterbury. The celebrant was the Rev. John O'Hanlon, who

[187] "The Empress Eugénie: 1870-1910." London: Harper and Brothers. New York: Charles Scribner's Sons. 1910.

[188] Paris: Ollendorff. 1911.

[189] His official title was "Commissaire Spécial, attaché aux Souverains étrangers en France," a post which he resigned nearly two years ago.

told me he was born and brought up at Dumfries, less than a dozen miles from Closeburn, the home of the Kirkpatricks, from whom, through her mother, the imperial lady descends. The Empress walked up the steep road leading from Cowes Pier to St. Thomas's Church. An observant spectator wrote of her: "Except for a slight lameness, the Empress has the activity and vigour of a well-preserved woman of sixty. The glorious chestnut hair, though now iron-grey, is still abundant, the eyes are bright, the features finely chiselled. The Empress, who once led fashions for all Europe, is now content to follow far in their wake, for the skirt of her simple costume was much ampler than those lately seen on the Royal Yacht Squadron's lawns, while her coat had sleeves of a bygone fashion." In the afternoon the Empress visited Princess Henry of Battenberg, at Osborne Cottage. On the following day (August 15, the date of the great fête in the Empire period) Princess Henry and Princess Christian took tea with the Empress on the *Thistle*, which remained in the Solent for several days. The Queen of Spain and Princess Victoria of Schleswig-Holstein were other visitors. The Empress was seen walking on the parade at Cowes, but no one noticed the "slight lameness" referred to, which, in fact, is non-existent.

On February 4, 1911, the daily papers announced the death of John Brown, of Southwold, aged seventy-four, "a pensioner of the Empress Eugénie"; and it was added that Brown "brought the Prince Imperial's body home." This was incorrect. Colonel Pemberton had charge of the remains from the Cape to Woolwich. The body was brought to England by the *Orontes*, and transhipped at Portsmouth to the *Enchantress*, which conveyed it to Woolwich. On board those vessels, besides Colonel Pemberton, were the Abbé Rooney, the Prince's valet (Uhlmann, who died some four years ago), and two grooms (Lomas and Brown).

In January, 1911, the Empress's friends read in the Paris papers the somewhat disquieting announcement that MM. André de Lorde and A. Binet had written a play called "Napoleon III.," in which both the Emperor and the Empress Eugénie will figure. French dramatists have hitherto, I think, refrained from presenting the august lady on the stage, and it is only within the last five years that the Emperor was impersonated in a piece entitled "La Savelli," by M. Max Maurey, produced by Mme. Réjane at her new theatre, Rue Blanche, in December, 1906. In the part of the Emperor M. Buguet acted with much distinction. His "makeup" was surprisingly good.

Very different was the treatment of the Emperor on the German stage, as recently narrated by M. Jules Claretie: "I was disgusted at seeing, at a Berlin theatre, in an adaptation of an old French féerie, Napoleon III., caricatured by a low comedian, dancing a cancan, his breast adorned with the grand cordon of the Légion d'Honneur."

In December, 1907, MM. Julien and Marcel Priollet selected "Napoleon III." as a title for their piece, produced at the Comédie de l'Époque, "amidst the bravos of the public."

THE LATE COMTESSE DE MERCY-ARGENTEAU
(*née* **COMTESSE CARAMAN-CHIMAY**).

From a private and unpublished photograph, courteously presented to the Author in 1911 by the Comte de Pimodan, the well-known author of a recently-issued valuable work on the Comte F. C. de Mercy-Argenteau, counsellor and confidant of Marie Antoinette.

The Prince Imperial was dragged on the stage as a consequence of the "romantic" story first told to his detriment in 1879.[190] So persistently was the rumour spread that the Prince Imperial had lost his heart to an English girl that a German play was written on the subject and produced at the theatre at Kreuznach within a month of the Prince's death in Zululand. In this amazing piece, which the German Government allowed to be performed at the fashionable watering-place (where the Empress Eugénie had "made a cure" some time after the war of 1870, and by whose inhabitants she was consequently well known), the Prince Imperial was portrayed in love with a gamekeeper's daughter, "Miss Mary." A rival tried to shoot the Prince, who escaped by the aid of a German servant, "Reinecke." The story, as unfolded on the stage, showed that, when the Prince had made up his mind to go to the Cape, the Empress offered a bracelet to "Miss Mary," who, regarding it as an attempted bribe, refused it, declaring melodramatically that woman's love was "not to be bought with gold." The dramatist made the most of the Zulus' "surprise" of the reconnoitring party, numbering nine all told, led—or assumed to be led—by Lieutenant Carey, 98th Regiment; and the attack, the abandonment of the Prince by his comrades, and his cruel slaying by the savages were all enacted. The scene of the last act was described as "the crypt of the Catholic Church, Chislehurst," and the Empress Eugénie was seen giving her dead son's last letter to "Miss Mary," who revealed to the imperial lady that she had been really married to the "little Prince" before he left for the Cape.

Not long after the tragedy of the First of June some Zulus were exhibited in Paris, and for fourpence, in a booth, illumined by oil lamps, M. Proudhon saw "how the Prince Imperial was killed"!

These fragments are pieced together for the sole purpose of completing the record of the history of the Empress given in my first volume. Such a record, imperfect as it may be, will not be found elsewhere. To be able to infuse into the narrative a note of gaiety is most agreeable to me, as I hope it will be to my readers at home and abroad.

One glorious summer afternoon[191] I roamed through rhododendron land. Oh the beauty of it!—the joy of living in so fair a world, a Paradise terrestrial! Through leafy mazes I wandered into gardens, where the air was laden with the perfume of roses and honeysuckles. For miles, and miles, and miles all was forest—dense, impenetrable forest. Unwillingly I left this scene of enchantment and entered a park. My brief midsummer day's dream was over. I was invited to mount one of quite a "stable" of prancing steeds, galloping in a circle—"patronized by the Royal Family and the English aristocracy." I was urged to "try my skill" in the art—say, rather, the science—of casting wooden rings over clocks, vases, and Lowther Arcade prettinesses in general. I was tempted by roundabouts, swings, "hooplas," cocoanut shies, Aunt Sally, and "numerous side-shows." "Zara," the "celebrated Palmiste," offered me "peeps into the future—the past laid bare"—"Zara," whose

---

[190] When this monstrous tale of an alleged liaison was widely published eight years later—in January, 1887—I denied it in the *Pall Mall Gazette,* on the authority of Monsignor Goddard. In 1911 it was again revived.

[191] June 7 and 8, 1911.

"remarkable character readings" were guaranteed to "astonish you" (I felt sure of it). "Afternoon, 2s. 6d.; evening, 1s." I could not, unfortunately, stay until the evening, or perhaps I might have made "Zara's" acquaintance—at the reduced fee.

And what else? A Pastoral Play—scenes from "As You Like it," presented by the "Marlboro' Players"; a Venetian play, "The Honour of the Joscelyns"; a Vaudeville entertainment, by "The Bluebirds," an "amateur association of ladies formed for the purpose of providing entertainments for the poor in winter, and also assisting deserving organizations"; a concert; Morris dances; a "display" by 100 boy scouts; daylight and evening fireworks.

It was a two days' Coronation Fête, given at Farnborough Hill, "by kind permission of H.I.M. the Empress Eugénie," in aid of the funds of the county branch of the National Service League. Farnborough had never seen the like, and rose to the occasion. I imagine that this garden festival "at the Empress's" will be, as it deserves to be, writ large in Hampshire history.

Since the appearance of my first volume,[192] "the Empress's Church"—St. Michael's, Farnborough—has received an addition. While the Empress was on her unwontedly long cruise in the *Thistle* during part of May and the whole of June and July, 1910, a striking scene was being enacted within the walls of St. Michael's. For some months the quiet which ordinarily reigns in the Mausoleum was disturbed. Sculptors and masons—French and English—appeared, masses of stone were hauled into the church, and the sound of mallets and chisels reverberated through the great crypt, which extends beneath the choir and transepts. Entering the crypt, I gazed at the transformation which had been effected. I saw a third tomb! It is a graceful arch, rising from the back of and surmounting the high altar. All who have visited the Catacombs at Rome will recall the "table" tomb and the "arched" tomb, and will not need to be told that the latter, from its shape, is the arcosolium. These tombs differ only in the form of the surmounting recess. In the "table" tomb the recess above, essential for the reception of the entombed body, is square. In the arcosolium, a form of later date, the recess for the tomb is semicircular, as at Farnborough. These modes of interment were adopted by the early Christians. I leave it to the archæologists to tell us whether or no the Empress Eugénie's arcosolium is unique in this country. I cannot recall anything resembling it. A space behind the altar is occupied by a massive block of masonry, with a flat surface, flush with the side walls from which the arch springs, and upon this the Empress's sarcophagus (assuming it should take that form, and so harmonize with the granite tombs of the Emperor and the Prince Imperial) will rest.

Here, then,

> "In God's own time, but not before,"

Eugénie de Montijo, Empress, will sleep her last long sleep with her beloved Dead—Exiles all.

The historian who comes after us will find in this place of Napoleonic sepulture ample materials for a moving chapter. He will have to re-narrate, with

[192] "The Empress Eugénie, 1870-1910." London: Harper and Brothers; New York: Charles Scribner's Sons. 1910.

the assistance of my modest records, the amazing rise and the more astounding downfall of an Emperor and the deplorable end of a Prince. But he will "use his best ink" in the endeavour to limn a faithful portrait of her who held the world in thrall by her beauty, who has endured her martyrdom with a resignation and fortitude so admirable as to have compelled the affectionate solicitude of the nation whose honoured guest she has been for forty-one sorrowful, yet not wholly gloomy, years.

As I write these closing lines the air is full of processional melody, the Town gay with colour. I think, not of the EMPRESS, when she, like our own beloved Albert Edward and Alexandra, was the centre of adulation, but of the WOMAN, in the not unkindly winter of her life, kneeling before a tomb—her own. It is All Saints' Day—the Jour des Morts[193]—and in the crypt she mingles her prayers with the Benedictines' "pour tous les fidèles défunts." So I had seen her aforetime, and some words I heard then will not be kept back when the sluices of memory are opened:

> ... And now, as in a strain of music, the theme comes back again, and we end with the first notes with which we began, so, if our thoughts have for a while run in another channel, they fall back into the great deep of sweet sorrow, and, I will say, of thanksgiving, for that noble, princely youth who has passed before our eyes with the brightness of a ray of light, and from this world has disappeared for ever.... What a morning in life it was when that beautiful youth entered into this world! What a mother's joy! If ever son was worthy of a mother's love, it was he. And if ever mother loved a son as an only son can be loved, it was she. What a desolation now! The solitary home. All alone. Yet not alone; for they who believe are never lonely. They have come unto "Mount Sion, and to the City of the Living God; to the company of many thousands of angels; to the Church of the first-born, who are written in the heavens; to God, the Judge of all; to the spirits of the just made perfect"; to the great cloud of witnesses ever about them. And as the Mother, who, when her Divine Son was in the grave, looked on with certain confidence to the glory of the Resurrection, to the future recognition in personal identity, and in the restored bonds of Mother and of Son in all the perfection of maternal and filial love glorified in eternity, so is it now. And this will be her consolation.... And what is the longest life of waiting but a little while at last?[194]

> The light beats down, the gates of pearl are wide:
> And she is passing to the floor of peace.
> And Mary of the seven times wounded heart
> Has kissed her lips ... the Light of Lights

---

[193] November 2, 1910: St. Michael's, Farnborough.

[194] "In Memory of the Prince Imperial." Sermon at St. Mary's, Chislehurst, on Sunday, July 13, 1879, by Henry Edward, Cardinal Archbishop.

Looks always on the motive, not the deed,
The Shadow of Shadows on the deed alone.

THE TIME WILL COME WHEN WE SHALL BE ABLE TO UNVEIL THE WHOLE TRUTH TO THE WORLD.

I SHALL CONTINUE TO HOPE FOR A FUTURE OF TRUTH AND OF JUSTICE.

THE EMPRESS EUGÉNIE.

THE PRINCE IMPERIAL
(THE POET LAUREATE'S SONNET)

FELIX OPPORTUNITATE MORTIS.

Exile or Cæsar? Death hath solved thy doubt,
And made thee certain of thy changeless fate;
And thou no more hast wearily to wait,
Straining to catch the people's tarrying shout
That from unrestful rest would drag thee out,
And push thee to those pinnacles of State
Round which throng courtly loves, uncourted hate,
Servility's applause, and envy's flout.
Twice happy boy! though cut off in thy flower,
The timeliest doom of all thy race is thine:
Saved from the sad alternative, to pine
For heights unreached, or icily to tower,
Like Alpine crests that only specious shine,
And glitter on the lonely peak of Power.

ALFRED AUSTIN.

June, 1879.

INDEX

A

B

H

I

M

N

O

P

Lector House believes that a society develops through a two-fold approach of continuous learning and adaptation, which is derived from the study of classic literary works spread across the historic timeline of literature records. Therefore, we aim at reviving, repairing and redeveloping all those inaccessible or damaged but historically as well as culturally important literature across subjects so that the future generations may have an opportunity to study and learn from past works to embark upon a journey of creating a better future.

This book is a result of an effort made by Lector House towards making a contribution to the preservation and repair of original ancient works which might hold historical significance to the approach of continuous learning across subjects.

HAPPY READING & LEARNING!

LECTOR HOUSE LLP
E-MAIL: lectorpublishing@gmail.com